COMMUNITY HEALTH AND SOCIAL SERVICES

MODERN NURSING SERIES

General Editors
A. J. HARDING RAINS M.S., F.R.C.S.
MISS VALERIE HUNT S.R.N., S.C.M., R.N.T.

AT PRESENT AVAILABLE AS PAPERBACKS

Textbook of Medicine with relevant physiology and anatomy
R. J. HARRISON Ch.B., M.D.

Obstetrics and Gynaecology for Nurses
GORDON W. GARLAND M.D., F.R.C.O.G.
JOAN M. E. QUIXLEY S.R.N., R.N.T.
MICHAEL D. CAMERON M.A., M.B., B.Chir., F.R.C.S., M.R.C.O.G.

Principles of Medicine and Medical Nursing
J. C. HOUSTON M.D., F.R.C.P.
MARION STOCKDALE S.R.N.

Principles of Surgery and Surgical Nursing
SELWYN TAYLOR D.M., M.Ch., F.R.C.S.

Physiology for Nurses
DERYCK TAVERNER M.B.E., M.D., F.R.C.P.

Psychology and Psychiatry for Nurses
PETER DALLY M.B., F.R.C.P., D.P.M.
HEATHER HARRINGTON S.R.N., R.M.N.

Emergency and Acute Care
A. J. HARDING RAINS M.S., F.R.C.S.
VALERIE HUNT S.R.N., S.C.M., R.N.T.
KEITH REYNOLDS M.S., F.R.C.S.

Midwifery
JEAN L. HALLUM B.Sc., M.D., D.Ch., F.R.C.O.G.

Orthopaedics and Accidents
MARGARET MILLER R.G.N., S.C.M.
JAMES H. MILLER M.B., Ch.B., F.R.C.S.

COMMUNITY HEALTH
AND
SOCIAL SERVICES

BRIAN MEREDITH DAVIES
M.D. (LONDON), F.F.C.M., D.P.H.

DIRECTOR OF SOCIAL SERVICES, CITY OF LIVERPOOL

Lecturer in Clinical (Preventive) Paediatrics, University of Liverpool.
Formerly Director of Personal Health and Social Services, City of Liverpool and Lecturer in Public
Health, University of Liverpool.

HODDER AND STOUGHTON
LONDON SYDNEY AUCKLAND TORONTO

ISBN 0 340 21436 8 Boards
ISBN 0 340 21437 6 Paperback

First published as *Preventive Medicine for Nurses and Social Workers* 1965
Second edition 1972, reprinted with extensive revisions 1975
Third edition 1977

Filmset by Elliott Brothers and Yeoman Limited,
Woodend Avenue, Speke, Liverpool L24 9JL,
and printed and bound in Great Britain
by Biddles of Guildford,
for Hodder and Stoughton Educational,
a division of Hodder and Stoughton Limited,
Mill Road, Dunton Green, Sevenoaks, Kent.

EDITORS' FOREWORD

The scope of this series has increased since it was first established, and it now serves a wide range of medical, nursing and ancillary professions, in line with the present trend towards the belief that all who care for patients in a clinical context have an increasing amount in common.

The texts are carefully prepared and organized so that they may be readily kept up to date as the rapid developments of medical science demand. The series already includes many popular books on various aspects of medical and nursing care, and reflects the increased emphasis on community care.

The increasing specialization in the medical profession is fully appreciated and the books are often written by Physicians or Surgeons in conjunction with specialist nurses. For this reason, they will not only cover the syllabus of training of the General Nursing Council, but will be designed to meet the needs of those undertaking training controlled by the Joint Board of Clinical Studies set up in 1970.

PREFACE TO THIRD EDITION

Two major changes have occurred since the publication of the Second edition in 1972—the reorganization of the health services and of local government.

In this Third edition, these alterations have been described. At the same time, many changes in detail and presentation have been introduced.

The main characteristics of the book have been retained and it is still presented in two parts:

(1) Community health services;
(2) Social services.

During the past three years, there is evidence of increasing connections between these two services and this is understandable and desirable because health and social services have come to rely more and more on each other to achieve their best results. An excellent example of this interdependence is seen in non-accidental injury in children and it is now clear that the prevention of· this distressing condition depends on a multi-disciplinary team approach between health and social services and many other bodies.

Chapter 1 has been greatly extended since the revised 2nd edition and deals in detail with the new structure of the health services.

This reorganization resulted in the responsibility for hospital social workers being passed to social services departments. At the same time, medical support for various local authority services (social services, education and environmental health) must be given by the new health authorities through their Specialists in Community Medicine and this is described in Chapters 4, 5, 11 and 12.

Another chapter which has been completely remodelled is Chapter 2 which deals with the measurement of health. At times of financial constraint, the determination of relative priorities becomes even more important and, if this is to be done logically, services should be judged on their effectiveness to prevent disease or social problems. This chapter now includes more examples of how this can be done and many of these are taken from valuable reports such as the Hospital In-Patient Enquiry and Hospital Activity Analysis and Social Trends.

The latest figures on maternal mortality are discussed in Chapter 3 and it is interesting to note that more than half such deaths are still considered preventable. The section of family planning has been extended (to include new legislation) and now is attached to this chapter.

In the chapters dealing with children, non-accidental injury is mainly dealt with on pages 158–162, but Chapter 3 includes more on safety in the home, and the relationship between the incidence of congenital abnormality and the age of the mother. Further reference has been made to the new classification of educationally sub-normal children and the abnormality of dyslexia has been introduced.

The chapter on communicable diseases (this new description is used rather than infectious diseases) deals with the remarkable decline in smallpox—this disease is on the threshold of extinction from the world as only a small area in the highlands of Ethiopia remains infected. However, both rabies and cholera now present greater threats and are discussed in more detail.

In the chapter on non-communicable disease, more information is given on the likely causes of some bladder cancers and on the factors leading to ischaemic heart disease. Three distinct types of obesity have recently been identified by a Medical Research Council report (with quite different implications for treatment) and these are described.

The second part of the book dealing with social services has been extended in many ways. Although most of this section describes local authority social services, brief reference is made to probation services and voluntary organizations, both of whom work very closely with social services departments.

Chapter 13 dealing with the care of children in need has been lengthened to deal in depth with non-accidental injury, alterations in community home procedures, court proceedings for juveniles and the changes to be introduced by the Children Act 1975 which affects many aspects of adoption, fostering and child care practice.

In the chapter on physical disability, attendance and mobility allowances are described fully and a description has also been given of the new aids centres now established in London, Liverpool, Newcastle and Birmingham.

There is a new section dealing with alcoholism in Chapter 15 and this recognizes the increasing health and social problems created by this condition.

The problems of the aged worsen yearly as the elderly population increases and as this vulnerable section of society faces the difficulties of inflation and increased costs. New features in Chapter 16 describe home care programmes for those recently discharged from hospital and the role of day hospitals. In addition the section on hypothermia has been considerably extended to include a more detailed description of the diagnosis, prevention and treatment of this dangerous condition.

The efforts being made in many cities to reduce homelessness by the greater involvement of housing departments are described in Chapter 17. The work of hospital social workers (now members of social services departments) is described briefly for the first time in this chapter.

The final section dealing with social security seems to become more complicated yearly but it is still essential for every nurse to understand the basic concept of social security. The details change so rapidly that it will always be important to check with social security offices the up-to-date rates and qualifications.

The reorganization of the health services has dulled the differences between hospital and community health and the primary health care team.

With the greater emphasis being placed on helping ill or vulnerable people in their own homes, a new dimension has now been added and it is important *that health and social services recognize how interdependent they are becoming.* Although primary health care teams (which include health visitors, home nurses and midwives) have always realized the social aspects of disease, it is now equally important for nurses in hospital and industry to understand how factors within the home of the patient can determine eventual success or failure in many instances. The increasing use of day surgery and other advances (such as community hospitals) has made the distinction between hospital and community nursing less apparent.

It is hoped that this short book will give a simple and readable introduction to community health and social services. It is intended to be of help to both the trained nurse (who is increasingly coming into contact with the new social services) and the nurse in training to understand the aims and structure of these services.

I would like again to thank my wife for all her patient and helpful correction of the proofs, the compilation of the index and for her constant encouragement.

Brian Meredith Davies

CONTENTS

1 THE STRUCTURE OF THE REORGANIZED HEALTH SERVICES

Before discussing the various parts of the community health services and the ways in which disease is prevented, it is important that the structure of the health services is fully understood.

The National Health Service in the United Kingdom was introduced in 1948 and was completely reorganized in 1974. It is an essential part of a much wider system of social security in which the whole state makes compulsory provision for various inevitable happenings in life, including the prevention of disease and the treatment of illness. The National Health Service is a comprehensive health service covering the whole country and its benefits and services are available to everyone. There is no contracting out of the service and it is financed centrally from both Exchequer general taxation and specific levies paid within National Insurance contributions.

The annual cost of the National Health Service has risen to over 4400 million pounds and of this amount, roughly 90 per cent comes from direct and indirect taxation and the remainder from National Health Service contributions. The financing of the service, although not the concern of this book, is a major part of the national budget (roughly 8.6 per cent of public expenditure) and the control of this enormous expenditure is under the Secretary of State for Social Services.

Health services are now provided as one integrated service and the original division into hospital, preventive and general practitioner services has been changed. In its place, the local health services are provided on a geographic basis with all major services being organized by 90 Area Health Authorities in England, 14 single Health Boards in Scotland and 8 Area Health Authorities in Wales.

In England, in addition there are 14 Regional Health Authorities who each co-ordinate from 3–11 Area Health Authorities. Although general practitioner services are part of the integrated health services provided by Area Health Authorities, an independent committee called the Family Practitioner Committee has been set up to deal with all contractual matters for general practitioners. The Family Practitioner Committtee covers the same geographic area as Area Health Authorities.

Function of the Secretary of State for Social Services

The Secretary of State for Social Services retains under health services reorganization full overall responsibility for the health and social services. The Secretary of State is responsible directly to Parliament and is a member of the Cabinet. The responsibilities of the Secretary of State for local social services undertaken by local authorities are discussed on page 142.

Under the National Health Services Reorganization Act, 1973, the responsibilities of the Secretary of State are to provide to an extent which he considers necessary:

(1) Accommodation for any services under the National Health Service Acts (clinics, health centres etc.).

(2) Hospital accommodation.

(3) Medical, dental, nursing and ambulance services.

(4) Facilities for the care of expectant and nursing mothers and very young children.

(5) Facilities for the prevention of illness and after care of persons suffering from illness. These include vaccination and immunization and a full range of rehabilitation services (including physiotherapy and occupational therapy).

(6) Such other services which are required for the diagnosis and treatment of illness (this includes full pathological, bacteriological, blood transfusion and mass radiography services).

(7) School health services (in conjunction with Local Education Authorities).

(8) Family Planning Services.

The Secretary of State has certain expert committees to advise him, the most important of which is the *Central Health Services Council*, an expert committee of medical, nursing and allied professions representing all the important fields of the health services. In addition, there are a number of *Standing Advisory Committees* (such as the Standing Advisory Committee on Prevention of Disease by Immunization) to which the Secretary of State may refer various specific problems. From time to time, particularly pressing problems occur which need very careful study. The Secretary of State may then arrange for them to be examined in detail by a special *ad hoc* Expert Committee. An example of an Expert Committee at present studying a problem is the committee set up under the chairmanship of Professor Court to consider the future of child health services. Such a committee would collect evidence from various sources, study that evidence and recommend a course of action. It then becomes the responsibility of the Secretary of State for Social Services to assess the report and decide whether to recommend Parliament to implement the changes suggested.

In some instances, it may be essential to consider changing the whole law relating to health. In this case, the Secretary of State, through Parliament, may first appoint a *Royal Commission* to study the whole subject and report to him and Parliament. An example of such action was the Royal Commission on the law relating to Mental Illness which was set up in 1955. Its report in 1958 was the first stage leading to the whole law on mental illness being changed by the Mental Health Act 1959.

In addition to these expert committees, the Secretary of State has a large staff of experts to advise him, based at the Department of Health and Social Security in London and locally in various regional offices. These include administrators, doctors, nurses and architects who deal with the detailed administration.

METHOD OF CONTROL EXERCISED BY THE DEPARTMENT OF HEALTH AND SOCIAL SERVICES

The method used to control health services locally varies. Although all day to day administration of the health services is dealt with locally (mostly at Area Health Authority and District levels), the Department of Health and Social Security has three methods of controlling overall development.

(1) *Financial*

This is the most important method. All the finance needed for the health services is supplied from the Department of Health and Social Security and covers running costs (*revenue expenditure*) and new buildings (*capital expenditure*).

The Department of Health and Social Security passes regional budgets for each Regional Health Authority which then allocates finances to each individual Area Health Authority. In allocating finance to Regional Health Authorities, the Department of Health and Social Security will take regard to special developments which it wishes to encourage. In this way, the Department of Health and Social Security will be able to encourage (by providing the finances necessary) services which urgently need developing.

As regards capital, in the past the Department of Health and Social Security has provided capital for hospital building on a 'once and for all' basis and not on any loan basis. It is likely that this will become the usual method of financing all capital in the future. In future all new health centres will be financed centrally and this should ensure a more uniform development of health centres.

(2) *Advisory*

Advice on the development of all aspects of the health services is constantly being issued by the Department of Health and Social Security in the form of memoranda and circulars. In many instances, the advice covers both health and social services. In the publication 'Better services for the mentally ill' issued in 1975, the whole question of the levels of services for the mentally handicapped was discussed and included recommendations of the type and amount of development in hospital and community services and covered the health and social services. In 1974, a special circular was issued on 'non-accidental injury in children'. This circular advised the way such services should be organized locally and asked for each area to report on its progress in setting up a new system of control through Area Review Committees (see page 160 for further details).

(3) *Planning and Policy*

The development of an integrated national health service calls for careful planning to ensure that the most urgent needs are met and that services are balanced between the different parts (*i.e.* between hospital, general practice and the community). It is, for instance, no use advocating a reduction in the number of hospital places for a certain group of patients (for example—the mentally ill) if there are not enough community services to help these patients when discharged from hospitals.

In the reorganized health service it is hoped that future planning will be more carefully carried out and will involve local staff of all types through the *Health-Care Planning Teams* (see below). It is hoped that a future long range plan for all the health and social services will be developed each year so that carefully integrated and balanced development will take place. In particular the planning aspect should always consider the *effectiveness of health services* as judged by their benefit to the ordinary people—i.e. are the health services managing to produce better health and less disease and is the health of the majority of the population better?

The Department of Health and Social Security acts as a master planner for the health and social services. By various methods, the Secretary of State is

Fig 1.1   **NATIONAL HEALTH SERVICE REORGANISATION ACT, 1973 – ENGLAND**

Officers
Central and Regional Staff of
Department of Health & Social
Security (D.H.S.S.)

Secretary of State for Social Services

(advised by Central Health Services Council and
Department of Health and Social Security)

Regional Team of Officers (R.T.O.)
Regional Medical Officer
Regional Nursing Officer
Regional Works Officer
Regional Administrator
Regional Treasurer

14 *REGIONAL HEALTH AUTHORITIES (R.H.A.)*
(each responsible for 3–11 A.H.As)
Planning and Priorities
Appointment of consultants (except in A.H.A.(T))
Allocation of resources between A.H.As
Capital building
Postgraduate medical, dental and nursing training
Ambulance services (delegated to Area Health Authorities)

monitors

Area Team of Officers (A.T.O.)
Area Medical Officer
Area Nursing Officer
Area Administrator
Area Treasurer

90 *AREA HEALTH AUTHORITY (TEACHING) (A.H.A.(T))*

or

AREA HEALTH AUTHORITY (A.H.A.)
(each responsible for managing the following:)
Hospital services
Community health services
Ambulance services

Also appoints consultants

monitors

District Management Team (D.M.T.)
Chairman and Deputy Chairman of
Medical Committee (family doctor
and consultant)
District Community Physician
District Nursing Officer
District Administrator
District Treasurer

155 *DISTRICTS* (day to day running of services)
District General Hospital
Maternity and child health
Domiciliary midwifery
Health visiting
Home nursing
Vaccination and immunization
Prevention of disease, care & after care
School health services
Health centres

FAMILY PRACTITIONER COMMITTEE (F.P.C.)
General medical, dental, optical
and pharmaceutical services
(including family doctors)

HEALTH-CARE PLANNING TEAMS

COMMUNITY HEALTH COUNCILS
Represents the consumer's
interests

able to exert an indirect control over the services—strengthening them where they are weakest and constantly encouraging an improvement in standards of care.

Parliamentary control

Because the Secretary of State is answerable to Parliament for the conduct of the health services, it is always open to any member of Parliament to raise any question, however detailed, and this must be answered by the Secretary of State verbally at question time or in writing.

In very serious instances, the Secretary of State can set up an Inquiry which then considers all aspects of the question and reports to the Secretary of State who then presents that report to Parliament. Recent examples have included fires in certain hospitals and allegations about the maltreatment of patients in mental hospitals.

A further method of control introduced by the National Health Service Reorganization Act 1973 has been the setting up of a Health Service Commissioner for England and a separate one for Wales (see page 15).

ADMINISTRATION OF THE NATIONAL HEALTH SERVICE

The simplest way to understand the functioning of the National Health Service is to look at the plan of its administration (see fig. 1.1).

It will be seen that:

(a) in England the Secretary of State and the Department of Health and Social Security are responsible nationally

(b) peripherally, a two-tier system of control is maintained by 14 Regional Health Authorities and 90 Area Health Authorities

(c) each Regional Health Authority has its own officers controlled by the Regional Team of Officers

(d) each Area Health Authority is managed by an Area Team of Officers and may be either

(i) one tier where there is only 1 District General Hospital.

(ii) two tiers where there are 2 or more District General Hospitals. This second tier is managed by the District Management Team.

Regional Health Authorities

Generally the Regional Health Authority is responsible for the main planning of health services, for capital building programmes, for postgraduate medical, dental and nursing training and for the allocation of financial resources between its constituent Area Health Authorities. In all but the 19 Area Health Authorities (Teaching), the Regional Health Authority also appoints all consultants and Senior Registrars. The one point to remember is that the Regional Health Authority is NEVER involved with the ordinary day to day running of the health services.

Area Health Authorities

Area Health Authorities generally are responsible for the main management of the health services but as regards the general practitioner services, contracts of service are handled by the Family Practitioner Committee (to ensure the independence of general practitioners).

All hospital and community health services are the responsibility of the Area Health Authority or the District Management Teams who are therefore in charge of:

District General Hospitals

Maternity and child health services

Domiciliary midwifery

Health visiting

Home nursing

Vaccination and immunization

Prevention of disease, care and after care (health education, chiropody, tuberculosis after care, occupational therapy and some types of convalescence)

School health services (in conjunction with the corresponding local education authority)

Health Centres

Ambulances (in large conurbations one Area Health Authority is responsible)

There are 19 Area Health Authorities which are also the centres for medical teaching (in conjunction with the medical schools of the corresponding University) and are specially designated *Area Health Authority (Teaching)*. One interesting additional responsibility which all such authorities have is that they appoint consultants and senior registrars. (In the rest of the service, the appointments of consultants and senior registrars are undertaken by the Regional Health Authorities.)

Within each Area Health Authority (unless it is small and only contains one District General Hospital) there is a further division of responsibility. There is a group of officers at Area level responsible for the health services generally for the Area as a whole and at District level for the day to day management of the hospital and community health services. There is usually one District for the geographical area served by each district general hospital. An Area Health Authority, which therefore includes three district general hospitals, will normally have three Districts each controlled by a District Management Team of Officers.

Much of the day to day management of the clinical and nursing services will be arranged on a district basis. Therefore the *District Nursing Officer* will normally be in charge of all nursing staff in the relevant district general hospital as well as the midwives, home nurses, health visitors and school nurses working in the locality.

LOCAL ADMINISTRATION OF THE HEALTH SERVICES

A general outline of the new health services has already been given but this section goes into greater detail and describes:

(a) Regional Health Authorities and Regional Team of Officers

(b) Area Health Authorities and Area Team of Officers

(c) District Management Teams

(d) Health Care Planning Teams

(*e*) Community Health Councils
(*f*) Family Practitioner Committees

(a) Regional Health Authorities and Regional Team of Officers

There are 14 Regional Health Authorities in England and their distribution is shown in fig. 1.2. Each has at least one University providing medical education within its boundaries. The Chairman and members of each Regional Health Authority are appointed by the Secretary of State after consultation with the universities, the large local authorities providing social services and the main health professions. Membership cannot include any current member of any Area Team of Officers of an Area Health Authority within that Regional Health Authority.

The responsibility of the *Regional Health Authority* includes:
(1) The development of strategic plans and priorities based on the needs identified by its Area Health Authorities.
(2) The allocation of financial resources between its constituent Area Health Authorities.
(3) Monitoring the performance of the Area Health Authorities.
(4) The development of a regional plan for specialist services.
(5) Postgraduate medical, dental and nursing teaching.
(6) Responsibility for encouraging research within the Regional Health Authority.
(7) Provision of an ambulance service—the day to day control is usually delegated to the Area Health Authority (except in Metropolitan Counties (i.e. Merseyside)).
(8) The design and construction of all large capital building developments (new hospitals etc.).

The *Regional Team of Officers* contains five staff:
Regional Medical Officer
Regional Nursing Officer
Regional Works Officer
Regional Administrator
Regional Treasurer

The main tasks of the Regional Team of Officers are:
(*a*) to prepare a Regional Development Plan dealing with distribution of medical specialities, development of medical manpower and the scheduling of major capital building projects.
(*b*) to monitor Area Health Authority programmes.

Each member of the Regional Team of Officers is of equal standing. One will act as Chairman and the chairmanship will rotate. Although the Regional Team of Officers monitors the performance of its Area Team of Officers, it is NOT managerially in charge of the Area Teams of Officers (which are consequently professionally independent).

The Regional Team of Officers is responsible for recommending regional policies to the Regional Health Authority. This is done by the preparation of a *Regional Development Plan* which deals with:
(1) distribution of medical specialities
(2) development of medical manpower
(3) scheduling of major capital building projects.

FIG. 1.2 England Regional Health Authorities and the Welsh Health Authority

(b) Area Health Authorities and Area Team of Officers

There are 90 Area Health Authorities in England and eight in Wales. Each *Area Health Authority* acts as the operational authority for the main hospital, community health and (with the Family Practitioner Committee which it must appoint) the general practitioner services. There are two types of Area Health Authorities—those with substantial teaching facilities (Area Health Authorities (Teaching)—and those without. The Chairman of each Area Health Authority is appointed by the Secretary of State. Each Area Health Authority has 15 members—four are appointed by the corresponding local authority and in the Area Health Authority (Teaching) by the university. The remaining members are appointed by the Regional Health Authority after consultations with the main health professions and other organizations (there is always a minority of doctors on any Area Health Authority).

Each Area Health Authority is serviced by an *Area Team of Officers* consisting of:

Area Medical Officer
Area Nursing Officer
Area Administrator
Area Treasurer

The Area Team of Officers does the planning and evaluation work for the Area Health Authority. The Area Team of Officers, who are of equal standing, draws up planning guidelines for each District and reviews and monitors district performance. It also advises the Area Health Authority on the development of health services in the area.

The *Area Medical Officer* reviews the health care needs of the area and recommends to the Area Health Authority health care policies. He also coordinates the preventive and other services including the clinical preventive work in child health clinics and health education. Attached to his staff are three *Specialists in Community Medicine* dealing with:

(*a*) child health
(*b*) social services and planning
(*c*) environmental health

The responsibility of these three specialists is to provide the corresponding local authority with medical advice and help in the school health services, social services and environmental services. Each of these specialists act independantly in giving advice to the local authority.

The *Area Nursing Officer* usually has less executive control as most of the day to day control of nursing services in hospitals and in the preventive field is undertaken by the District Nursing Officers. (The exception is in the case of the 29 smallest Area Health Authorities which each contain only 1 District General Hospital). The responsibility of the Area Nursing Officer is to advise the Area Health Authority on all nursing matters and as a member of the Area Team of Officers to examine District plans for nursing. She therefore is very much concerned with the planning and evaluation of nursing services as well as ensuring through the district nursing staff and others that the local authority obtains nursing advice especially in the school health service. On the staff of the Area Nursing Officer there is an Area Nurse (Child Health Services) who is responsible for the school nursing services.

(c) District Management Teams

Within 61 of the 90 Area Health authorities, there will be smaller districts (153 in all). Where appointed, the majority of the day to day running of the health services is delegated to a *District Management Team* consisting of six officers:

2 Clinicians (1 Consultant + 1 general practitioner)
District Community Physician
District Nursing Officer
District Administrator
District Treasurer

As with the Regional and Area Teams of Officers, all members of the District Management Team are jointly responsible and are equals in the management sense. A chairman is chosen and changes regularly.

The *District Community Physician* reports directly to the Area Health Authority (not through the Area Medical Officer) and coordinates service planning—assesses the community's need for health care, identifies gaps in the services, coordinates health-care planning teams and organizes or conducts special studies in health care services for the District Management Team. He also controls the preventive medical work undertaken by clinical medical officers attached to him by the Area Medical Officer. Apart from metropolitan districts and the 29 small single district Area Health Authorities where the Area Specialist in Community Medicine (Environmental Health) acts in this capacity, the District Community Physician also acts as 'proper officer' in the investigation of notifiable disease and food poisoning and therefore works closely with the local authority.

The *District Nursing Officer* manages the nursing services of the community and hospital nursing services. She is therefore in charge of all nursing staff in the district general hospital and the midwives, home nurses and health visitors in the community. She gives nursing advice to the District Management Team; she reports directly to the Area Health Authority (not through the Area Nursing Officer). She also takes part in the health-care planning teams in the District.

(d) Health-Care Planning Teams

Health-Care Planning Teams are multi-disciplinary working parties of officers set up in each District to analyse and assess the needs of the health services. There will be two types of Health-Care Planning Teams:

(1) permanent teams continuously dealing with the following:
children
maternity service
mentally ill
mentally handicapped
elderly

(2) 'ad hoc' teams set up specially to consider a special subject. Such teams may be disbanded after they have studied and reported on a specific subject. They will cover many aspects and examples would include:
review of primary health care services
introduction of day surgery in hospitals
diagnosis, treatment and prevention of non-accidental injury in babies ('battered babies').

It is intended that each Health-Care Planning Team should contain a wide range of professionals in the health service—general practitioners, consultants, hospital and community nursing staff (midwives, home nurses and health visitors), para-medical staff—radiographers, physiotherapists, occupational therapists, chiropodists, hospital social workers and social workers from the corresponding local authority. The Health-Care Planning Teams will provide an opportunity for views on special subjects within each district to be studied in detail and to be presented to the District Management Team and from there to the Area Health Authority and Regional Health Authority and to the Department of Health and Social Security. The Area Health Authority through the Joint Consultative Committee (see below) will discuss with the local authority the views of the Health-Care Planning Teams.

Joint Care Planning—Health and Local Authorities

Because services provided by local authorities (particularly those of the social services departments) have a considerable impact on health services and vice versa, it has been decided by the Department of Health and Social Security that effective arrangements should be made for joint planning.

Joint Care Planning Teams have therefore been set up by all Area Health Authorities and the relevant local authorities (including social services and education departments). Joint planning will cover all aspects of health and social services but is particularly important to ensure the correct balance of services for the elderly, the disabled, the mentally handicapped, the mentally ill, children and families and for socially handicapped groups such as alcoholics and drug addicts.

Joint Consultative Councils

Every Area Health Authority and the matching local authority must set up a *Joint Consultative Committee* which has the responsibility of advising on the planning and operation of the health services and the social, environmental and education services run by the local authority. The aim of such a committee is to improve cooperation.

In all metropolitan districts, a single Joint Consultative Committee is set up to deal with all aspects. In non-metropolitan counties there are two Joint Consultative Committees, one for social services and education set up with the county council and one for environmental matters set up with the local district councils in the area, which are responsible for environmental health matters.

(e) Community Health Councils

Community Health Councils have been introduced into the health service by the National Health Service (Reorganization) Act, 1973. There are about 153 Community Health Councils in England—one for each District. Their main function is to represent the local consumers' interests and to ensure that the development of the local health service does take regard of local opinion. Each will contain 18–30 members, one third of whom will be drawn from voluntary bodies active within the district. About half the members will be appointed by the corresponding local authority and one sixth by the Regional Health

Authority which will provide any permanent staff). No member of a Regional Health Authority, Area Health Authority, Family Practitioner Committee, nor any doctor or other National Health Service employee may serve on a Community Health Council.

Each Community Health Council has the following list of matters which it can investigate:

(1) consider the effectiveness of the health services in that District
(2) planning of health services
(3) variations in local health services—closure of hospitals or hospital departments
(4) collaboration between the health services and the local authority environmental health, education and social services
(5) standards of service—number of hospital beds in the district and the average number of patients on family doctors' lists
(6) patient facilities including hospital out-patients, open visiting of children, waiting times, amenities for hospital patients and arrangements for rehabilitation of patients
(7) waiting periods for in-patients and out-patients' treatments and for domiciliary services
(8) quality of catering in hospitals and in other health service institutions
(9) complaints (*not* individual complaints from patients, see below) but the general type of complaint
(10) advising individual members of the public how and where they should lodge a complaint and the facts that should be provided.

Each Community Health Council must issue an annual report which must then be sent to the Regional Health Authority and Area Health Authority. It is hoped that these Community Health Councils will provide a chance for local people using the health services to keep a careful watch over their development.

(f) Family Practitioner Committee

Although each Area Health Authority is also responsible for the family doctor services, the status of the general and dental practitioners, ophthalmic medical practitioners, opticians and pharmacists as independent contractors has remained unchanged. A special committee has to be set up called the *Family Practitioner Committee* which deals directly with the Department of Health and Social Security on all contractual matters. This committee contains 30 members, half of whom are appointed by the professions and, of the remaining 15, 11 are appointed by the Area Health Authority and 4 by the corresponding local authority. Its chairman is appointed by the committee from its own members.

All doctors providing family doctor services in the area have a contract to do so with the Family Practitioner Committee. The buying and selling of goodwill has been abolished and doctors wishing to join the service as principals must apply to the Family Practitioner Committee.

There is a special machinery set up nationally by the Secretary of State—the *Medical Practices Committee*—which is constantly assessing the number of general practitioners in any area compared with its population. It then classifies each area into one of four types:

(i) *Designated area*—an area in which there is an inadequate number of doctors, where the average number of patients per doctor exceeds 2500. Doctors are encouraged to practise in such an area and will receive a special inducement payment of £750 per year.

(ii) *Open area*—an area with a fair number of doctors where the doctor/patient ratio is between 1/2100 and 1/2500. Permission will always be granted to practise in such an area.

(iii) *Intermediate area*—an area with the doctor/patient ratio between 1/1800 and 1/2100. Applications to practise in such areas will never automatically be granted and each area is considered on its merits with special reference to the trends in the area.

(iv) *Restricted area*—an area which is over-doctored and where the number of patients per doctor is below 1/1800. Permission is never granted to start a new practice in a Restricted Area and entry can only be obtained by applying for a vacancy or partnership or assistantship.

Size of practice and choice of patient and doctor

A limit of 3500 is fixed on the total number of patients any single doctor may have on his list. If the doctor employs an assistant (he must have the permission of the Family Practitioner Committee to do this), the limit is raised by a further 2000 patients.

The public have a completely free choice of doctor and the doctor also has a free choice of deciding whether or not to accept the patient on to his list. Once the patient has been accepted by the doctor, he is required to render to him all proper and necessary treatment. If the doctor has also agreed to give maternity medical services, then this treatment will include such services for which he will receive additional payment. In addition the doctor must arrange further medical treatment for his patients such as the admission to hospital or attendance at outpatients. Every general practitioner is responsible for ensuring adequate medical cover during his absence on holiday or for sickness.

Medical List

Each Family Practitioner Committee is required to keep a list of all doctors practising in the area, called the *Medical List*, which must indicate separately the general medical practitioners who undertake maternity services. This list is available at the local Family Practitioner Committee headquarters and main Post Offices, where it may be examined by any member of the public to help in his choice of a doctor.

If a patient has difficulty in finding a doctor to accept him, he can apply to the Allocation Committee (another sub-committee of the Family Practitioner Committee) which will then allocate the patient to a convenient doctor. There are facilities for a patient to change his doctor if he wishes to do so, or for a doctor to indicate that he no longer wishes to look after a particular patient.

Methods of controlling medical practice

Local Medical Committee

One of the most important committees of any Family Practitioner Committee is the *Local Medical Committee* of doctors which acts as the local medical advisory committee to the Family Practitioner Committee. Any difficulties connected with particular practices or with local policies are referred to the Local Medical Committee who then advises the Family Practitioner Committee. In the case of a doctor who is considered by the Secretary of State to be prescribing excessive drugs and appliances for his patients, the Local Medical Committee has the task of carrying out an investigation. If, as a result of their enquiry, the Local Medical committee come to the conclusion that there has been excessive prescribing, then they must report the case to the Family Practitioner Committee who may then recommend the Secretary of State for Social Services to withhold a certain sum from the remuneration of the doctor, as a penalty. Usually such action is rarely taken, a warning first being given to the doctor.

Other similar expert committees help in the administration of the dental service—the *Dental Service Committee,* with the pharmaceutical services—the *Area Chemists Contractors Committee,* or with the ophthalmic services—the *Ophthalmic Service Committee.*

Methods of Controlling General Practice

A *Medical Services Committee* appointed by the Family Practitioner Committee investigates any serious complaints raised by a patient about the services to him by his doctor. This consists of the Chairman of the Family Practitioner Committee plus six other members of which three must be from the Local Medical Committee. There is a set procedure laid down for the investigation of such complaints. Minor complaints can be investigated by the Administrator to the Family Practitioner Committee and major complaints by the Medical Services Committee. Also the hearing is always in private and the doctor's name is never made public. The Medical Services Committee reports its findings to the Family Practitioner Committee which then sends its decision to the Secretary of Sate. The doctor may also appeal to the Secretary of State. In the case of a proved complaint, a doctor may be warned, have a special limit as to the number of patients on his list imposed, or have a sum withheld from his remuneration. There is no appeal beyond the Secretary of State whose decision is final.

In very serious cases, the Family Practitioner Committee can refer the case to a central *Tribunal* set up by the Secretary of State for Social Services, with a chairman who must be a barrister or solicitor of at least ten years' standing. The Tribunal holds an inquiry and, if satisfied that the case is serious enough, can order the removal of the doctor *from general practice in the Health Service.* In such a case, there is a right of appeal to the Secretary of State. This is quite different from action by the General Medical Council which can determine the fitness for a doctor to practise in *any medical field.*

Value of general medical services

There is little doubt that, although the hospital and specialist services cost so much more, the standard of medical service provided for each individual patient depends as much on the standard of the general medical services as on any other factor. Although there is no compulsion on any person to register with a doctor, the vast majority of people have so registered—about 98–99% of the population.

Charges to patients

There is no additional cost to the individual in obtaining all the medical services provided by hospitals or by general practitioners. Small charges are levied for prescription (20p per item in 1977). Prescriptions for the following people can be obtained without charge by completing the declaration on the back of the prescription form: children aged 15 years and under, women aged 60 and over and men aged 65 and over, and people holding exemption certificates. These are issued to expectant and nursing mothers, people suffering from certain medical conditions, persons and their dependents receiving supplementary benefit and family income supplement. A part charge is made for all dental treatment and other charges are levied for dentures, but these are free for young persons (anyone under 16 or in full-time attendance at school) and expectant and nursing mothers. Charges are also made for spectacles.

HEALTH SERVICE COMMISSIONERS

Health Service Commissioners for England and Wales have been introduced by the National Health Service Reorganization Act, 1973, to investigate complaints against the relevant health bodies.

Both these commissioners are only removable on an address from both Houses of Parliament and their salaries are paid directly out of the Consolidated Fund. They are therefore in the same independent position as High Court Judges.

The main functions of these Health Service Commissioners are to investigate:

(1) An alleged failure in a service provided by a relevant health body—Regional Health Authority, Area Health Authority, Family Practitioner Committee, Public Health Laboratory Service Board or any special body appointed before and after 1 April 1974.

(2) An alleged failure of a relevant body to provide a service which it was a function of that body to provide.

(3) Any other act taken by or on behalf of a relevant body in a case where it is alleged any person has sustained injustice or hardship in consequence of the failure or of maladministration.

It is important to note that the Health Service Commissioner is specifically excluded from dealing with:

(1) Professional complaints against decisions of individual doctors or nurses in regard to individual patients.

(2) Any action which is dealt with by the Tribunal set up to deal with serious complaints (see page 14).

(3) Any complaint which is subject to action in a court of law.

SCOTLAND

The reform of the health services in Scotland was introduced by separate legislation, the National Health Services (Scotland) Act, 1972. The general principles of the new legislation are the same—the removal of all community health functions from local authorities and the establishment of a unified health service. The main difference between the reform in Scotland and that in England is that a single tier system has been chosen. There are 14 Health Boards which will deal with the running of the health services.

The Secretary of State for Scotland is responsible to Parliament and the Scottish Health Services Planning Council advises the Secretary of State and reviews the development of health services in Scotland. A series of national consultative committees formed from members representing the professions providing health care and treatment, advise the Scottish Health Services Council.

A new body called a *Common Services Agency* provides the Scottish Health Services Council, the Scottish Health and Housing Department and the 14 Health Boards with certain executive and advisory services including:

(1) major building project control,
(2) complex management service provision,
(3) health service staffing and training,
(4) secretarial services for the Scottish Health Services Council.

In the Scottish health services reorganization much emphasis has been laid on *integration of services at patient level* and not only at senior management level. There is also emphasis on the need to plan health services to meet the needs of patients and to make the best possible use of the staff, money and physical resources. Team work in all aspects of the health services is stressed as well as the involvement of doctors and clinical workers in management matters.

There are two important new advisory committees introduced in the Scottish health services reorganization:

(1) A University Liaison Committee which advises on undergraduate and postgraduate teaching and research.
(2) An Area Consultative Committee representing doctors, dentists, nurses, midwives, pharmacists and ophthalmic and dispensary opticians which advises on all professional matters.

WALES

Although the health reorganization in Wales was introduced by the same legislation as in England—the National Health Service (Reorganization) Act, 1973—there are important differences between the health services in England and in Wales. No regional tier of authorities has been set up in Wales. The Secretary of State for Wales has overall responsibility to Parliament for the health services in Wales. In addition he has four main duties:

(1) to determine health policies in Wales,
(2) to allocate resources between the eight Area Health Authorities,
(3) to ensure that objectives are achieved,
(4) to ensure the standards of the health services in Wales are satisfactory.

The *Welsh Health Technical Services Organization* is a new body that has been set up and is directly accountable to the Secretary of State. It has three main functions including:

(1) The designing and building of all major hospital and other capital works.
(2) The running of a central computer service for the health services in Wales.

(3) The negotiation of central supply contracts.

There are 8 Area Health Authorities in Wales. Each consist of 15 part-time members who are responsible to the Secretary of State for planning and providing health services. There is a District organization similar to the English pattern (see page 10). Area Teams of Officers are appointed but, in addition, a senior member of each health profession has been appointed to give advice to the Area Team of Officers and to the Area Health Authority about matters which are relevant to his/her profession.

2   THE MEASUREMENT OF HEALTH

The measurement or assessment of the health of a community is an important feature of any preventive health programme. Rarely is it possible to attempt to carry out all desirable preventive health work in any area at once. It is, therefore, essential to be able to assess the fluctuations in the health of the community from time to time, and to decide which are the worst problems so that they may be tackled first. It is also valuable to be able to compare the health of say one city or country with another. Often, in this way, marked variations will be shown in the health of different places and then a search can be started to discover the reasons behind such differences.

The assessment of the health of any group of individuals may occasionally be made by a series of medical examinations held on all the people in say a factory or a school. But this is only possible where there is complete control over the persons involved and is never practicable for a whole community such as a city, town or country. The measurement of the health of such populations is only possible by indirect methods, by studying various factors such as mortality of the population from different diseases and studies of the incidence of disease. The collection and interpretation of such information is called the study of *Vital Statistics*.

Most of these studies concern either the incidence of disease (*morbidity*) or the proportion of persons within the community dying from disease (*mortality*). Although accurate records of incidence of disease are the more valuable, it is rarely possible to get such figures as there is no method of ensuring that all or even a fixed proportion of cases are reported. It is, however, necessary to know completely the cause of all deaths (for legal purposes), and mortality statistics are usually very complete and certainly more reliable when dealing with very large communities. But even with mortality statistics, difficulties may arise from different standards of diagnosis and from introduction of a new form of treatment which may change the mortality completely. An example of this is typhoid fever. The mortality rate of this disease has fallen over 10 per cent to 1 or 2 per cent following the introduction of ampicillin treatment. Thus, the present mortality rate cannot be used as a reliable indicator of the incidence of this disease.

It is obviously desirable to refer to all statistics in terms of the same unit of population and this is normally per 1000 persons. Thus the *Crude Death Rate* is the number of persons who *die per year per 1000 persons*. The *Infant Mortality Rate* is the number of infants under the age of 1 year who die per 1000 births per year. The *Maternal Mortality Rate* is the number of women who die from causes associated with childbirth *per 1000 total births*.

It is essential to know the population accurately to calculate these various death rates. A *Census*—when the population is counted—is undertaken every ten years and was last carried out in April 1971. The Registrar General calculates the estimated population of all areas in the intermediate years between each Census.

Age Distribution of the Population

The distribution of the various age groups within the population is of interest:

Table 2.1   Age and Sex Structure of Population, England and Wales 1975

	Males		Females		Total	
Age groups	Thousands	Per cent	Thousands	Per cent	Thousands	Per cent
0–14	5829	24.3	5522	22.9	11351	23.1
15–44	9831	41.0	9531	37.7	19362	39.3
45–64	5605	23.4	5936	23.5	11541	23.4
65–74	1926	8.0	2554	10.1	4480	9.1
75+	779	3.2	1710	6.8	2489	5.0

Note that although there are large numbers of males in the population at the younger age groups, the reverse occurs in old age—there are many more old women alive than old men. In 1975 there were 779,000 men aged 75 years and over compared with more than twice as many women—1,710,000.

The proportion of old people in the population has been rising steadily throughout this century. In 1901 only 4.7 per cent of the community was aged 65 years and over compared with 14 per cent today.

The **Birth Rate** is the number of children born per year per 1000 of the population. This is affected by many factors such as the numbers of persons of reproductive age within a population—the higher their proportion, the higher is likely to be the birth rate. The social habits of a country will cause great changes in birth rate—the rate in Poland (a Roman Catholic country with many young persons) is 26.1 (1969) compared with the rate in England and Wales in 1976 of 12.0.

The accompanying graph of the Birth Rate in England and Wales from 1900 to present day shows many fascinating changes. It will be seen that the rate fell steadily to the very low figure of 14.4 in 1933; it fell during the second world war, rose to a peak in 1947, and fell again, only to rise once more to the figure of 18.5 in 1964. Since that year it has steadily fallen to 12.3 in 1975. These changes tell one much about the pattern of human life in those seventy-five years. The high rate in 1900 was associated with a very high death rate among children (15 per cent died before their 1st birthday) so that although the birth rate was high a much smaller proportion of children reached adult life than today. The low rate of the 1930s was connected with the very unstable living conditions between the two world wars. The 1947 peak was the result of many families being re-united after the war. The 1965 high figure is dependent upon many factors, including earlier marriage and greater prosperity. During the last ten years, increasing use of effective contraceptives (the pill), abortion and less prosperity have all played an important part in reducing the birth rate.

The **Crude Death Rate** (the number of persons dying per 1000 population) is of little value, as the relative population in towns is never known accurately. When there is a large number of aged inhabitants, the number of deaths in such a community is bound to be higher, irrespective of the living conditions in that area. More important is the **Standardised Mortality Ratio** (S.M.R.) which makes allowances for changes in the age structure of the population (1968 = 100). In 1975 the S.M.R. was 93.

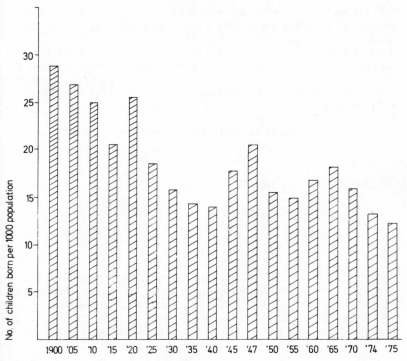

FIG. 2.1 Birth rate, England and Wales

The **Infant Mortality Rate** is the most useful death rate to give an indication of the living conditions of any area. The infant mortality rate is the number of infants who die under 1 year of age per 1000 live related births. It is a measure of the number of children who die before reaching their first birthday per 1000 born alive. In 1976 in England and Wales the rate was 13.9 which means that 1.39 per cent of infants born alive, died in their first year of life.

The improvement in the infant mortality rate, and consequently in the living conditions in England and Wales, is shown by the following table:

Table 2.2   Infant Mortality Rate per 1000 live births, England and Wales

1900	138
1910	112
1920	84
1930	60
1940	56
1950	29.6
1960	21.8
1965	19.0
1970	18.2
1974	16.3
1975	15.7
1976	13.9

If a graph is drawn of this improvement (see fig. 2.2), it will be seen that there has been a general improvement throughout the last sixty years. There have, however, been periods such as the 1930s when the change was very slow due to the slowing down of the improvement in the living conditions. The infant mortality rate is a very sensitive indicator of changes in the living conditions. It can, for instance, be used to compare the living conditions of large cities in the same country. The rates for many large towns in England were as shown in Table 2.3.

Table 2.3   Infant Mortality Rate per 1000 live births, 1971

Solihull	10
Northampton	13
Reading	15
Bristol	17
Nottingham	21
Liverpool	22
Preston	26
Rochdale	29

Many people find it difficult to believe that the excellent paediatric services available in some cities do not improve matters. They do play their part in keeping the deaths lower than they might otherwise be, but the main factors affecting an infant's health are the conditions in the home. An increase of unemployment leading to deterioration of living conditions would increase

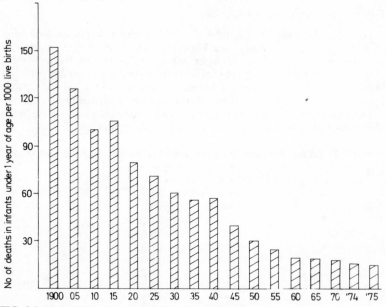

FIG. 2.2   Infant Mortality Rate, England and Wales

infant deaths. Also, a political decision relieving unemployment might do more to prevent infant deaths than many medical improvements. In other words, this is a good example of how social factors must always be considered as well as medical factors among the most valuable preventive health influences.

A very important part of the infant mortality rate is the number of infant deaths which occur in the first four weeks of life—the *neonatal mortality rate.* In 1976 this was 10.7 per 1000 live related births showing that two thirds of the first year deaths occur within the first 4 weeks of life.

The majority of neonatal deaths occur in the first week of life and this is now called the early neonatal mortality rate. Thus in 1976 the neonatal mortality rate was made up as follows:

Early neonatal mortality rate	8.4
Late neonatal mortality rate	2.3
	10.7

The **Perinatal Mortality Rate** is a combination of the number of *stillbirths* and of *deaths* that occur within the first week of life, per 1000 total births—early neonatal death rate.

In 1976, in England and Wales the perinatal mortality rate was 18.0. (9.6 stillbirth rate plus 8.4 deaths in the first week of life.)

The value of the perinatal mortality rate is that it gives a very good indication of the hazards to a baby immediately before and after birth. The gradual fall of the perinatal mortality is shown in Table 2.4.

Table 2.4   Perinatal Mortality (England and Wales) 1950-76

1950	37.4
1955	37.4
1960	32.8
1965	26.9
1970	23.5
1971	22.3
1974	20.5
1975	19.0
1976	18.0

The **Maternal Mortality Rate** is another very interesting death rate which is the number of women who die from causes associated with childbirth per 1000 total births. It is a measure of the risk attached to childbirth, as deaths are only counted if they are directly related to the pregnancy.

Examination of the maternal mortality rate shows that since 1900 it has improved dramatically. In 1975 it was 0.11 compared with 4.81 in 1900. But examination of the way in which this rate has improved shows that it did so quite differently compared with the infant mortality rate. Comparison of the two graphs shows that the infant mortality rate gradually and steadily improved throughout the last sixty years, whereas the maternal mortality rate hardly altered from 1900 to 1930 and at the beginning of the 1930s had actually risen to 4.1. It then fell very quickly after 1937. The reason for this difference is that the maternal mortality rate is affected by entirely different factors—whereas the infant mortality rate is mainly connected with living conditions, the *maternal mortality rate is related to the standard of obstetric practice.* An advance in obstetrics, particularly the introduction of chemotherapy and antibiotics cut down the dangers of deaths from puerperal infection so dramatically after 1937. It was later followed by further advances reducing the danger of toxaemias and haemorrhage.

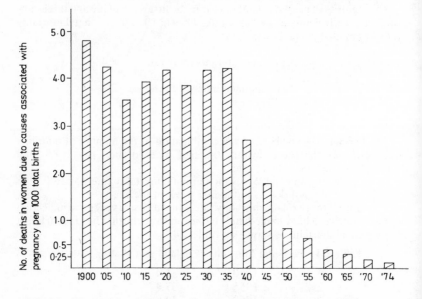

FIG. 2.3   Maternal Mortality Rate (including abortion), England and Wales

The way in which these statistics have helped to suggest improvements in obstetrics and thus prevent much illness is described in detail in the next chapter.

STUDIES INTO THE INCIDENCE OF DISEASE

Morbidity Measurement

Many different methods of measuring the incidence of disease (morbidity) are currently being perfected. Some of the most interesting of these have been connected with hospital records in special studies now undertaken called Hospital In-Patient Enquiry and Hospital Activity Analysis. Studies have also concentrated upon the certificates of sickness received from general practitioners. Examples of these are now given:

Table 2.5 Discharges and deaths from hospital due to non-psychiatric illnesses in Great Britain per 100 000 population in 1971

Order	Males		Order	Females	
1	Other causes	2541	1	Pregnancy, childbirth and puerperium	4003
2	Disease of digestive system	1189	2	Other causes	3292
3	Diseases of respiratory system	1089	3	Diseases of digestive system	914
4	Injuries (other)	846	4	Diseases of respiratory system	781
5	Diseases of heart	640	5	Neoplasms, malignant	572
6	Neoplasms, malignant	622	6	Injuries (other)	567
7	Disease of peripheral circulatory system	475	7	Disease of peripheral circulatory system	502
8	Fractures, dislocations, sprains	450	8	Diseases of heart	452
9	Disease of musculo-skeletal system	346	9	Diseases of musculo-skeletal system	402
10	Diseases of nervous system	181	10	Neoplasms, benign	368
11	Neoplasms, benign	137	11	Fractures, dislocations, sprains	336
12	Tuberculosis	54	12	Diseases of nervous system	175
			13	Tuberculosis	35

[From report on Hospital In-Patient Enquiry (England and Wales) 1971—Department of Health and Social Security.]

It is interesting to note the differences between the sexes although there are many general similarities. Apart from pregnancy in women, and 'other causes' in both sexes, the next two commonest conditions in hospital are diseases of the digestive and respiratory systems. In men injuries other than fractures come next, but in women malignant neoplasms although these do not reach the level of this cause in men. Diseases of the heart represent a level of 566 in men, but only 412 in women, but benign neoplasms in women are much higher, 403 compared with 157 in men. This is almost certainly due to the large number of benign tumours of the uterus-fibroids necessitating hospital treatment. In both sexes, tuberculosis is the last in order, but men total 54, but in women, only 35. This is due to the incidence of almost 2:1 men:women in this disease.

Another interesting method of illustrating statistics is given in the diagram (fig. 2.4, p. 26) demonstrating the average number of beds occupied daily in hospitals in Great Britain in 1973.

This diagram emphasizes the large number of hospital beds occupied by mental disability, 45 per cent (mental illness 29 per cent and mental subnormality 16 per cent). Although in number of discharges (see Table 2.5) pregnancy is the largest in women, the total maternity beds number only 4 per cent due to the short stay in hospital of many such cases.

An analysis of the causes of sickness certified is another useful way of studying disease morbidity. The following tables (pp. 26–7) are taken from the Digest of Health Statistics for England and Wales published by the Department of Health and Social Security.

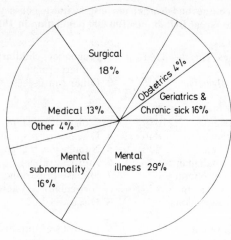

FIG. 2.4   Average number of beds occupied daily by cause, Gt. Britain, 1973.

There are two main ways of presenting such returns:
(1) new spells of sickness (rate per 1000 at risk (Table 2.6)),
(2) days of sickness per 1000 persons at risk (Table 2.7).

Table 2.6   The 12 Commonest Causes of New Spells of Certified Incapacity, 1970 (rate per 1000 persons at risk)

Males		Females	
1. Influenza	109.6	1. Other diseases of the respiratory system	126.7
2. Other diseases of the respiratory system	88.3	2. Influenza	95.2
3. Bronchitis	46.1	3. Symptoms and ill-defined	60.1
4. Symptoms and ill-defined	42.9	4. Infections and parasitic diseases	44.0
5. Diseases of digestive system	38.1	5. Diseases of digestive system	31.0
6. Infection and parasitic diseases	36.1	6. Bronchitis	30.1
7. Accidents	32.6	7. Mental illness	22.3
8. Arthritis	27.4	8. Accidents	20.1
9. Sprains and strains (joints)	20.8	9. Arthritis	17.4
10. Other diseases of musculo-skeletal system	15.2	10. Diseases of urinary system	15.9
11. Skin diseases	14.2	11. Skin diseases	14.4
12. Mental illness	13.3	12. Sprains and strains (joints)	9.6

Table 2.7   The 12 Commonest Causes of Days of Certified Incapacity, 1970 (rate per 1000 persons at risk)

Males	Days Lost	Females	Days Lost
1. Bronchitis	2249	1. Mental illness	2439
2. Symptoms and ill-defined	1623	2. Symptoms and ill-defined	2091
3. Other diseases of the respiratory system	1419	3. Other diseases of the respiratory system	1548
4. Ischaemic heart disease	1419	4. Arthritis	1265
5. Mental illness	1372	5. Influenza	1161
6. Influenza	1366	6. Bronchitis	1020
7. Arthritis	1142	7. Other diseases of the circulatory system	851
8. Diseases of the digestive system	1132	8. Diseases of the digestive system	847
9. Other diseases of the circulatory system	1018	9. Diseases of the nervous system	842
10. Accidents	864	10. Ischaemic heart disease	681
11. Diseases of the nervous system	810	11. Other diseases of the musculo-skeletal system	475
12. Other diseases of the musculo-skeletal system	572	12. Diseases of breast and genital system	466

It is most interesting to compare these tables and to note the differences between the sexes. In some diseases although the number of spells of sickness is small, the number of days lost is very large. Ischaemic heart disease is not among the 12 commonest causes of new spells of sickness, but is third in importance in days lost in males and tenth in females. The importance of mental illness in women is immediately emphasized, being first in days lost (fifth in men) and seventh in spells of sickness (twelfth in men). Bronchitis causes more than twice the number of days lost in men (2249) compared with women (1020). This may well be a reflection on the problems caused by excessive smoking in men compared with women.

Communicable diseases

Before any effective preventive measures can be planned, it is essential to know the levels of incidence of the disease in question.

Most serious communicable diseases must be notified to the 'proper officer'. In metropolitan districts, single London districts and in single district Area Health Authorities, this will normally be the Area Specialist in Community Medicine (Environmental Health). In other areas, it will be the appropriate District Community Physician. This allows the disease to be completely investigated and its source of infection discovered, as well as allowing a complete record of the incidence of the disease to be maintained. The story of the virtual disappearance of a disease like *Diphtheria* is told by its notifications.

Table 2.8   Diphtheria, England and Wales

Year	No. of cases notified	
1942	41 404	←Mass immunization
1943	34 662	programme started
1944	23 199	
1945	18 596	
1946	11 986	
1947	5 609	
1948	3 575	
1949	1 881	
1950	622	
1954	173	
1958	80	
1962	16	
1966	20	
1970	22	
1972	5	
1974	3	
1975	9	

Statistics clearly show that the disease is no longer a major problem and also illustrates the success of the immunization scheme introduced in 1942 and continued ever since.

Another interesting record is the fall of new cases of *tuberculosis* over the last 27 years:

Table 2.9   Notification of Tuberculosis, England and Wales 1950-70

Year	Males	Females	Total
1950	26 969	22 389	49 358
1952	26 558	21 536	48 093
1954	23 694	18 654	42 348
1956	20 683	14 821	35 504
1958	17 955	11 883	29 838
1960	14 351	9 254	23 605
1962	11 749	6 096	17 845
1964	10 013	5 006	15 019
1966	8 257	4 109	12 366
1968	7 705	4 623	12 328
1970	6 998	4 282	11 280
1975	6 541	4 277	10 818

Another useful feature which these records emphasize is that the *problem of tuberculosis in men and women is changing in proportion.* In 1950, the ratio of male and female cases was 1.2 to 1. But by 1964, the cases in women had fallen much faster and now the ratio is 2.0 to 1.0, men to women. By 1974, it had changed again to 1.6 to 1.0. An accurate knowledge of how the problem changes is essential to ensure that preventive health measures are concentrated where they will be most useful. In the example given above, it is clear that more effort is now called for to attack the problem of tuberculosis in men than women. A fuller discussion of how the problem of tuberculosis in men is concentrated in the ages 45 years and older is given in Chapter 7.

Non-communicable disease

The value of a study into the incidence of non-communicable diseases is that it emphasizes the relative problems of different diseases and stimulates research into factors which are connected with their incidence. Very often special research studies are started in this way and lead to important preventive factors being demonstrated. A good example of this is given by *cancer of the lung*, which has increased so alarmingly from 6439 deaths in 1940 to 33 000 in 1974 (see fig. 2.5) that research has been undertaken to find out the reasons for this increase. From 1962 to 1970 the Royal College of Physcians studied this problem and their reports stated that cigarette smoking is an important cause of lung cancer. The latest report goes much further and indicates clearly the risks involved in cigarette smoking. Although a study of the statistics of cancer of the lung shows that it could be reduced by persuading people to stop or not to

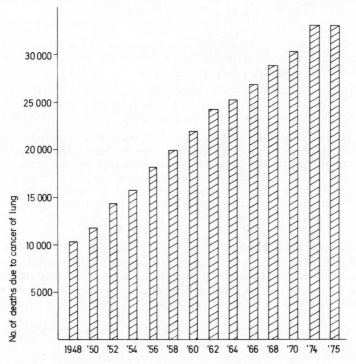

FIG. 2.5   Deaths from cancer of lung, England and Wales

start smoking—the actual ways in which the nation can be persuaded are more complex. The Chief Medical Officer's Report of the Department of Health and Social Security for 1970 estimates that four out of every ten deaths in men could be prevented by the abandonment of cigarette smoking.

Further studies using statistics have shown that cancer of the lung has also increased in city dwellers compared with those living in the country due to the excessive atmospheric pollution in cities. The differences are not nearly as great as between cigarette smokers and non-smokers but sufficient to lead to further research.

The incidence of *Ischaemic Heart Disease* is another problem in which statistics are being utilized widely in promoting research into possible causative factors. During the last fifteen years there has been a marked rise in the number of persons in England and Wales who die from this cause. The rise in the number of persons dying from ischaemic heart disease is startling as seen by the following table:

Table 2.10　Deaths from Ischaemic Heart Disease 1961-74 England and Wales

Year	Males	Females	Total
1961	66 400	50 100	116 500
1966	75 300	54 800	130 100
1970	80 800	58 500	139 300
1974	87 900	65 500	153 400

It will be seen that recorded deaths from ischaemic heart disease have increased by nearly 50 per cent in the last 15 years. The actual increase may not be as great as suggested because:

(1) the population in 1974 contains a larger proportion of elderly eople and this group is one in which death from ischaemic heart disease is high;
(2) the level of diagnosis may have improved.

To make certain that all factors are understood, investigations are taking place into the incidence of ischaemic heart disease. Many different factors are being investigated, such as the effect of increased exercise, diet, or the stature of individuals. Many of these researches will take a long time to complete but it is hoped that they will eventually lead to a much better understanding of the various factors which cause ischaemic heart disease and thus to methods by which it can be prevented.

Social factors in disease

A further method that can be employed to study disease is to compare the incidence or mortality of illness by grouping the family by occupation. The Registrar General divides the population in England and Wales into five different social classes on the occupation of the father or each family as follows:

Class I Professional (Lawyers, Doctors, Clergymen, Bank Managers, Company Directors)
Class II Intermediate (Farmers, Teachers, Nurses, Local Government Administrative Officers)

Class III Skilled (Mineworkers, Clerical Workers, Shop Assistants, Typists, Skilled Industrial Workers)
Class IV Semi-skilled (Agricultural Workers, Semi-skilled Industrial Workers)
Class V Unskilled (Building and Dock Labourers, Estate Labourers, Porters, Costermongers)

Studies have been made by the Registrar General into the mortality of these five social classes in different diseases. The results show marked variations. They are usually given in a form called *Standardized Mortality Ratio*. This is given as a ratio of 100 in the number of deaths expected in a group for a specified year. A group experiencing exactly the same deaths as expected would have a Standardized Mortality Ratio of 100. If the Standardized Mortality Ratio is 75, then the group only has 75/100 or 3/4 of the expected mortality (it is enjoying less mortality than expected). If the Standardized Mortality Ratio is 200, it means the mortality is 200/100 or twice as great as normal.

Examples of how the deaths from various diseases vary widely with social classes (expressed as S.M.R.s) is given below in Table 2.11.

Table 2.11 Standardized Mortality Ratio in men aged 15-64 by Cause and Social Class 1961 (England and Wales)

	Social Class				
	I	*II*	*III*	*IV*	*V*
Tuberculosis	40	54	86	108	185
Diabetes	81	103	100	98	122
Ischaemic Heart Disease	98	95	106	96	112
Malignant Neoplasm (all sites)	73	80	104	102	139
All causes	76	81	100	103	143

In the case of tuberculosis, the mortality is much lower in Social Class I and II than in V. This is because the chance of this disease spreading is greater in persons with inferior living conditions. With ischaemic heart disease the variations between social classes is slight. However it is interesting to note that social classes I and II have improved their position in the last ten years particularly when compared with social class V.

When all cancers are considered together, there is an increase with social class, and study of cancers at different sites of the body shows other differences between the Social Classes.

When the mortality from all causes is considered, it will be seen that Class I enjoys the least mortality with 76 per cent of normal and Class V the worst with 143 per cent.

Value of vital statistics

Each day in the wards, the nurse will constantly be concerned with various measurements to assess the health of the individual patient—taking temperatures, collection of specimens, assisting with biochemical or radiological investigations.

She should look upon vital statistics in their various forms in the same way, for they represent the most reliable means available to measure the health of the community. No nurse needs become an expert in vital statistics, but a simple knowledge and understanding of their uses will make her work more interesting. Community health problems change continuously and if the rudiments of the subject are understood, then the effects of these changes will mean so much more.

3   MATERNAL HEALTH SERVICES

In England about 600 000 births occur each year and the task of caring for the health of each mother is an important part of the preventive and curative health services.

Unlike almost any other speciality in medicine, the care of women in their pregnancy is mainly a physiological one—there is nothing abnormal in the process itself. This has helped to create a very strong preventive service and the emphasis of all the maternity services is to avoid and prevent abnormalities occurring, and to recognize and diagnose them early so that if they do occur, their effects are minimized.

The maternity services are more closely co-ordinated than almost any other type of medical care in this country. This is essential as the maternity service is shared between hospitals and the domiciliary services.

HOSPITAL CONFINEMENTS

The proportion of mothers having their babies in hospitals varies with the area but in 1975 over all England 96 per cent had their confinements in hospital or nursing home and 4 per cent at home. However, there were many variations and many towns showed a hospital delivery rate between 95 per cent and 98 per cent. The tendency throughout the country has been for the proportion of hospital confinements to rise. A priority system to determine who should have hospital confinement is usually operated. The following are the groups of mothers who should *always be delivered in hospital*:

(1) Those in whom there is an abnormality (such as toxaemia of pregnancy or malpresentation, e.g. breech).
(2) Mothers with four or more children.
(3) Mothers over the age of 35 years.
(4) All *primigravidae* (mothers in their first pregnancy).
(5) Mothers living in poor home conditions and for other serious social reasons.

In all areas, it is standard practice for all mothers in one of the above five priority groups to be admitted to a maternity hospital. It is also usual to admit other normal mothers where beds are sufficient, provided, of course, that in doing so, no priority group is excluded.

The ideal minimum time for each mother to spend in hospital after her confinement is ten days. However, there is an increasing tendency for mothers to be discharged earlier than this. By 1975 70 per cent of mothers delivered in hospital were discharged home on or before the 7th day of confinement. The indications are that this tendency will be increased and in 1975 19.4 per cent of mothers were discharged home as early as 48 hours after delivery. There are many social and domiciliary care problems created by such early discharge, for no mother is fit to look after her home at such an early stage of the puerperium and must have special help.

33

DOMICILIARY MATERNITY SERVICES

There is very strict control maintained over all maternity services by a central authority created for the purpose—the **Central Midwives Board**. This body lays down rules for the conduct of all midwives. In addition, under the Midwives Acts, all unqualified persons, who are not either midwives or doctors (or students in training to become midwives or doctors) are prohibited from attending any woman in childbirth except to assist under the personal direction of a midwife or doctor, except in a sudden or urgent necessity. This rule prevents unskilled and untrained persons attending women in childbirth and so ensures indirectly that every woman is looked after by a fully-trained qualified person.

The rules of the Central Midwives Board are supervized locally by the Regional Health Authority who usually delegates this responsibility to the Area Health Authority. These rules include:

(a) Supervision over all certified midwives practising in the area. This covers midwives in maternity hospitals as well as those in nursing homes or employed as domiciliary midwives; in practice, the detailed supervision of midwives in maternity hospitals is left to the senior staff of those hospitals. The area health authority supervises midwives in nursing homes and domiciliary practice. No midwife may practise until she has given her notice to do so to the local supervising authority.

(b) Power to suspend a midwife from practice if it appears necessary to do so, to prevent spread of infection, e.g. it would be dangerous for a midwife who was a nasal carrier of pathogenic streptococci, to continue midwifery.

The Central Midwives Board itself lays down a code of practice and rules for all midwives. These specify the records she must keep, the standards she must follow in her midwifery practice, the drugs she may use, the anaesthetics she shall use, as well as making it quite clear in what medical emergencies she has a duty to call in medical aid. In addition, the Central Midwives Board insists that every practising midwife shall attend a refresher course once every five years.

The rôle of General Practitioner and Midwife

If the mother is to be delivered at home there are three possibilities open to her:

(a) In a minority of cases, her own general practitioner carries out the antenatal care, delivers the patient and the midwife acts as a maternity nurse. Post-natal care also is undertaken by the general practitioner.

(b) In most cases, the general practitioner does the ante-natal care but the midwife delivers the patient calling him only in case of need. The midwife reports delivery to the general practitioner who then completes the post-natal care.

(c) She may choose to be delivered solely by a midwife who, in this instance, accepts full responsibility for looking after the patient in the ante-natal period and in her confinement.

In practice, it is usual for the mother to choose alternatives (a) or (b) as her own doctor is in an excellent position to help and advise his patient in the event of complications. General practitioners who have had special experience in midwifery and who undertake regular domiciliary midwifery, are placed on the 'obstetric list'. They are remunerated at a higher rate for each confinement than doctors who are not on the list.

Organization of a domiciliary midwifery service

Each area health authority employs the midwives who carry out the domiciliary work. At present there are very few private midwives practising.

The midwife can best be described as an expert practitioner of normal child bearing in all its varied aspects. At present, it is recommended that each midwife undertakes no more than 40 home deliveries a year if she is working on her own or 60 if she has, in addition, a pupil midwife assigned to her. She works very closely with the health visitor who should wherever possible be introduced to the mother during her ante-natal care (see page 49).

Each area health authority arranges an adequate midwifery coverage for the whole area. Often each midwife is provided with a house or flat from which to practise, and it is usual for the midwife to have a car for her use. This is particularly important as often she has to reach her patients quickly at any hour of the day or night, and to carry heavy equipment (including mobile gas and oxygen or Trilene analgesia equipment).

Maternity outfits, which include all the necessary sterile dressings for the confinement and puerperium, are supplied free to each mother. It therefore should not be necessary for the general practitioner to have to supply extra dressings for the confinement.

All midwives are trained in giving either Trilene or gas/oxygen analgesia. A medical certificate of fitness for analgesia must be obtained from the patient's own doctor during the pregnancy. An adequate form of analgesia is available today to all mothers confined at home who wish to use it. Modern apparatus is very reliable and is designed to allow the patient to give herself (after tuition), her own gas/oxygen anaesthetic during the first stage of labour. The patient lies on her side, presses the mask with a pressure valve on it over her nose and breathes a mixture of gas and oxygen. As she loses consciousness, her grip relaxes, the mask falls away shutting off the valve and the supply of gas is cut off. She regains consciousness and may repeat the cycle if necessary.

ANTE-NATAL CARE

The prevention of many of the complications of pregnancy rests more with careful ante-natal care than with any other factor. It is the responsibility of the midwife to ensure that adequate ante-natal care is carried out on all her patients.

The mothe r who is to be delivered in hospital usually receives ante-natal care by that hospital. In cases in which it is difficult for the mothers to attend the hospital ante-natal clinic, arrangements are usually made for her to attend her own doctor for ante-natal care.

The pressure on most hospital ante-natal clinics is so great that it is not possible to carry out health education or mothercraft clinics in the hospitals, and the usual arrangement is for the mothers to attend a special health education mothercraft clinic for this purpose. The first ante-natal examination usually takes place at the time of confirmation of the pregnancy, at about the third month of pregnancy.

A complete general medical examination must then be undertaken to ensure the woman has no undetected illness. At this time, a complete record should be obtained of past medical history paying particular attention to any past history of tuberculosis, diabetes and any virus infections from which the patient may have suffered. Chest X-rays are now only carried out if history or symptoms indicate that this would be wise.

The next stage is for a complete obstetric history to be taken of any previous pregnancies paying particular attention to any difficulties and abnormalities which may have occurred, either in her own or the baby's health. In all cases, blood tests should be taken and sent to the laboratory and include:

(*a*) A *Wassermann* or similar test to make certain that the mother *has no hidden infection of syphilis*. If it is found that she has a latent syphilitic infection at the third month of pregnancy and immediate treatment is started, *then a possible congenital infection in the infant can be avoided*.

(*b*) *Haemoglobin* estimation to check the level in each mother. If this is lower than normal, immediate treatment must be started. This is important as haemorrhage may occur later, and the results of such haemorrhage are bound to be more serious in cases where the haemoglobin level is lower than normal.

(*c*) *Blood Group* should be estimated and recorded. In an emergency, such information will be invaluable to enable a blood transfusion to be given quickly.

(*d*) *Rhesus factor* estimation should be carried out. If the mother is Rhesus positive then no problems will arise. If, however, the mother is Rhesus negative, difficulties may occur later affecting the health of her second and subsequent children. If the father is also Rhesus negative then all will be well. If, however, the father is Rhesus positive, which is more likely, then a further blood examination must be undertaken at the 34th week of pregnancy to check whether antibodies have developed in the mother's blood. If they have, then it is likely that the baby will develop serious haemolytic jaundice after birth and may need an exchange transfusion. For this reason, the patient must be delivered in hospital and the neighbouring paediatric unit should be alerted before the birth.

Even when antibodies are absent from a Rhesus negative mother's blood, blood from the baby's umbilical cord should be collected at birth and sent to a laboratory to be tested for antibodies.

Prevention of Rhesus incompatibility by immunization

It is now possible to prevent many of the problems of Rhesus incompatibility by immunization with Anti-D immunoglobulin of Rhesus negative women immediately after their first confinement or miscarriage. The problem in Rhesus incompatibility is due to red blood cells from a Rhesus positive child crossing the placental barrier and entering the mother's blood stream. Shortly after the birth of the first child, the Rhesus negative mother manufactures antibodies against these Rhesus positive red blood cells of her child which, in this way, are then destroyed. In second and subsequent pregnancies, these antibodies increase and, when they recross the placenta barrier and enter the baby's blood stream, they lead to massive destruction of the baby's blood cells usually after birth, but in serious instances, before birth which may lead to a stillbirth.

Immunization with Anti-D immunoglobulin should be given *immediately following the first delivery* of a child or after *a first miscarriage or abortion.* An Anti-D immunoglobulin then destroys the Rhesus positive red blood cells of the baby within the mother's blood stream and there is not time enough for the mother to develop antibodies. Therefore a consequent pregnancy will be like a first pregnancy and no problems will arise. It is, however, necessary in such cases to *reimmunize the mother after all subsequent pregnancies or miscarriages to prevent antibody formation.*

Recommendations in regard to treatment are as follows:

(1) In all cases the Anti-D immunoglobulin should be given within 60 hours of delivery or termination of pregnancy (miscarriage or abortion).

(2) All Rhesus negative women giving birth to a Rhesus positive baby after the 20th week should be screened for fetal cells so that women who have large trans-placental haemorrhages can be given large doses of Anti-D immuno-globulin.

(3) The usual dose of Anti-D immunoglobulin for all Rhesus negative women having had Rhesus positive babies regardless of parity or ABO group, should initially be 100mg. Further doses may be necessary for cases in which large transplacental haemorrhages have occurred.

(4) A standard dose of 50mg should be provided for all women known to be Rhesus negative, having therapeutic abortions up to and including the 20th week of pregnancy, except for those who are sterilized at the same operation. Rhesus negative women whose pregnancy with a Rhesus positive fetus is ter-minated after the 20th week, should receive a dose of 100mg.

(5) The decision to use Anti-D immunoglobulin for Rhesus negative women having spontaneous abortions should be left to the individual clinician.

Dental care in pregnancy

Dental care in pregnancy is very important as the mother's teeth can deterior-ate rapidly at this time. Every mother should, therefore, have a dental exami-nation carried out immediately after the first ante-natal visit and arrangements made for any dental treatment needed to be done at once. Because care of the teeth is so important in pregnancy, special arrangements are made to treat, at no cost, all pregnant and nursing mothers (up to 1 year after confinement)—this free treatment includes the provision of dentures if needed. Area Health Authorities arrange for this dental treatment to be car-ried out by their own dental staff at clinics.

Health education in pregnancy

The first ante-natal visit should be concluded by arranging for the mother to attend various health educational clinics as are available, to learn *mothercraft.* This is especially important to the mother having her first child (primipara) and gives her the opportunity to meet the health visitors who will help care for her baby after its birth.

A visit should next be paid by the midwife or health visitor to the home of the woman to assess whether it is suitable for a confinement. At this meeting, there should be frank discussion about many aspect of the pregnancy. Advice should especially be given concerning the diet for the mother.

Recent research has emphasized that there is a greater risk to the baby of a mother who smokes during pregnancy. In 1974 a health education campaign run by the Health Education Council spelt out these extra risks and pointed out that over 1500 babies annually might not have died if their mothers had given up smoking when they were pregnant. It also emphasized that smoking by the mother can lead to underweight at birth.

Prescription charges are waived to expectant mothers and until their baby is one year old. A Family Practitioner Committee Exemption certificate is needed; this is obtained by filling in Form FW8 obtainable from the doctor, midwife or health visitor.

Diet for pregnancy

A well-balanced diet with a good proportion of high-class protein is required. Many mothers have queer ideas about diet in pregnancy and the midwife must be patient and make certain that the diet required is fully understood. At least a pint of milk should be drunk per day and food-stuffs rich in iron, calcium, phosphorus and vitamins should be eaten. 1 or 2 eggs and a good helping of meat, fish poultry or liver should be eaten per day. Cheese is also a most valuable food in pregnancy.

Vitamin preparations either in the form of tablets or orange juice and cod-liver oil may be obtained from the local clinic, or alternatively these may be taken in the diet by fresh fruit and various fats.

Good well-balanced meals will reduce the likelihood of unexplained prematurity and the incidence of toxaemia of pregnancy.

Maternity Grant and Allowance

These are dealt with in Chapter 18 (see page 228).

Free milk

An expectant mother with two or more children under school age is entitled to free milk, regardless of her family income. The claim should be made on Form FW8 for seven pints of liquid milk or one pack of national dried milk per week.

Free milk is also available to expectant mothers and all children under school age where the family income is below a certain level and to all handicapped children aged 5-16 who are not registered at school and to children attending a registered day nursery.

Continued ante-natal care

Further ante-natal examinations are regularly carried out during pregnancy—at least once a month until the 28th week and then every two weeks until the 36th week and, from that time until delivery, once a week. At each visit an abdominal examination is carried out. The position of the child is carefully observed and recorded during the last weeks of pregnancy and, particularly in the primipara, the *early engagement of the head in the pelvis* is checked. At each visit, the *blood pressure is examined*—it should never rise above 130/90 during pregnancy. In addition, the *urine is tested for albumin* and the legs palpated for oedema.

A careful *record is kept of the weight gain* during pregnancy, especially between the 20th and 30th weeks. If the weight gain exceeds 7 lbs (3.3kg) in this period, especially in young primipara, this should be regarded as an early sign of toxaemia of pregnancy. Such patients should be treated accordingly with a high-protein low-carbohydrate diet and observed very carefully at frequent intervals. If other signs of impending toxaemia develop, especially a raised blood pressure and/or development of albuminuria, the patient should be put to bed and given strict bed rest. She must be admitted to hospital for further treatment, if, in spite of bed rest, signs of toxaemia persist.

Value of ante-natal care in preventing serious abnormalities of pregnancy

It cannot be emphasized too strongly that good ante-natal care can reduce very markedly the dangers of serious abnormalities of pregnancy. Early in the ante-natal care programme of any mother, the posible danger of an ectopic pregnancy must be borne in mind. Ectopic pregnancy was the fourth commonest cause of maternal death in England and Wales in 1970–72 and accounted for 34 deaths. Half of these occurred at home or in the ambulance during transfer to hospital. 7 died in hospital awaiting operation. *Immediate operation* is most important as soon as the diagnosis has been made. Resuscitation should *not* precede operation but be co-incidental with it.

The main dangers of *toxaemia* and *haemorrhage* can both be greatly reduced by careful ante-natal care which leads to early recognition of a developing toxaemia or highlights a possible placenta praevia which could later lead to a dangerous haemorrhage.

Any abnormality discovered in ante-natal work must be completely investigated. The following are a few of the more important abnormalities shown up in ante-natal work:

(*a*) a raised blood pressure
(*b*) albuminuria
(*c*) oedema
(*d*) a loss of blood per vaginam even if this is only slight—a 'show'—may be a sign of placenta praevia.
(*e*) signs that the head of the child has not fully engaged into the mother's pelvis.

This is a very important factor in the primipara in whom the head should be fully engaged by the 36th week and often earlier. If the baby's head in the primipara is not engaged by this time, there is usually an abnormal reason. Either the presentation is faulty (persistent occipito posterior), or there may be an abnormally small pelvis, which is rare today except in immigrant populations, or the pelvis may already contain the placenta—placenta praevia.

As the pregnancy nears its end it becomes even more important that ante-natal examinations continue to take place regularly. It is essential *if a patient defaults from attending* an ante-natal visit, that the *doctor or midwife call on the patient* to find out the reason. In many instances, the reason may only be slackness on the part of the patient but it may be that she has developed some symptom which she does not recognize as serious but which gives her the excuse to postpone her visit. If this symptom is a serious one of say impending toxaemia, the midwife's visit may well be instrumental in ensuring that proper treatment is carried out promptly, which could make all the difference between, in extreme cases, a live child plus healthy mother, or the tragedy of a maternal death with probably a stillbirth.

Pulmonary embolism is the second commonest cause of maternal mortality (after abortion). Its risk rises with age and parity of the mother and is increased by Caesarean section. It is important that early signs are not missed— not infrequently pleuritic pain is present but its significance is often not recognized and the patient is treated with antibiotics. Such pain in pregnancy should always be treated seriously as it may indicate a pulmonary embolism.

Preventive aspects of maternal mortality

At present one mother per 9000 pregnancies loses her life as a result of child-bearing. *Each maternal death is very carefully investigated to find the cause and whether there were any preventable factors in that death.* This enquiry is carried out by a consultant obstetrician and the community physician. The most recent series of such investigations collected together by the Department of Health and Social Security (1970–72) show that of present-day maternal deaths 53.9 per cent have some clear preventable factor. In other words, 53.9 per cent of the deaths caused by childbearing could have been avoided if some mistake or omission had not occurred. The types of 'preventable factors' vary from mistakes and omissions on the part of the doctors and midwives to lack of co-operation on the part of the patient herself.

When the great improvement over the last thirty-five years in the safety of child bearing is examined (1 mother per 230 pregnancies died in 1936), it is easy to be complacent, but the fact remains that if all the preventable factors were reduced, and theoretically this is quite possible, only 1 in (approximately) 19 000 women would die, not 1 in 9000 as at present. Detailed examination of the types of mistake which lead to most of these deaths show that lack of adequate ante-natal care was the most important reason.

The seven most common causes of maternal mortality in the 1970–72 survey of maternal deaths in England and Wales were:

1.	All other causes	139
2.	Abortion	81
3.	Pulmonary embolism	61
4.	Toxaemia	47
5.	Ectopic pregnancy	34
6.	Sepsis	32
7.	Haemorrhage	27

MANAGEMENT OF LABOUR IN DOMICILIARY PRACTICE

although only 4 per cent of births now occur at home, the following account is still given in detail as all home deliveries may present special hazards for the mother and child.

Whether or not a doctor has been booked, usually the midwife is first notified when labour starts. She then visits the mother, examines her and if she confirms that labour has started, arranges for the care of the mother. The midwife will bring to each patient the anaesthetic apparatus plus all the equipment for the labour.

As explained earlier, the mother may give herself a whiff of anaesthetic either using gas and oxygen or Trilene. Of the two forms, Trilene is a little more popular for domiciliary practice today. Its advantages are:

(a) that the apparatus is very light to carry;
(b) that a longer period of analgesia is obtained;
(c) that there is less danger to the child.

The midwife reports that labour has started to the doctor. As most doctors have to carry on their busy practices, it is usual for the midwife to continue to look after the mother, only calling the doctor in if some difficulty occurs.

A high degree of surgical cleanliness is maintained by using sterile gowns, masks, cap and sheets. Increasing use is being made of disposable sterile materials, and these now include disposable towels, masks, caps and syringes. Sterile gowns used remain at the patient's house to reduce any risk of carrying infection from patient to patient.

Midwives may leave the patient for a short time in the first stage of labour. They can give either pethidine or more commonly pethilorfin which has less depressant effect upon the child. Because labour often progresses rapidly after giving such drugs, no midwife should leave the patient after administering pethilorfin.

After delivery, the midwife may have to resuscitate the child. She has a special mucus sucker to clear the air passages of the child and also a sparklet oxygen resuscitator. This is a most valuable and neat apparatus which supplies oxygen at a measured rate for the baby to breathe and has made the problem of resuscitation much safer and surer.

If, during the labour, the midwife meets with any abnormality, she must send immediately for medical aid whilst staying herself to continue the delivery. Some Area Health Authorities provide their midwives with portable radio transmitters so that they can summon medical aid without having to leave their patient. In most cases, medical aid will be provided by the doctor who is booked, but, if no doctor has been booked, the midwife sends for the nearest doctor who is on the obstetric list.

In more urgent and serious problems, the midwife may send for a special mobile hospital team, the 'flying squad'.

Use of hospital emergency team (flying squad)

Each maternity hospital has a mobile team (flying squad) consisting of an experienced obstetrician (consultant or registrar) plus an anaesthetist and an experienced hospital midwife, who will go to the home of a patient to deal with any emergency in labour. Usually such a team is taken to the patient's home by an ambulance. The most usual reasons for the flying squad to be sent for are:

(1) *Sudden haemorrhage* (particularly post partum haemorrhage). In this instance the flying squad helps to resuscitate the patient and for this purpose they carry blood and plasma for transfusion. They may also have to control bleeding and deal with its cause (say retained placenta). It is much safer to resuscitate the patient first and then move her to hospital.

(2) *A complication of labour*—an example would be difficulty in the second stage of labour such as unexpected breech presentation.

Flying squads have proved themselves to be most valuable especially in large cities. One of their great values is that they are readily available at all times. The general practitioner may be out on his rounds when help is urgently needed and it is reassuring to the midwife to know she can always obtain skilled help by calling out the flying squad.

In a recent survey, it was found that the flying squad was called out to 1 in 70 domiciliary births—the causes being for haemorrhage in a third of the cases, for retained placenta in half the cases and for varying difficulties in the remainder.

The co-operation card

Although domiciliary midwifery usually does not involve the hospital service, co-operation, as shown by the value of the flying squad, is of great importance. One of the most important features of co-operation between the services, is that every woman whether booked to have her baby in hospital or at home *should always carry a special co-operation card with her.* This is a simple record of her ante-natal care, containing all the information which is invaluable in an emergency. If a patient booked for home confinement suddenly requires urgent hospital admission, this co-operation card is of great value in arranging for prompt and proper treatment. It records the results of all tests carried out including blood group, and, therefore, valuable time is saved.

Post-natal care

Six weeks after delivery a full post-natal examination should be carried out either at the hospital where the baby was born or at the doctor's surgery or at the clinic. By this time the health visitor should be acting as one of the most important advisors to the mother (see Chapter 4).

Care of the unmarried mother

The care of the unmarried mother in pregnancy is a special problem. At present approximately 8.8 per cent of all births occur in mothers who are unmarried. Illegitimacy produces many difficulties and, from the preventive health point of view, the most serious immediate problem is that the disturbed social circumstances surrounding an unmarried mother produce greater hazards to both mother and child. These are mainly connected with the fact that no ante-natal care may be carried out because of concealment of the pregnancy, or the mother may be forced to leave her home due to unsympathetic parental reaction. The extra hazard to the baby in an illegitimate birth is shown quite dramatically in an increased infant mortality rate of 24 for illegitimate births compared with a rate of 16 for legitimate births.

Wherever possible, arrangements are made to help the unmarried mother to stay at home. If the rift so often created between parents and the mother-to-be can be healed, problems tend to be reduced and hospital delivery and possible early adoption may provide the best result possible.

In about half of the cases, however, the unmarried mother cannot and does not wish to stay at home. In such instances the best solution is for her to be helped by a social services department who can usually arrange a suitable hostel or similar unit, many of which are run by church or voluntary organizations. After the birth of the child in hospital many unmarried mothers need time to decide whether they wish to care for the child or arrange adoption. An increasing number now care for their children and are accommodated in flats or sheltered housing (see below).

Sheltered housing for unmarried mothers

Independent accommodation for the unmarried mother where she can live with her baby for 1½–2 years after confinement has been introduced in a few areas and has proved very successful. By using day nursery services the mother is able to go out to work and lead a more normal independent life than is possible in hostels. Later permanent housing is often arranged and with the help of a day nursery run by the social services department the mother can undertake a full-time job.

German measles and pregnancy

An attack of german measles (rubella) during the first three months of pregnancy can result in harmful effects to the child in utero. These include a higher proportion of abortion and stillbirths and an increased incidence of congenital abnormalities, especially congenital cataract in the child, congenital heart disease or deafness. Research has also shown a much higher infant mortality in children of mothers who develop rubella during the first three months of pregnancy. Active immunization is advocated for all girls aged 11–13 years (see page 76). Vaccination of women of child-bearing age is not recommended routinely. If an adult woman wishes vaccination, a serological test, which can be carried out by the Public Health Laboratory Service should always be undertaken. Vaccination should only be offered to those who are seronegative (approximately 10 per cent of adult women without a history of rubella). *It is most important that a woman is not pregnant at the time of the vaccination, and does not become pregnant for at least two months after protection.*

Any mother who has never had german measles or has not been immunised and who comes into contact with the disease during the first three months of pregnancy should be promptly *immunized with immunoglobulin*. This normally prevents an attack of german measles developing and protection lasts for six weeks and so avoids subsequent congenital deformities in the child.

It is, however, essential to realize that any danger from german measles *only occurs within the first three/four months of pregnancy* and that a later attack does no harm. Therefore, reassurance is often needed when this occurs.

FAMILY PLANNING

Under the National Health Service (Family Planning) Act, 1967, Area Health Authorities have power to provide family planning advice together with the issue of contraceptive substances and appliances *on medical and social grounds.*

The National Health Service (Family Planning Amendment) Act, 1972 placed vasectomy on the same basis as other contraceptive services which the

Area Health Authority may provide. Advice from the Department of Health and Social Security stressed:

(1) The importance of counselling by a doctor experienced in family planning before operation.

(2) That there should be adequate facilities for operation (including access to inpatient beds should a complication arise).

(3) That adequate follow-up should be provided including an alternative method of contraception *until a negative semen has been obtained on two occasions at an interval of one month.*

Family planning services are based on three important principles:

(1) Comprehensive family planning advice should be available free of charge to all who wish to have it. It is hoped to increase clinic provision and more advice will be given to maternity and abortion patients. The domiciliary service is very important and arrangements are made to give such advice in the patient's own home if it is unlikely that she will attend a clinic.

(2) General health education should include information on family planning.

(3) Free contraceptive supplies should be available for those who need them (with the exception of the condom). This category includes those with a special social need who would otherwise be unlikely to undertake effective contraception and those with a financial need.

People with a *medical need* for family planning pay the standard prescription charge. Others pay the full cost of their supplies.

General practitioners also have a very important rôle in family planning and such advice should be offered by general practitioners and health visitors without waiting for people to ask for it. General practitioners can prescribe contraceptive pills on prescription forms EC 10. (Recent advice from the Committee on Safety of Drugs has emphasized that oral contraceptives with a low oestrogen (20–50 mcg) were associated with a lower incidence of thromb-embolic complications than earlier pills.)

A new development is that a few progressive authorities have developed a special domiciliary family planning service for women who suffer from ill health, live in poor social circumstances and are overburdened with too many children and who do not find it easy to attend a clinic. Southampton and York pioneered this service which is now being started in other areas. Such domiciliary family planning services have been shown to be of great value in helping to prevent deterioration in such problem families.

Abortion

Since the introduction of the Abortion Act, 1967, abortion is now legal in the United Kingdom where it can be shown by two doctors that the physical or mental health of the mother or children would be seriously affected by the birth.

The abortion (except in an emergency) must be performed in a National Health Service Hospital, in one of the approved services hospitals, or in a place for the time being approved by the Secretary of State for the purposes of the Act.

By the end of 1976, there were 61 approved nursing homes in England. During 1976, 101 000 abortions were performed in England.

Considerable variation has been shown to occur throughout the country dependent upon the attitude of gynaecologists and other doctors in different areas. The details of the present law are capable of considerable variations of interpretation: pregnancy may be terminated by a doctor if two registered medical practitioners are of the opinion, formed in good faith:

(a) that the continuance of the pregnancy would involve risk of the life of the pregnant woman or of injury to the physical or mental health of the pregnant woman or any existing children of her family, greater than if the pregnancy were terminated, or

(b) that there is a substantial risk that if the child were born it would suffer from such physical or mental abnormalities as to be seriously handicapped.

In assessing (a) account may be taken of the pregnant woman's actual or reasonably foreseeable environment.

4   PREVENTIVE CHILD HEALTH SERVICES

CARE OF THE NEO-NATAL PERIOD (birth to 28 days)
The first month of any child's life, the neo-natal period, is one of the most critical, for it is then that the majority of infant deaths occur. In 1975 the number of infant deaths under one year per 1000 live births was 15.7 but 11.0 was the rate for deaths in the first month (neo-natal mortality).

It is, therefore, very essential that great care is taken with the newborn child.

Haemolytic disease of the new born (see also pages 36–37)
Cases which are not immunized with Anti-D immunoglobulin
At birth every baby of a Rhesus negative mother should have some blood removed from the umbilical cord to test for antibodies which, if present, will gradually destroy the baby's red blood corpuscles by haemolysis. If a blood test shows antibodies to be present, the baby must be immediately admitted to hospital for treatment which may include an exchange blood transfusion, which sets out to dilute continuously the antibodies and thus reduces the danger of blood destruction.

A simple perspex device for estimating quickly the depth of jaundice in a newborn child (an icterometer) should be carried by every midwife and is useful to help judge the depth of jaundice. It is especially useful to record the intensity of jaundice in premature babies.

Neo-natal cold injury
Although for many years it has been widely recognized that the very small premature baby is liable to suffer from chilling, only recently has it been shown that this is also a hazard in normal children. If any baby, in its first life, becomes seriously chilled, its body temperature may fall dangerously low to 32.2°C (90°F) or lower. The baby then becomes quiet and difficult to rouse and feed, and is cold to touch, and later oedematous. It may have a deceptively florid red complexion.

The prevention of this serious neo-natal cold injury is to make certain that the *temperature of the room in which the baby is sleeping does not fall below 18°C (65°F)*. Each midwife has a wall thermometer which she leaves near the baby's cot to record the present temperature and the minimum temperature. This check and control is most important in winter but is still needed in summer, when unexpectedly low air temperatures may occur at night.

CARE OF THE PREMATURE CHILD (low birth-weight baby)
The majority of illnesses and death occur in that group of small babies called *premature babies*. As it is never possible to say with complete accuracy the length of any preganancy, a baby whose birth weight is less than 5 lb 8 oz (2.5

kg) is classified as a premature birth. About 6.8 per cent of all births are premature.

The chance of survival of a premature baby falls rapidly as the birth weight falls. With babies between 5 lb (2.25 kg) and 5 lb 8 oz (2.5 kg) birth weight 1.2 per cent die within 28 days but, for premature babies whose birth weight is under 3 lb 4 oz (1.5 kg), 39 per cent die within 28 days.

The special hazards for a premature child is shown by the neo-natal death rate (deaths within first 28 days of life) for such children is 8-9 times greater than for all children.

The reduction of mortality from prematurity can be achieved in two ways:
(a) by avoiding prematurity
(b) by improving care facilities for premature babies when born.

Avoidance of prematurity

In many instances the exact cause of prematurity (of labour starting when the child is smaller than normal) is unknown. However, in some cases it will be associated with severe toxaemia of pregnancy, and first-class ante-natal care which reduces the incidence of toxaemia will also reduce prematurity.

Another important cause is chronic malnutrition in the mother and this is why the diet of each mother in pregnancy should be carefully watched. Other general poor living conditions, overwork, increased frequency of infection, are also associated with a larger incidence of prematurity. There is a greater frequency of unexplained prematurity in women from Social Class IV and V (unskilled labourers, etc.) than in Social Class I and II. Improvements in living conditions will help reduce the incidence of prematurity.

Care of premature babies

It is convenient to subdivide all premature babies into two groups—those under 4 lb 8 oz (2 kg) and who should be admitted to a special premature baby unit, while the second group, from 4 lb 8 oz (2 kg) to 5 lb 8 oz (2.5 kg), can be looked after at home, provided the home is satisfactory, and there is a special premature baby nursing service.

Premature baby units

Special baby care units for premature babies should be provided in all large maternity departments. Such units are usually designed to look after a small number of such infants. The care of the very small premature baby calls for skilled nursing using many modern techniques.

Incubator care will be needed for the very small premature babies. The value of the incubator is that it makes it easier to control the atmosphere in which the baby lives. There are three main factors:
(1) The *temperature* of the incubator should be maintained so that the baby's temperature is kept *constant* at just below 36.6°C (98°F).
(2) There should also be a *constancy* in the *relative humidity* within the incubator. It is best to keep the relative humidity (level of water vapour in the air) constantly at 60 per cent.
(3) The *supply of oxygen* should be controlled. As many tiny premature babies

have difficulties in pulmonary ventilation, oxygen can be most helpful, but *great care must be taken not to increase the level of oxygen too high,* for if this is done, there is danger of damaging the retina of the new-born child and producing blindness (retrolental fibroplasia). Thus, the level of oxygen is always kept at the lowest which will give adequate relief to the child.

Feeding

There are many different methods of feeding used. Because of the effort of sucking, breast feeding is rarely possible for very tiny premature babies. But human breast milk may be used from a human *breast milk bank* which is set up at the largest paediatric centres

Various forms of artificial feeding are used—often carefully graduated weaker feeds of dried milks. These are always given more frequently than usual, two or three hourly, and often given by nasal catheter, allowing the measured feed to flow by gravity.

Prevention of infection

To all premature babies, *infections* represent their greatest hazard. The development of a respiratory infection in a small premature baby may be so sudden and dramatic that death may result after a few hours. The prevention of infection is, therefore, one of the most important tasks of the nurses in charge of a premature baby unit. Strict rules must always be observed. No one (other than the parents) should enter a premature baby unit unless his presence is essential. No one should enter if suffering from an infection (cold or upper respiratory infection). Everyone must wear sterile cap, mask and gown. Hand washing must be scrupulously carried out.

Great care must be taken not to carry infection from one cot to another and very high nursing standards are essential. New admissions, especially if admitted from home, should be separated from those already being nursed within the unit.

In some units, air sterilization is practised using ultra-violet light filters.

Domiciliary care of premature babies

Larger premature babies, between 4 lb 8 oz (2 kg) and 5 lb 8 oz (2.5 kg) weight can be looked after quite adequately at home provided the home is reasonable and that there is a *domiciliary premature baby service.* This is run by the area health authority and consists of specially trained nurses, who may also be midwives, whose task it is to look after the premature baby at home. The nurse has special equipment such as cots, feeding equipment and thermometers, which can be loaned to the mother. The nurse then teaches the mother all the necessary information especially about feeding problems, and follows this up by daily or twice-daily visits to each baby, to ensure that care is continuing properly. In this way, continuous advisory help is available to the mothers of premature babies and it also ensures that, if any difficulty or illness occurs in the premature baby, it can be promptly treated. In many cases ignorance plays a large part in producing problems in the premature baby looked after at home. The great value of the domiciliary premature baby service is that it reduces the effects of such ignorance.

The nurses who staff the service must do nothing else and must be careful to avoid introducing infection within the home. Visitors to see the premature baby must be as carefully controlled as in hospital. In practice, infection is not as large a problem in the domiciliary premature baby service as in the hospital premature baby unit as there is much less danger of cross infection from other patients and staff, as the human contacts with the premature baby at home are so limited.

CARE OF THE NORMAL BABY

Rôle of the Health Visitor in home care

The standard of care and help given to the mother within a month after her confinement in helping with the care of her child is most important. It is during this period that the basis of sound health in the child can be formed.

The care of the child immediately after birth will be by the staff of the maternity ward, if a hospital birth, or by the midwife who delivered the baby, if the birth took place at home. When the mother leaves hospital after delivery, the midwife will take over the care of the baby for a few days. After the 14th day, the main adviser to the mother, apart from the family doctor who is usually only consulted if some illness or extreme difficulty occurs, is the *health visitor*.

The health visitor is a highly trained nurse who, after gaining her S.R.N. and at least Part I Midwifery examination, must then attend a year's full-time course in social and preventive medicine and qualify by examination for her Health Visitor's Certificate. Her main task is to ensure that all the family and especially the children are as healthy as possible. She achieves this by a continuous process of health education and strives to become the welcomed adviser to the mother and family in all health matters.

If possible, the health visitor meets the mother during her pregnancy at mothercraft classes so that she gets to know her. She takes over from the midwife the responsibility of the mother and child at the 14th day after delivery. It is best if this can be done by midwife and health visitor meeting at the mother's home on the 14th day. Increasingly it is becoming usual for the link up between the general practitioner and health visitor to be closer and closer and so the health visitor today will usually be working with the general practitioner who is also in charge of the patient.

Infant Feeding

The first important factor upon which the health visitor concentrates is the feeding of the child. Wherever possible, breast feeding is recommended. To establish breast feeding much patience and encouragement are needed. The temptation to give up the effort because of difficulties is often great and much anxiety is felt by mothers who fear the baby is not getting enough milk on the breast. Recently a national committee was set up (under the chairmanship of Professor Oppe) to look into present day practice in infant feeding. Its report expressed unanimous opinion that the best food for babies is human breast milk, and that, when successfully managed, breast feeding of 4 to 6 months duration offers many advantages to both mother and infant. Since the risks of ill health are greater when the baby is very young, breast feeding for even as short a period as 2 weeks is an advantage.

It is difficult to be certain of the proportion of babies that are breast fed today. Recent investigations have shown much variation but the proportion is about 25 per cent of all children at 4 months. The increased tendency for some mothers to return to work after two months, the ease and convenience of artificial feeding both have tended to reduce breast feeding. It is, however, important to realize that the infant who is breast fed for five to six months has the best possible start in life. There is a lot of evidence that the incidence of all types of infection is lowest in breast fed children. In outbreaks of infantile gastroenteritis, which can be a dangerous disease in young infants, the breast fed child almost invariably escapes. There is also evidence that the personal bond between mother and child is never closer than between the mother and her child whom she has breast fed.

Health visitors therefore do all they can to encourage breast feeding. If, however, this is not possible, then the health visitor constantly helps the mother by giving her advice regarding artificial feeding. Today the majority of artificial feeding is by use of dried milks which are reconstituted just before the baby's feed. There are many different kinds. Suitable dried milks are available at area health authority maternity and child health clinics at low cost. It is also usual to sell other proprietary baby foods at such clinics.

The health visitor also advises and helps the mother with all the small day-to-day problems of bringing up a baby. Frequency of feeding, clothing to be used, temperature of room, general hygiene and the sleep patterns of babies, are all dealt with. A most important aspect of a health visitor's work is that she visits the home of the mother and there can give practical advice and health education in the mother's own environment, which the mother herself will have to use. She can make certain the mother fully understands all the intricacies attached to caring for a small baby. Each health visitor hopes that the mother will look forward to her visits as those of a friend and adviser.

Child Health Clinics

By the end of the first month, it is expected that the feeding of the baby will be progressing satisfactorily and the mother is invited to bring her baby along to the nearest child health clinic.

The child health clinic is the local headquarters of the preventive medical services for children and is designed as a place to which the mother can bring her baby at any time for help and advice.

No ill child should ever be taken to such a clinic but should be seen by the general practitioner. In cases of doubt, the health visitor will call to see the baby at home. It is important to avoid bringing ill babies to child health clinics because of the risk of spreading infection.

Each child health clinic is staffed by the same health visitors who do the home visiting in the area. The functions of the clinic include:

(a) *Education in mothercraft*—this is carried out by individual tuition to mothers or group tuition with help of leaflets, posters, lectures and films. All health education topics are discussed, including the avoidance of accidents in the home.

(b) *Sale of infant foods* including:
 (i) Suitable dried milks
 (ii) National Cod-Liver Oil

(iii) Concentrated Orange Juice

(iv) Vitamin A and D tablets for expectant and nursing mothers (these also contain calcium, phosphate and iodine)

(v) Certain other baby foods.

Mixed feeding in infants usually starts any time between 12 and 15 weeks. There is a wide variety of special baby foods now available which are usually sold in tins or jars and are made up from many types of strained baby foods made from many meats and vegetables. There are also many different cereals available so that any baby now gets used to a wide variety of new tastes.

(c) Routine medical inspection—A doctor attends the clinic and sees the mother and examines the child on her first visit and usually at three months, six months and one year, and subsequently annually. The doctor is also available if the health visitor or mother wishes to see him in between their routine examinations, the purpose of which is to check that the baby is perfectly fit and to discover any abnormalities as soon as possible.

(d) To give advice on minor problems as they arise. Much of this will be done by the health visitor during home visits but mothers are also encouraged to visit the clinic if they have problems in between home visists. Feeding problems and difficulties connected with the development of the child are usual reasons for such visits.

(e) To give protective immunizations to infants. These immunizations which can also be given by the general practitioner in his surgery, are fully discussed in Chapter 6 and include immunization against whooping cough, diphtheria, tetanus, poliomyelitis and, in girls, rubella.

SCREENING TESTS TO DISCOVER UNSUSPECTED ILLNESS

During the first few months of a baby's life, it is important to carry out various checks on the health of the child to make certain that all abnormalities are spotted (such tests are called 'screening' tests).

Phenylketonuria

This is a rare metabolic disease (incidence approximately 1 in 10 000) in which the metabolism of the infant is faulty and poisonous phenylalanine metabolites are produced which eventually lead to a marked retarded mental development, and the child develops severe mental subnormality. If treatment is started when first symptoms of mental subnormality show themselves, it is too late. However, if the disease can be diagnosed within a few weeks of birth, and the child given a special diet, this mental deterioration can be avoided.

Every child has a simple blood test—the Guthrie test—carried out on a specimen of blood taken from the baby between the sixth and fourteenth day of life. Several spots of blood from the young infant are collected from a heel prick on to specially absorbent filter paper. In the laboratory a small disc is punched out of each of the blood impregnated filter papers and up to 100 individual discs are placed on a special agar plate containing a spore suspension of *Bacillus subtilis*, and an inhibitory substance Phenylalanase acts as an antagonist to the inhibitor; after incubation in positive tests growth of the organism will be observed around the blood disc.

In 1975 about 95 per cent of babies born in the United Kingdom were tested for phenylketonuria.

Congenital dislocation of the hip

Another good example of a condition which, if diagnosed very early, can be quite simply and completely treated, but which, if diagnosed later, is difficult to treat and may lead to permanent disability, is *congenital dislocation of the hip.*

It is now known that the main cause of this condition is inadequate development of the acetabulum of the pelvis.

There is a simple test (eliciting Ortolani's or von Rosen's sign) which the midwife or health visitor should carry out on all babies at birth and at monthly intervals until the child is 4 months old. In this test, the hip of the child is manipulated from the adducted to the abducted position while the thigh is flexed. A positive result is indicated by a 'click' or 'snap' being produced during the test and corresponds with the dislocated femoral head moving into the proper position in the acetabulum.

If the test is abnormal, the child should be referred without delay to an orthopaedic surgeon. Treatment is simple and consists of maintaining the hips continuously in abduction until the subluxation has been corrected. The constant pressure of the head of the femur in the centre of the acetabulum causes it to deepen and develop normally. After treatment for six to nine months, the danger to the infant of congenital dislocation of the hip disappears.

Special screening examination for 'at risk' infants

Many more specialized screening tests, such as detailed examination of an infant a few months old for deafness, are more complicated and take longer. The vast majority of such congenital disabilities occur among about 13–14 per cent of infants in whom the family history, the obstetric history, or post-natal history is in some way abnormal. Infants in this group are referred to as the 'at risk' groups. These include infants in whom:

(1) *Family history is suggestive of*
Any deafness, blindness or cerebral palsy
Any known congenital abnormalities
Mental disorder

(2) *Obstetric history* is abnormal. These include any illness or abnormality of the mother in pregnancy—rubella, excessive vomiting, threatened abortion, toxaemia, multiple pregnancy, premature birth, asphyxia, prolonged labour.

(3) *Post-natal problems* including difficulties in sucking, convulsions or any serious illness in the first few months of life.

For all children coming within this 'at risk' group, special attention should be paid during the first five years of life. Certain additional screening examinations should be carried out and these include testing for deafness. Such tests take place continuously but specially at age 8–11 months and 2–2½ years. Health visitors do these at home and in the clinic.

The follow-up of children in the 'at risk' groups is the responsibility not only of the health visitor but also the general practitioner and special paediatric departments. If only all these are warned of the greater possibility of all forms of congenital abnormalities in the 'at risk' groups, the danger of late diagnosis of abnormalities will be very largely avoided.

CARE OF NORMAL CHILDREN, 6 MONTHS TO 5 YEARS OF AGE

The preventive care of children from six months to five years of age continues along similar lines. Periodic visits are made to the child's home and his progress is checked from time to time at the child health clinic or by visits to his own doctor. The two approaches which are followed are:

(a) checking that normal progress is being maintained,

(b) complete investigation of any illness or abnormality discovered.

Normal stages of development in children

Normal progress in any child is checked by watching the various stages of growth reached, and checking that these are not late in appearing. The normal baby should be expected to sit with support by 3rd or 4th month and by 7th month to sit alone. By the 8th or 9th month he can usually stand with support and he probably will stand without support between the 10th and 14th months. Walking will follow shortly after he can stand without support. Crawling or creeping usually occurs about 9th or 10th month but may not always be shown.

In the past, probably too much attention was paid to a baby's weight as indicating progress. It is still useful in indicating change in progress—a sudden loss of weight or halting in the gain in weight always calls for further investigation. However, no reliance should be placed on tables giving 'normal' weights for children of different ages due to the wide variations commonly seen in normal children.

Usually a *baby will double his birth weight by five months and treble it by twelve months.* Sudden changes in weight—say suddenly ceasing to gain weight—are indicators to be used as other signs and symptoms for further full investigation. There is much individual variation. In particular, care must be taken not to stress to the mother too much the baby's weight, for it should never be her main guide to his progress. It is interesting to note that some of the fittest babies who have been breast fed are often lighter than average but are usually very active and alert.

The general behaviour of the child is an important guide—he should be a happy active child constantly exploring his home in an inquisitive way. That he should feel secure in his home is important.

Sphincter control of the bladder of a baby is slow to develop. It usually does so at the end of the first year and may not be completely reliable until the child is 2½ to 3 years old. It is important that the mother realizes this for futile attempts to train the baby too young may only cause undue irritation and tensions, and may later produce the opposite effect in enuresis. These and other problems should be freely discussed between the mother and health visitor and, in this way, most of the difficulties will be avoided.

Weaning from either breast milk or from bottled feeds commences between three and six months of age. Today, with the many specially prepared foods for weaning (including tinned foods) this is simple. In many clinics, such foods are sold and the health visitor is always there to advise on their use.

The development of speech in a child is a very important stage. The first primitive efforts to produce speech start at 7 or 8 months of age. The child begins to imitate what he hears and to associate persons and objects with the sounds he makes. By 1½ years of age, he should be using simple words and simple sentences.

A very slow development of speech should always lead to a careful re-testing of hearing. The completely deaf child hears nothing to imitate and unless taught by special methods, will never speak. The other important reason for severe retardation of speech is lack of normal mental development. Further examination in such a case will show retardation in other stages of physical development.

Clothing and shoes

As the child begins to walk, it is most important that his clothing and shoes always fit him. Many crippling deformities of the feet have been produced by ill-fitting shoes at all ages. As far as possible, shoes with wide fitting toes should be selected. It is also important to make certain that the child's socks are the correct size. If they are too short, they will exert a constant pressure on the toes and may lead to overlapping of toes and other deformities. Because no two children have similar shaped feet, it is always wise not to pass on shoes to younger children of the same family. This can, however, be safely done for loose fitting wear such as wellington boots.

A constant watch should be kept on the way in which the feet of the toddler are developing. Minor deformities such as flat feet, pes cavus and rigid feet, can be spotted easily. All respond much more readily to treatment at this age than later. Early diagnosis can thus do much to prevent subsequent problems.

Intestinal infestations

Minor infestations with *threadworms* are quite commonly seen at this age. The worms often migrate from the rectum to the buttocks at night time leading to much itching and irritation. This is often the cause of toddlers sleeping fitfully. Diagnosis is easy—examination of the anus shows the tiny migrating worms. Once diagnosed, treatment with modern drugs is easy using piperazine phosphates, and prevents further problems.

SAFETY OF YOUNG CHILDREN

As the child grows up, he becomes more and more inquisitive and thus may become more liable to accidents and illnesses.

In England and Wales just over 1,000 children aged 0–14 years are killed in accidents each year *excluding traffic accidents*. 593 of these die from accidents within the home and about one third of these are infants under one year of age.

Temperature

Excessive heat or cold can be dangerous (see also page 46 for neo-natal cold injury). Older babies can also be affected to a lesser degree; no infant should go out of doors in very cold or foggy weather. Babies also ought to avoid intense heat and a pram can become a heat trap. The hood should be kept down in sunny weather and a sun canopy should be used. Under no circumstances should a baby be left in an unventilated car in summertime.

Prams

The brake must be tested regularly. Cat nets must be used as a cat may snuggle against a baby's face for warmth and suffocate him. A baby harness should be used later in a pram for all infants sitting up.

Cots and bedding

Pillows are unnecessary and dangerous to young babies for their use may lead to suffocation. Under no circumstances should a cot be painted using lead paint as the child may later suck the sides of the cot and be poisoned.

Feeding

It is possible for a baby to choke on a bottle propped up in a cot or pram. No baby should ever be left alone with a bottle and all feeding must be carefully supervised.

Prevention of home accidents

The most common accidents include:

(1) Inhalation of food or other objects leading to obstruction and suffocation
(2) Mechanical suffocation
(3) Fire
(4) Falls
(5) Poisoning.

Each year children under five years of age die as a result of such accidents in the home. All are preventable and continual efforts are made by health visitors to reduce these casualties. Mothers are taught the dangers of letting young children play with unsuitable objects, such as plastic bags, the importance of fireguards and flameproof clothing, the dangers of unprotected stairs and of brightly coloured medical tablets, many of which are poisonous to young children, and which look so like sweets to them.

Some area health authorities have gone as far as introducing a special loan scheme for fireguards and all are constantly engaged in health education efforts to reduce the needless loss of life and invalidism caused by these tragic home accidents.

Care of acute illness in the child aged 1 to 5 years

In families, it is not unusual for the younger children to become infected with the common childhood infectious diseases, measles, whooping cough, scarlet fever. Treatment is similar to that of older children but it is always important to remember that such illnesses may be the starting point for various chronic minor inflammatory and catarrhal conditions such as tonsillitis, sinusitis, or otitis media.

With modern chemotherapy and antibiotic treatment many of the serious chronic conditions such as otitis media can be avoided *provided that early diagnosis is made and treatment started.* It is important that such acute infections in children are treated promptly.

The treatment of the child with enlarged tonsils depends:

(i) on whether the child has successive attacks of tonsillitis;
(ii) whether there is associated respiratory obstruction from enlarged and inflamed adenoids;
(iii) whether infection spreads to involve the ear.

If any of the above three are present, tonsillectomy should be carried out as soon as the child is well again. Prompt removal of the adenoids in such children is likely to prevent serious otitis media. Tonsils today are rarely removed just because they are enlarged.

Various squints may become obvious in this age group and the doctor or health visitor should always check if there is any sign of such defects. Early diagnosis and effective treatment will do much to reduce the likelihood of chronic and serious problems later.

Notification of congenital abnormalities

Congenital abnormalities have been made notifiable by local health authorities to the Office of Population Censuses and Surveys since 1967. This followed the demonstrations that pre-natal infections such as rubella or the use of drugs in pregnancy such as thalidomide, have caused congenital abnormalities. It was felt that it is essential to maintain some continuous observations in the country on the level of congenital malformations so that any increases will be noticed at once.

In 1974 in England 12 143 infants were born with some congenital abnormality (2.3 per cent of all births). Many of these abnormalities are slight. The commonest abnormalities reported are: talipes, hydrocephalus or spina bifida, anencephalus and cleft lip or palate.

The mortality among babies born with a congenital abnormality is higher than normal.

It is important to realise that the age and parity of the mother are significant features in determining the levels of incidence of congenital malformations; the highest rates are in older women with four or more children (see Table 4.1).

Table 4.1 Incidence of notified congenital malformations by parity and age of mother, England and Wales 1971.

Age group of mother	Rate per 10 000 total births	Parity of mother	Rate per 10 000 total births
Under 20	190.2	0	171.6
20–24	163.7	1	139.6
25–29	153.9	2 & 3	173.4
30–34	164.0	4+	222.9
35–39	186.3		
40+	251.9		

Co-ordination of child health services and education and social services

At all times, it is essential to ensure co-ordination between the child health services and the education and social services. Health visitors and social workers should work closely together (see page 150) and both should undertake domiciliary care for children who are either handicapped or have special problems.

In many handicapped children, the special education (see page 64) which they need should start as early as 2 years of age. Such children when they reach the age of 17 years will become the responsibility of the social services, although all education authorities continue to have some responsibility as regards continuing education until they reach the age of 21.. By arranging a well co-ordinated service involving health visitors, teachers and social workers, continuity of care will make certain that the best possible success in each individual is achieved.

NON-ACCIDENTAL INJURY (Battered baby syndrome)

Another area in which co-operation between child health, education and social services departments is essential is in the control of non-accidental injury. This is dealt with in detail in Chapter 13 (see pages 158–162).

5 HEALTH SERVICES FOR SCHOOLCHILDREN

The prevention of disease in schoolchildren is the concern of all branches of the health services, but special arrangements are made under the Education Act 1944 to safeguard the health of children at school. Each Area Health Authority must organize a comprehensive range of integrated health services for children including a *school health service* run in conjunction with the relevant local education authority. Each Area Health Authority must also appoint an Area Specialist in Community Medicine (Child Health) who is responsible to the local education authority for providing and organizing the health staff for the school health services. Many doctors are employed within the school health service by the Area Health Authority—some being specially trained to deal with handicapped children—and are usually employed full-time whereas others work part time on a sessional basis and in this respect increasing use is made of general practitioners.

The move of the child to school when aged five years is one of the most important changes in his life, for he leaves the comparative peace and security of his own home to mix with dozens of other children in the competitive atmosphere of the classroom and playground at school. Even for the child with brothers and sisters, the move to school is important, but, for the first or only child, the impact of school represents a very great change.

School life in all children covers the next eleven years, many remain at school until eighteen years of age when they move on to a University.

Preventive medicine for any child of school age must very largely be connected with school life. In order to help children to get the most benefit from their education, a highly developed preventive medical service has been built up in the *School Health Service* to ensure that every child's health is safeguarded throughout his school career.

There are two main functions of the school health service:

(a) To make certain that every child is *as fit as possible*. This includes many services designed to diagnose disabilities as early as possible, to allow for correction before they have a lasting effect upon the health of the child. This function also includes the promotion of *positive health*—it is not just sufficient to see that no disease occurs, but there must be a positive programme designed to make every school child as fit as possible.

(b) To arrange the educational programme for various groups of *handicapped children*.

Nursery school

The normal child can gain much from attending a nursery school when aged 3–5 years. The value of such schools which the children usually attend for half a day, is in the social contact made. The child gets used to working with others and this is specially useful for the child and makes the entry into primary school easier. The medical care of children in nursery schools is important and is undertaken by the school health service. Special care must be taken with outbreaks of communicable disease as conditions such as dysentery can rapidly spread in nursery schools if not recognized early (see page 95).

STEPS TAKEN TO ENSURE EVERY SCHOOL CHILD IS AS FIT AS POSSIBLE

The present method of medical examination in schools is a combination of *full routine medical examinations* on all children either just before or immediately after entry into school (5 years) combined with *selective medical examinations during school life.* Just before leaving school (15 years) there is another full examination including a fitness test for employment.

Occasionally the initial examination is replaced by a *pre-school initial medical inspection* at 4 years of age. This has the advantage that a dental examination is possible earlier (when conservative dentistry is more effective) and enables any medical defect discovered to be investigated fully and treated before entry to school.

Routine medical inspections

Each school is visited at least once a year by the team carrying out the routine medical inspection—the school doctor, the health visitor and/or school nurse, and a clerk to assist with clerical work. The medical examination takes place at school, if possible in the specially planned medical inspection room. Each parent is invited to be present and, of course, the presence of the parent is most important in all cases, but specially with the first medical inspection. It is best to summon the parents on a single appointment system so that they are kept waiting as little as possible. About 12 children are examined each morning and afternoon.

A very careful *medical history* is taken from the parent and this is supplemented by the records of the child from the child health service and other sources such as general practitioner records. These should provide a complete story of the child's progress from infancy with full details of any illness, medical problems, immunizations, as well as a brief record of the health of his parents and family. It is best if the health visitor who dealt with the child when a baby also looks after the school which he attends. This is not always possible but is usually the case, for the infant's school is normally in the same district as the child's home. To have the same health visitor working with pre-schoolchildren and with the infant and junior schools, means that she knows a great deal about the background of each child, for she knows the parents and their home.

Any unusual point in the medical history is noted and, if the child is within the 'at risk' group, he will need to be very carefully watched.

A full *medical examination* then takes place by the school doctor. All systems are carefully examined, including the special senses. Apart from testing for abnormalities, particular attention is paid to posture, nutrition and minor orthopaedic problems such as minor foot deformities—pes cavus, flat foot. The intelligence of each child is not tested routinely but, if the teacher raises any doubt about the child's mental ability, a special intelligence test is arranged at once.

Sight testing is carried out routinely on five-year-olds using the Keystone machine which tests visual acuity, colour vision and muscle balance. If any defect is found, a full ophthalmic examination is arranged.

Any child with a squint must be treated immediately. Treatment can be carried out at the nearest eye hospital or special orthoptic treatment can be arranged by the school health service.

The *hearing* of every child should be examined *individually* in the first medical examination when aged five. This can conveniently be carried out by a doctor or health visitor using a sweep test with a portable pure tone audiometer. This is a light portable machine which produces sound of varying volume at frequency ranges from 128 to 8000 cycles per second. Each ear of the child is tested independently—the child being given a small wooden mallet and asked to strike the table each time he hears a sound. Each frequency is tested starting with a loud volume of sound and gradually the volume is reduced until the child can no longer hear anything. This indicates the *threshold of hearing*—the lowest volume of sound at that particular frequency which the child can hear. This test is repeated for each frequency so that a pattern of hearing is established eventually for both ears and at a number of different frequencies. It is important to test hearing at different frequencies as occasionally there is a loss of hearing at one particular part of the sound scale (high-frequency deafness).

Testing the hearing of a five-year-old with this machine in expert hands takes between two and three minutes. About 5 per cent of those tested fail the tests. All who fail should be immediately retested and this usually results in about a third of those who originally failed the test, passing it on the second occasion (they failed the first time not because of hearing loss but because they failed to understand the test). This means about 3 per cent of the original group fail. These children must all be further investigated by an Ear, Nose and Throat Department to establish the cause of their hearing loss.

In many cases, the hearing loss is quite small and, without a special test, might never be discovered. It is, however, most important that any hearing loss, even if small, is discovered early, otherwise it is very likely to interfere with the educational progress of the child, because the child will probably not be working to his full potential. If he is an intelligent child, he may still be progressing quite well in class compared to other children, but he will not be learning as quickly as he ought.

All children with any hearing loss are carefully followed up and, where necessary, a hearing aid is prescribed by the hospital department. Those with minimal hearing loss are always put at the front of the class to make certain they have the best opportunity to hear each lesson.

If any illness or disability is discovered in the routine medical examination, the parent is told about it and a note sent to the child's own general practitioner who then arranges for treatment in the usual way. The school health service is really *a diagnostic service* and not a treatment service, although it is careful to check that the treatment ordered by the doctor is properly carried out by the child. In some cases, the treatment may affect the child's ability to play a full part in some of the activities of the school—such as games. Wherever possible, interference in this way is always kept to a minimum for it is most important that no child should ever think he cannot manage some activity unless this is essential. Close liaison must be maintained between the family doctor and school doctor in this respect.

After the school doctor has examined each child, he indicates those he would like to see again. Whenever any disability is discovered, arrangements are always made to see the child and parent again in a few weeks after treatment. This succeeding examination will take place at one of the follow-up school clinics held weekly. All children who have been found to have disabilities should be seen on the next routine medical examination which the doctor carries out at that school—this will normally be the following year. A perfectly normal child would not be seen by the doctor following the initial medical inspection at 4 to 5 years until the child is to leave school (15 years).

The exceptions to this would be if a sudden illness developed in the meantime or if the parent or teacher were worried about the health of the child—in this case, the child would be seen either at the next visit of the doctor to school or be referred to the follow-up clinic.

A few examples of how routine medical inspection works are given by:

(1) *Normal child*
The child is medically examined at school when aged 5 years and 15 years. In addition the health visitor/school nurse visits the school each term to check on minor illnesses and absentees. A questionnaire is completed by parent and teacher when the child is aged 8 years and 12 years. Selective medical examination is carried out where the answers cause concern.

(2) *Child with constant disability*
Child with defective vision, or some chronic disability such as a scoliosis. This child would be seen when five years old at school, and then on each *annual* routine medical examination carried out by the doctor on the next visit to the school. Also the child may be seen at any time at follow-up clinics.

(3) *Normal child on entry to school who later develops severe illness*
An example would be a child found to be quite normal on entering school at five years but who developed rheumatic fever when aged seven. This child would have been medically examined at five, found normal, and marked to be seen again at fifteen. However, when he developed rheumatic fever at seven, he would be referred immediately on return to school to the school doctor who would then see him regularly as needed and on each subsequent routine medical examination at the school.

This careful 'watching over' process of the health of all schoolchildren should always be carried out in such a way as to help and assist parents, general practitioners and teachers. Any child is seen after any recent serious illness, or if the teacher, parent or health visitor/school nurse is concerned because of unsatisfactory progress or difficulty of any kind.

OTHER FUNCTIONS OF SCHOOL MEDICAL OFFICERS
The good school doctor will visit his schools in between his more lengthy visits to carry out routine medical inspections to check up other points which are important to the health of the child. These include:
(a) Helpful advice about the hygiene in the school. This will include examination of buildings, heating plant, washing facilities and kitchen premises.
(b) Investigation of all communicable diseases. There are always likely to be outbreaks of communicable disease in schools, especially in infant and junior

schools. Much time can be saved by prompt and proper investigation. It is not usual today to quarantine large numbers of children, for it is known that this rarely achieves much prevention of disease and always means a great loss of education time. However, bacteriological investigations should be carried out on the close family contacts of certain communicable diseases (such as diphtheria, dysentery, salmonella or enteric infections) and may prevent much unnecessary disease by defining carriers who may spread the disease.

Whenever a case of tuberculosis occurs within a school, complete and careful examination of all contacts (staff and children) must be carried out to make certain that an unsuspected case has not been the cause.

It is best always for all such investigations to be undertaken by the regular school doctor and health visitor for they know so much about the school and its staff and children, and will thus be able to ensure the fullest investigations are undertaken with the minimum interference with school work.

(c) *Health education* should be one of the most important functions of the school health team. The aim is to promote positive health—to assist the teaching staff to improve the health of the child as far as possible. This means encouraging certain non-athletic and underdeveloped children to improve their physique in various ways. Every school doctor should take an interest in the games schedules of the school. But it is also important not to neglect that group of children in every school who, for one reason or another (say bad eyesight) never seem able to excel at traditional ball games. Other forms of active recreation should always be encouraged and special activities such as walking, camping, cycling, rock climbing, skiing, fishing, sailing, skating and riding should, wherever possible, be part of the sporting activities of any school. To benefit from such sports is within the compass of any school today, for the Central Council of Physical Recreation runs a multitude of excellent courses in all areas of the country especially designed to introduce the older school child to such activities. Such an introduction in school life may readily play an active part in maintaining the health of the adult later after he has left school.

Special subjects in health education must be tackled such as sex education, care of teeth and education to prevent children starting to smoke. None of these topic are easy to put over successfully and often more can be gained by example. In this respect, the behaviour of all the teaching staff is most important—a campaign to stop children from starting to smoke is unlikely to succeed unless the staff is also prepared to help. Attempts must always be made to see that health education comes into ordinary education wherever possible so that it is a continuously active process rather than a sudden strenuous campaign.

(d) *Immunizations* should always be encouraged in schoolchildren. Booster doses of diphtheria and poliomyelitis immunization should be given to those who have had prior courses against these diseases. For children who have never been immunized, primary courses of immunization should be arranged at school. The aim should be to make it as easy as possbile for the child to be immunized.

BCG vaccination against tuberculosis should be offered to all schoolchildren aged 12 to 13 years who are then Mantoux negative (see page 75).

Arrangements should be made to immunize all girls against rubella between the ages of 11 and 13.

(e) *The discovery or ascertainment of all groups of handicapped children* is another function of the school doctor who also has the important task of advising on the education of such children.

Cleanliness inspection

In addition to the health inspection visit, the health visitor visits each school frequently. She does this for these reasons:

(i) to note which children are absent from school so she can pay a home visit to help and advise;

(ii) to carry out certain screening tests—repeat any hearing tests and test the vision of seven-year old children;

(iii) to carry out regular cleanliness inspections on schoolchildren.

About 2 per cent of all schoolchildren are found to have evidence of infestation with head lice. These infestations are mainly in the form of nits—the eggs of the head louse. Arrangements are always made for the cleansing of the child at a convenient school clinic and for subsequent examination to make certain that there has not been a recurrence. It is also essential for the health visitor to visit the home, for often members of the family are involved and, in such cases, to treat the schoolchildren only will achieve little. Particular attention on such home visits must be paid to examine the hair of the older members of the family.

Another disease in which it is important to treat all the family and which occasionally is found in schoolchildren is *scabies.* Modern treatment with benzyl benzoate solution is most efficient and soon controls such infestations, provided *all infected members of the family are treated simultaneously.*

School clinics

School clinics are provided so that schoolchildren can attend follow-up clinics and have minor ailments treated without having to spend much time away from school.

Treatment is not really part of the school health service but there are so many problems connected with getting children's eyes tested for glasses that it has been found most convenient for an eye specialist to hold *an ophthalmic clinic* in a school clinic periodically. The Area Health Authority co-operate with the Education Committee in arranging this service.

Occasional special *orthopaedic clinics* are held in school clinics by orthopaedic consultants to treat and follow up the large number of minor orthopaedic problems always found in a school population. Such clinics are of special importance in country areas where attendance at a hospital outpatient department may be difficult.

Preventive dental treatment in schoolchildren

A comprehensive preventive dental service is an important part of the school health service.

Unlike the rest of the school health service, the school dental service is both a diagnostic and treatment service.

A visit is paid by the dental surgeon to each school every six months and every child is examined dentally and notes made of all defects. Each child is then called for individual treatment by the dentist in the following weeks. Treatment is usually carried out at the dental clinic which normally is attached to the school clinic. In remote country areas dental clinics may be mounted in a mobile caravan so that the treatment centre can be taken and parked at the school. This arrangement allows treatment of every child to be carried out without taking the children away from school for long periods.

Most school dental services have facilities to carry out orthodontic treatment, on children with crowded and misplaced teeth. Effective orthodontic treatment in the school child can prevent many dental problems later. It is, however, most important that orthodontic treatment is started early enough so that the permanent teeth can develop correctly.

There is a shortage of dentists in the school dental service and, to help overcome this, *dental hygienists* work under the personal direction of dentists tackling certain tasks such as the scaling of teeth and doing some fillings.

In 1973 a report of a study of the dental health of children 5–15 years in maintained schools was published. It showed that very few children avoid dental decay—7 out of 10 of the five-year-old children had evidence of past or present decay. Among teenagers the proportion was more than 95 out of 100. Some evidence of gingivitis was found in half of the children by the age of 17.

There was also marked regional variation and this may be connected with either the natural or artificial fluoridation of water supplies.

CARE OF THE HANDICAPPED SCHOOL CHILD

A subsidiary, but most important function of the school health service is to arrange for the most satisfactory education of all handicapped schoolchildren whether this handicap is physical or mental.

The individual problems of the different groups of handicapped schoolchildren are discussed below, but there are certain basic principles which apply to all handicapped children:

(1) Every care must be taken to make certain that the degree of handicap is diagnosed and discovered *as early as possible.*

(2) *Education and special care must be started early*—in some cases as early as two years of age and continued later than normal. With many handicapped young persons education may continue until the age of 21.

(3) Improvisation is always helpful, and the aim must be to make each child *as independent as possible.*

(4) The best solution for any handicapped child is always that one which is as *near normal* as possible. There are many ways by which a severely handicapped child can be educated:

In an ordinary school
In a special class in an ordinary school
In a special day school
In a special residential school
At home.

In some cases, it is necessary to start the handicapped school child in a residential special school, but the aim should always be to rehabilitate the child gradually so that if at all possible, he finishes his education in an ordinary day school. In this way, he will be better prepared to fend for himself when he finally leaves school and to earn his living as a handicapped child.

Handicapped schoolchildren can be divided into a number of different groups although recently there have been some doubts raised about the value of such a categorisation.

(i) Blind
(ii) Partially sighted
(iii) Deaf
(iv) Partially hearing
(v) Delicate
(vi) Educationally subnormal (Moderate)
(vii) Educationally subnormal (Severe)
(viii) Maladjusted
(ix) Physically handicapped
(x) Epileptic
(xi) Speech defect
(xii) Dyslexia

The details of these groups are as follows:

Groups (i) and (ii): Blind and partially sighted

Blind children have no useful sight and must be educated by non-visual methods. Education in nearly all cases takes place in a residential school except in the largest cities. Blind children often start their training at the age of two years in the Sunshine Homes run by the Royal National Institute for the Blind.

Partially sighted children have very poor eyesight but, with special assistance, they can be taught using visual methods. Classes must be very small, not more than ten in a class, and special equipment is needed. In most instances, partially sighted children can be taught in special day schools or special classes within day schools.

Groups (iii) and (iv): Deaf and partially hearing

Deaf children have no useful hearing and cannot be taught by auditory methods. It is essential that their training and education should start very young (as soon as diagnosed) and it is very specialized. By remarkable methods which have translated the teaching of sounds into visual tuition, it has been possible to teach speech to totally deaf children who have never heard human speech. In the absence of such teaching, the totally deaf child will also be dumb, as speaking is learnt by the child copying what he hears. Most deaf children are educated in special residential schools.

Partially deaf children can be educated in small classes using auditory methods provided special hearing aids are available. Such tuition usually takes place in special day schools but may be carried out in residential schools.

Group (v): Delicate children

This group is a large mixed group containing many medical and surgical conditions which interfere with a child's education. Chest diseases (such as asthma, bronchiectasis and tuberculosis), heart conditions (rheumatic heart or congenital heart disease), blood diseases, diabetes and alimentary diseases, make up this group which includes any rare disease of childhood which makes a child's education difficult.

Many of these children need at first to be admitted to a residential school to allow their medical and educational condition to be fully assessed. In many instances, the child's education will have been very badly interrupted by repeated illnesses and the child becomes very backward in his education. Many parents of such children worry so much about the child's health that they over protect the child.

Having assessed the child in a residential school and having introduced some degree of stability into his education, it is often possible later to return the child to a special day school.

In the case of a child undergoing a series of serious operations—such as a bronchiectatic child—the regime at a residential school will often build the child up and help his treatment as well as maintaining as far as possible, continuity with his education.

Group (vi): Educationally subnormal children (Moderate)

Educationally subnormal children are children of lower intelligence than normal and are divided into two groups; Educationally Subnormal (Moderate)—E.S.N.(M) and Educationally Subnormal (Severe)—E.S.N.(S).

It is possible to estimate the *Mental Age* of a child by carrying out an Intelligence Test which consists of a series of tests, questions and exercises designed to show knowledge gained and reasoning power.

The *Intelligence Quotient* $= \dfrac{\text{Mental Age}}{\text{Real Age}} \times 100.$

Examples

A child aged 10 years who has a mental age of 12 years would have an intelligence quotient (I.Q.) of 120.

$$\text{I.Q.} = \frac{\text{Mental Age}}{\text{Real Age}} \times 100 = \frac{12}{10} \times 100 = 120.$$

A child aged 10 years who has a mental age of 10 years would have an intelligence quotient of 100.

$$\text{I.Q.} = \frac{\text{Mental Age}}{\text{Real Age}} \times 100 = \frac{10}{10} \times 100 = 100.$$

A child aged 10 years who has a mental age of 8 years would have an intelligence quotient of 80.

$$\text{I.Q.} = \frac{\text{Mental Age}}{\text{Real Age}} \times 100 = \frac{8}{10} \times 100 = 80.$$

It will thus be seen that a perfectly normal average child would have an Intelligence quotient of 100. Above average intelligence gives an intelligence quotient over 100 and below average intelligence an intelligence quotient below 100.

Value of intelligence quotient

The intelligence quotient gives an indication of the level of intelligence. There are other important factors which must also be considered, especially emotional stability and personality.

Intelligence quotients vary roughly as follows:

	120–125+	University entrant
	115+	Bright school child
	90–115	Average school child
	80–90	Retarded school child
	55–79	Educationally subnormal (moderate)—E.S.N.(M)
Under	50–55	Educationally subnormal (severe)—E.S.N.(S)

It is, however, important to realize that *these levels are guides only* and that exceptions occur in this grouping.

In grading an unintelligent child, it is necessary to carry out probably two or more intelligence tests and also to try the child out with a highly experienced teacher before the final decision is made. A very careful search must always be made for any signs of an accompanying physical deformity, such as deafness, which could be responsible for the low result.

Educationally subnormal children need to be educated in either a residential or special day school where the curriculum contains a greater proportion of practical teaching, and where the pace of the teaching is slower than at a normal school

A child who does well in an educationally subnormal (moderate) school may later be able to move back to an ordinary school.

Group (vii) Educationally subnormal (severe)

Following the Education (Handicapped Children) Act 1970 the care of subnormal children attending junior training centres was transferred to the education services. The junior training centre becomes another special school (for educationally subnormal (severe) children).

A particular problem with all unintelligent children is that they are more likely to show behaviour difficulties than normal children. The rate of juvenile delinquency is always higher in such children and the school health and social services are always doing all they can to help reduce this problem. Educationally subnormal (severe) girls with low intelligence quotients are in greater moral danger as they are more easily led astray. It is, therefore, important that this aspect is fully discussed with their parents so that everything can be done to reduce this risk. Surveys of the intelligence of unmarried mothers have shown a greater proportion with low intelligence than in the population at large.

Group (viii): Maladjusted

The maladjusted child is one who is a 'problem child' showing many behaviour difficulties. Because of this, he may become retarded educationally, although his intelligence may be normal.

There are many causes of this problem. Some maladjusted children show emotional instability and even a pyschological disorder, but many just show unstable home conditions including marital difficulties between parents, divorce or separation of parents.

Complete careful diagnosis of the problem is essential. This is rarely a simple procedure. Often repeated visits of the child and his parents to the *Child Gui-*

dance Clinic where a psychiatrist and psychiatric social worker are in attendance, will be necessary before the complete causative factors are unravelled. It is usual for the social worker attached to the child guidance clinic to be a member of the Social Services Department so that there is maximum co-ordination between the social work undertaken in the child guidance clinics and the community social services.

Maladjusted children are always best educated in ordinary schools for they gain from contact with normal children. Any psychological disorders in maladjusted children must be treated appropriately. It will, however, be necessary to attempt to improve the home conditions. Because it is often hard or impossible to improve conditions in a divided home, treatment of maladjusted children is often difficult and calls for much patience. Relapses in behaviour occur and delinquency may complicate the picture. Continued encouragement and understanding by teaching and medical staff will sometimes eventually succeed.

Failure in the maladjusted child may have serious consequences later for these children may drift into criminal behaviour and may even become chronic criminals. There is no doubt that much crime could be prevented by more concentrated medico-social work upon maladjusted schoolchildren.

Group (ix): Physically handicapped

This group contains the very severely handicapped children. Many have serious handicaps often with paralysis and include children handicapped by such diseases as poliomyelitis, muscular dystrophies and other serious orthopaedic conditions. Many such children have never attended normal schools since their illness commenced. It is usual to educate such children in special residential or day schools in which the classes are very small where each crippled child can receive much personal attention.

In those diseases which are not progressive, it is important towards the end of the child's education to do everything possible to make such children as independent as possible. In this respect, it is always wise to try and arrange for the child to spend his last year of school life at an ordinary school even if this can only be arranged by much improvisation—such as arranging special transport. If the child can learn such independence, he is far more likely to succeed in finding and holding a job on leaving school.

Group (x): The child with epilepsy

The majority of children with epilepsy can be educated in an ordinary school provided that:
(*a*) the fits do not occur very often;
(*b*) there is no marked behaviour difficulty—i.e., the emotional stability of the child is reasonably normal;
(*c*) there is a good liaison between the school doctor and teacher who realizes that no other child in the class will come to any harm from witnessing the occasional epileptic fit.

In the case of very frequent major fits or of marked emotional instability, it is wise to arrange for the child to be admitted at once to a special residential school for epileptics for assessment and treatment. Such a school may be run in conjunction with an epileptic colony and its medical and teaching staff will have great experience of such problems. After assessment and correct treatment, in a proportion of cases, it will be possible for the child to return to an ordinary school.

It is, however, stressed that only a small proportion of children with epilepsy ever need to go to such a school, for they can be educated at an ordinary school quite satisfactorily.

Group (xi): Speech defect

Any defect of speech in a school child can be serious unless corrected. Such children may quickly develop emotional difficulties from the frustration of being unable to make themselves readily understood. This in turn will tend to aggravate their speech defect.

A most careful physical examination is needed to exclude a physical cause (defective hearing or deformities of palate) and then regular speech therapy must be started. Speech therapists are on the staff of each school health service to carry out this treatment by relaxation training and speech training.

It is most important that the child with a speech defect stays in a normal school with normal children. Special schools are, therefore, not needed.

Group (xii): Dyslexia

Dyslexia is an interesting condition in which there is a specific language difficulty which shows itself in a series of ways affecting spelling, reading and other language skills. There is always a marked discrepancy between the mental potential of the child (which is often normal) and his educational level despite conventional classroom instruction. The incidence of dyslexia is as high as 3 per cent although many minor cases are missed. In many instances the condition is not recognised until very late with consequent serious loss of learning potential. In many such cases these children may later become language disabled adults.

The cause of dyslexia is not fully understood but most agree that it is caused by a lesion in the central nervous system which has been either present from birth or shortly afterwards. Many children suffering from dyslexia do well if the condition is recognized early, and attend nursery schools and later receive *individual teaching* or teaching in very small groups in which it is possible to mould a teaching programme to an individual child.

Further care of handicapped schoolchildren

Great care is taken to provide special educational services for the handicapped schoolchildren. The eventual success of these special education facilities will depend on the ease with which the handicapped young adult is able to take his place in industry on leaving school.

Great care is needed to ensure that the handicapped child can be trained to carry out a skilled occupation on leaving school. All handicapped children should be carefully assessed as regards their potential at discussions between the specialist careers officers, the school medical officer and social workers of the Social Services Department as well as the disablement resettlement officer of the Employment Service Agency. This co-ordination should take place during the last three years of the handicapped child's school life so that continuity can be maintained in the care of the handicapped child. (See Chapter 14 for further rehabilitation and training available for the young adolescent handicapped person.)

6 PREVENTION OF DISEASE BY IMMUNIZATION

In many communicable diseases, an attack of the disease is followed by a varying period of immunity from further attacks. Not all communicable diseases are followed by an immunity (for example, the common cold is followed by only a very transient immunity) but in many, the length of immunity is substantial and may last many years or even a lifetime. Whenever a person develops an immunity in this way, he does so by manufacturing special disease resistant bodies called *antibodies*.

It is possible to copy this mechanism artificially by introducing into the human body modified bacteria, viruses or their products so that the individual does not suffer from the disease but does develop antibodies and, therefore, does develop an immunity to a natural attack.

Artificial immunization and vaccination relies on this principle. Immunity can either be *active* or *passive*.

In **active immunity** a special product of the bacteria or virus (antigen) is introduced into the body, often by injection, but occasionally by mouth, which stimulates the human body to manufacture its own protective antibodies. The patient himself makes his own protection. Immunity produced in this way is always more satisfactory as it lasts a long time. Its only drawback is that it often takes two to three months for the human body to build up such immunity.

Passive immunity is used when an animal, such as an ox, has first been actively immunized and has itself manufactured antibodies, which are then used to protect man. The great value of this method is that it gives immediate immunity, but this is very transient and rarely lasts longer than about four to six weeks. It is, however, very useful either to treat a patient suffering from the disease, such as diphtheria antitoxin, or to give a temporary immunity to a person who has been in close contact with the disease and who may be incubating it. A disadvantage is that the patient may easily be sensitized to the protein of the animal and suffer from serum sickness.

A more satisfactory passive immunity is obtained by using *immunoglobulin,* the active constituent of human blood which contains the antibodies.

In preventive medicine, great use is made of active immunization but little of passive immunization.

ACTIVE IMMUNIZATION

The dangers of communicable disease are in two main ways:

(i) by a direct invasion process of a certain part of the body. Examples include inflammation of lung in whooping cough, of the small intestine in typhoid or of part of the central nervous system in encephalitis.

(ii) by the bacteria producing a very powerful poison (toxin) as it grows in the body. Examples include diphtheria, tetanus or toxin food poisoning

The first group of diseases is usually protected by using an antigen which consists of either the dead bacteria or viruses concerned (typhoid prevented by Typhoid Paratyphoid A & B Vaccine (TAB), or whooping cough by whooping cough vaccine), or else by a modified or changed live bacteria such as Bacillus Calmette-Guérin (BCG) in tuberculosis, or live virus as in Sabin vaccine in poliomyelitis. In the latter two cases, the live bacteria or virus has been changed (undergone a mutation) which results in the modified bacteria or virus being unable to produce the real disease in the human, but it can produce a modified reaction which then will be followed by an immunity.

Some quite startling successes have been achieved by immunization. Diphtheria is probably the best example. In the ten years before immunization started in 1943, approximately 50 000 cases occurred each year. This meant that at that time, about one person in ten might ordinarily have been expected to suffer from diphtheria at some time during his life. After immunization was introduced, the incidence fell rapidly and by 1950 only 622 cases occurred. This improvement has contained and in 1975 only 9 cases were traced. Immunization has virtually eradicated the disease.

Although other diseases have not diminished so dramatically, there has been an similar improvement in poliomyelitis which has now become very rare.

.It is important to realize that people inherit different amounts of natural immunity. A few fortunate persons have a remarkable natural immunity while many others have little or none. When all people are immunized their natural immunity is added to very considerably. This means that, after immunization, there will still be considerable variation in the amount of immunity in any group which has just been immunized. Over a period of years, protection will gradually wear off. Obviously the person who had very little natural immunity will have his acquired immunity more quickly lowered in this way, to a level where a severe attack of the disease will not be averted.

It is for this reason that, even after immunization, it is never possible to guarantee complete protection against disease in all people. Most diseases are usually avoided in 90 per cent of people by immunization, and even in those who do develop an attack after immunization, it is usually a much milder attack.

Active immunization schedule for a child

Age	Immunization
6 months	Triple immunization (diphtheria, whooping cough and tetanus) plus oral poliomyelitis (1)
8 months	Triple immunization (diphtheria, whooping cough and tetanus) plus oral poliomyelitis (2)
12 months	Triple immunization (diphtheria, whooping cough and tetanus) plus oral poliomyelitis (3)
14 to 18 months	Measles
5 years	Booster: Diphtheria, tetanus and poliomyelitis (oral or inactivated vaccine)
11–13 years	(girls only) Rubella (german measles)
10–13 years	BCG vaccine (to protect against tuberculosis)
15 years	Booster: Tetanus and poliomyelitis (oral or inactivated vaccine)

Triple immunization against diphtheria, whooping cough and tetanus

These immunizations are combined for convenience. They are given first to the young baby at three or five months because of the importance of avoiding whooping cough early in life when it can be a dangerous disease. However, if immunizations are carried out before three months of age, the antibody response (and therefore effectiveness) is slight.

The diphtheria and tetanus portions of this immunization are *toxoids* protecting against the powerful toxins in both diseases. It is impracticable to inject toxin for it has many dangers. If, however, formalin is added to toxin, its chemical compositon is changed and the resultant toxoid is quite harmless, but fortunately it will act as an efficient antigen and produce a good immunity.

The whooping cough portion of the immunization is a true vaccine—it is a mixture of killed whooping cough bacteria. Injection of such vaccine leads to a good immunity for four to five years against attack. This means that immunization will postpone the danger of an attack of whooping cough until after the age of five years, so avoiding the dangerous attacks which occur in very young children under nine months of age.

Whooping cough vaccine should not be given to children with a personal or family history of convulsions, cerebral irritation in the neonatal period, epilepsy or any other disorder of the central nervous system.

The diphtheria immunization requires a booster dose periodically and this is given when the child is aged five years and fifteen years.

Tetanus immunization is boosted by inoculations at 5 and 15 years and afterwards when injury occurs and when consequently there is a danger of developing tetanus.

It is most important to realize that all three doses of the primary immunization at 6 months, 8 months and 12 months *must* be given to ensure complete protection. The first of these injections is followed immediately by hardly any protection—the first dose seems to prepare the body's mechanism for producing antibodies. The second dose is followed immediately by a fair protection while the third dose produces the most lasting protection. *For this reason, mothers must make certain that their children have all three doses.* A system of computerization of all immunization records helps to remind parents of the need for further immunizations in their children.

Poliomyelitis

This disease was a serious threat until widespread immunization was introduced in the early 1960s. Since then only occasional cases have been reported in the United Kingdom. The continued absence of this disease in any epidemic form is due to the success of poliomyelitis vaccination.

Originally dead inactivated (Salk) vaccine was used but in 1962 this was superseded by *Sabin oral* vaccine which has the following advantages:
(1) It is easier to administer—by mouth rather than injection;
(2) It produces an immunity not only to a clinical attack of poliomyelitis, but also to a carrier state in the intestine;
(3) It can be given to close contacts of a patient with poliomyelitis to reduce the danger of an epidemic;
(4) It is free from dangers of allergic reactions.

There are three types of poliomyelitis virus—type I, II and III, and all three must be included in any vaccine.

The mechanism of protection in the oral vaccine is that with each dose the small intestine is seeded with one of the particular types of virus which then grows rapidly and colonizes the intestine. This is followed by a marked immunity to that type of virus.

Once the intestine has been seeded by virus of a particular type, it cannot be colonized again with the same type, so the second dose leads to colonization of one of the other types and the third dose with colonization and protection against all three types.

It is essential that three doses are given to ensure complete protection. The vaccine is given conveniently on a lump of sugar (3 drops) or in a sugar solution. Care should be taken to store it in a refrigerator to maintain its potency.

Smallpox

At the time of going to press the amount of smallpox in the world has fallen dramatically (see page 86). The following account of vaccination against smallpox is still given in full although the likelihood of a serious outbreak has clearly receded.

Smallpox was the first disease in which immunization was successful when Jenner in 1792 first discovered that the local and relatively mild disease cowpox is followed by an immunity against smallpox.

Vaccination against smallpox is still carried out using cowpox lymph and today is used to protect travellers or those who may be at special risk (doctors, nurses, public health inspectors or ambulance drivers). The drop of cowpox lymph is put on the skin, usually left upper arm, and the virus introduced into the skin either by the multiple pressure method or by scarification using a needle. About seven to eight days after vaccination a skin lesion develops which becomes indurated and swollen and finally pustular. There may be a slight general reaction but usually it causes little upset. The lesion has to be covered by a dry dressing and it should be kept as dry as possible. After two weeks, the vaccination lesion clears up leaving a small circular scar.

Immunity against smallpox after successful vaccination lasts from three to five years. From 1975, the United Kingdom requirement for a valid vaccination certificate is restricted to travellers coming within 14 days from a country any part of which is infected.

International regulations insist that revaccination is carried out every three years to ensure complete protection. The reaction on revaccination depends on the immunity state of the patient revaccinated. If he still has a good immunity to smallpox, no reaction will occur but if his immunity has worn off, he will get another primary reaction.

However, on successful revaccination the patient's new antibodies giving the patient more immunity are produced more quickly than after the first vaccination. It is for this reason that immediate revaccination of all close contacts of a case will protect them from developing smallpox and is a most important preventive procedure when a case of smallpox occurs.

Vaccination of contacts who have never been vaccinated before is also carried out and, in most cases, will prevent smallpox but not so certainly, because the immunity after the first vaccination always develops more slowly.

Evidence of vaccination against smallpox should be recorded. There is a specially recognized international certificate which must be signed by the doctor doing the vaccination, and then stamped with an official stamp of the Area Specialist in Community Medicine (Environmental Health) or District Community Physician who certifies such a doctor exists (it is a simple precaution to reduce the risk of forgery of international certificates).

Vaccine lymph is carefully manufactured in this country under licence and control of the Department of Health and Social Security. The life of cowpox vaccine is limited to fourteen days unless carefully kept in refrigerated conditions when it has a longer life. It is most important that great care is taken with the storage of all vaccine lymph and that outdated material is destroyed, otherwise the cause of failure to get a reaction on revaccination may be only due to the lymph having lost its potency and not due to the patient still having an immunity. A serious mistake in interpretation of results of vaccination in contacts could follow and lead to close contacts not being properly protected and unnecessarily developing smallpox.

To reduce the possibility of this occurring when revaccinating close contacts of smallpox, it is best to:

(a) revaccinate using fresh lymph wherever possible, i.e. with new supplies;
(b) do two insertions in each patient to reduce risk of faulty technique;
(c) repeat the revaccination four days after the first revaccination of all who fail to show a result.

Tuberculosis

Immunization against tuberculosis is undertaken using a live vaccine of the Bacillus Calmette-Guérin (BCG) type. This strain of bacteria is named after the two Frenchmen who first developed it at the beginning of the century. It is a *modified or attenuated strain* of tubercle bacillus which has lost its power to cause the disease in man but can produce a small trivial skin lesion after injection. This local skin infection later leads to an immunity against tuberculosis.

BCG immunization is only used on persons who have no skin sensitivity to tuberculin as shown by the tuberculin test. Three main groups of persons are immunized against tuberculosis:

(1) Close contacts (e.g., other members of the family) of a case of tuberculosis. This group includes the new-born baby born to parents, either of whom has had tuberculosis in the past.
(2) Schoolchildren who are tuberculin negative aged 10–13 years (in 1976, 8 per cent of schoolchildren were negative). With the parent's consent, all children aged 12 years are given a skin test at school. Those who are tuberculin negative are then vaccinated with BCG.
(3) Persons who in their occupation are liable to run a greater risk of infection from tuberculosis—examples include nurses and doctors in training. It is usual to give a tuberculin test to all new nursing and medical students and to give BCG vaccination to any who are negative. With the increase of routine BCG vaccination to schoolchildren aged 12 years, fewer and fewer nursing and medical students need BCG vaccination on entry.
(4) Children of certain immigrants in whose communities there is a high incidence of tuberculosis (especially those from Pakistan, Bangladesh, India and Africa).

After vaccination with BCG, a small skin lesion develops and may suppurate for some weeks and may not clear up until a few months after vaccination. This is quite normal and all that is required is a dry dressing to cover the lesion. Sometimes BCG vaccination is followed by an axillary adenitis. This is rare and usually clears up without complications.

Measles

Immunization against measles is carried out using live vaccines (Scherz strain) given by a single injection at the age of 1 year or shortly afterwards. This usually produces a satisfactory immunity. No child suffering from active tuberculosis or with an allergic history should be immunized against measles.

Rubella (german measles)

Vaccination against rubella should be given to girls aged 11–13 years to avoid any danger later of infection during early pregnancy. Freeze-dried live attenuated virus is used of the Cendehill strain. A single dose is used.

Routine vaccination of adult women is *not* recommended as it is not known whether the strain of virus can reach or harm the fetus. If vaccination is requested, a screening serological test should first be carried out by the Public Health Laboratory Service and vaccination should only be offered to those who are seronegative (approx. 10 per cent). *It is most important that a woman is not pregnant at the time of vaccination and does not become pregnant for at least 2 months after immunization.*

Rabies

Considerable concern is being felt at the present time in the United Kingdom because of the spread of rabies on the continent. Although it is hoped to limit this danger by the Rabies Act 1974 (see page 99), it is important that nurses know that although rabies can be prevented by *early* active immunization immediately after contact with a rabid animal, the course of injections is long and painful.

Human diploid cell vaccine should be used and the course consists of 14 daily injections into the abdominal wall with a booster dose 10 days later and a final booster 20 days after that.

For persons at special risk (handling animals that may be rabid) 2 immunizations of duck embryo vaccine are given 4–6 weeks apart. Booster doses are given 6 months later and then every 3 years.

Anthrax (see also page 98).

Immunization against anthrax has now been introduced for all workers at risk. Three doses of killed vaccine is used with 2nd and 3rd injections after 6 and then 20 weeks. A single booster injection is given annually.

Consent to immunizations

As legally an injection is an assault on the person, it is necessary to obtain the written consent from a parent or guardian before immunizing any child or young person under the age of 16 years. Consent is not required in the case of adults.

With oral immunization, consent is not so important although in the case of children it is usual to obtain the consent of the parent.

Consent can conveniently be obtained by circulating letters from school. Recently there has been a move to obtain consent to cover all immunizations necessary for a child, and this practice is likely to spread as it is a much simpler arrangement.

Immunizations for persons travelling outside this country

Apart from smallpox vaccination which has already been discussed, there are three further diseases in which immunizations are given for protection:
(1) Typhoid fever
(2) Yellow fever
(3) Cholera.

(1) *Typhoid fever*

Typhoid and paratyphoid fevers can be prevented by giving a course of Typhoid Paratyphoid ABC vaccine (TAB) which is a suspension of killed bacteria.

Two doses are given at not less than ten days apart or more than two months. Booster doses should be given every two years.

TAB immunization should be given to all persons who are going to travel in countries in which primitive water supplies are used. These include all tropical countries, and Italy, Spain and N. Africa. It is also a wise precaution if camping in Europe.

It is usual to suffer from a mild reaction after TAB inoculations—the patient complains of a headache and has a slight pyrexia for a few hours.

(2) *Yellow fever*

Yellow fever is a serious tropical virus disease which is limited to a narrow band of country in mid-Africa and central South America. A most effective immunization is given by injection of a live attenuated strain of virus which produces immunity. Very stringent storage conditions are essential for this vaccine which is freeze dried. For this reason, special centres have been set up in this country to give yellow fever vaccination and it can only be given at such centres.

Immunization is only necesary for persons visiting those parts of Africa or South America where the disease occurs. For all such travellers, immunization against yellow fever is compulsory.

(3) *Cholera*

Immunization against cholera is only necessary for travellers who are visiting certain parts of India or other far eastern countries in which cholera occurs.

The immunization is by means of a vaccine (suspension of killed cholera bacteria) and consists of two inoculations with at least two weeks in between each dose. Moderately severe reactions may follow this inoculation.

Vaccination however has proved relatively ineffective against the El Tor strain.

PASSIVE IMMUNIZATION

Reference has already been made to the use of diphtheria antitoxin and tetanus antitoxin which can be used to prevent attacks of those diseases in close contacts who may be incubating them. In diphtheria only, antitoxin is a valuable therapeutic agent in the early stages of the disease.

Another form of passive immunization is valuable which uses the active part of human blood—immuno-globulin—which contains the antibodies of infectious diseases. *Immuno-globulin,* to be of any value in active immunization, must have been separated from the blood of a person who has either suffered from the disease in the case of measles or rubella, or from a person who has recently had a smallpox vaccination.

Examples of the use of immuno-globulin to prevent disease include:

Rubella (german measles)

This is a trivial communicable disease and the only reason for ever wishing to prevent an attack is in the case of a woman who is in the early stage of pregnancy. This is because an attack of rubella during the first three months of pregnancy will often result in either a miscarriage or the birth of a congenitally malformed child.

For this reason, if any woman in the first three months of pregnancy is known to have been in contact with a case of rubella and, if she has never suffered from the disease, and has not previously been actively immunized against rubella (see page 43) she should at once be given 2.0 g of immuno-globulin. This will protect her for about six to eight weeks, which is long enough to avoid the danger of any birth complication.

There is only a danger of congenital malformations in the child from an attack of german measles in the first three/four months of pregnancy. An attack later in pregnancy is harmless and, therefore, there is no need to immunize a woman contact of german measles after this period of pregnancy.

Measles

Active immunization against measles is discussed on page 76.

Immuno-globulin is occasionally used to prevent an infant or young child (who has not previously been immunized actively against the disease) catching measles because of the special dangers in individual cases and especially when measles occurs within a paediatric ward which contains a number of ill children who have not yet developed measles. The sudden additional complication of an attack of this disease would be undesirable for it might prove dangerous in an already ill and debilitated child. To prevent this, the other ill children within the ward are immunized with immuno-globulin (collected from persons who have suffered from measles) and this immediately gives them an immunity for about six weeks. The usual dose in a child under two years is 0.4 g and 0.75 g in older children. This allows enough time to isolate the case (and any further cases) and is a valuable preventive health measure.

Smallpox

Vaccination is still the most usual method of protecting persons who have been in close contact with a case of smallpox. But occasionally, it is not possible to vaccinate contacts to produce immunity. In this case, immuno-globulin, collected a few weeks after successful vaccination (*hyper-immune immuno-globulin*) will give protection if inoculated into the contact in large enough doses. The recommended dose is 1.5 gm.

The Army has a store of hyper-immune immuno-globulin which is collected from voluntary recruits shortly after the vaccination.

Infective hepatitis

It is possible to protect a small vulnerable population (such as those attending a day centre for physically or mentally handicapped persons) against an epidemic of infective hepatitis by using immuno-globulin. In a recent outbreak, success was achieved by actively immunizing those at the centre and newly admitted entrants during the 50 days following the outbreak. The dosage used was 500 mgm for everyone except those under the age of 10 years who received 250 mgm.

Rabies

Human antibodies immuno-globulin should be used in the post-exposure treatment of persons who are manifestly sensitive to equine antiserum as shown by a skin test. Eventually it is planned to use human antirabies immuno-globulin exclusively.

Arrangements for giving immunizations

Immunizations for children can be given:
(*a*) by the family general practitioner at his own surgery;
(*b*) at area health authority child health clinics when mothers attend with babies.

There is no advantage in the immunization being undertaken at child health centres and general practitioners often arrange a special weekly time at their surgeries for immunizations, so that mothers may then bring their children there for immunization without having to mix with ill persons attending ordinary surgery sessions. The doctors have to give immunizations free as part of their service but are paid a small fee for the record card of each completed immunization or vaccination.

7 PREVENTION OF COMMUNICABLE DISEASES

Methods of prevention have been more highly developed in those diseases which are communicable or infectious (which can be passed from person to person or from animal to person) than in other illnesses.

Two generations ago, it was felt that isolation of the patient was likely to be the most valuable single factor, and strict isolation of the patient and their contacts (quarantine) was widely practised. With more and more information as to the exact methods by which these diseases spread, it was realized that isolation is of little value in many communicable diseases.

The rôle of the infectious disease hospital has completely changed in the last thirty years. When isolation was considered to be essential in all infectious disease, large infectious disease hospitals were built, often in out of the way districts, so that the isolation of the patients treated in them was more complete. Today the main reason for arranging admission to an infectious disease hospital is not to isolate the patient, but because the patient needs hospital treatment as he cannot have adequate treatment at home. This is usually because:
(a) treatment of the disease requires specialized techniques—such as severe cases of food poisoning, typhoid fever, anthrax, diphtheria or special complications of measles, whooping cough, scarlet fever or tuberculosis.
(b) the home and social conditions are inadequate to look after the case. Under this heading, any infectious disease may have to be treated in an infectious disease hospital if the home conditions are unsuitable.

In the case of smallpox, complete isolation in a special smallpox hospital is still essential. It is the one exception because this disease is extremely infectious.

Dangers of treating communicable diseases in ordinary wards
It is very undesirable to treat any case of infectious disease in an ordinary ward or even in a side ward of an ordinary ward in a general hospital. Treatment of the patient can quite easily be carried out in an ordinary ward but the danger is that the infection is likely to spread to the other patients (cross infection).

Because of this difficulty, modern hospital practice is to have small single bedded infectious disease units—say two wards each containing twelve single rooms attached to a large central hospital. It is also very helpful to have such units attached to a large paediatric hospital. Then any sudden infection in a patient already in the hospital can be treated in the infectious disease unit without interrupting the treatment of the main condition, as the same consultant paediatrician can continue to look after the patient.

Methods of spread of communicable disease
Before the methods of prevention for individual diseases can be discussed, it is necessary to study generally the methods of spread of infectious disease in the United Kingdom.

(1) *Airborne* or droplet infection
  Streptococcal infections—scarlet fever, erysipelas, puerperal fever, tonsillitis
  Staphylococcal infections—pemphigus neonatorum
  Pneumococcal infections—pneumonia
  Diphtheria
  Meningitis
  Smallpox
  Tuberculosis
  Common childhood infectious diseases—measles, whooping cough, mumps, rubella.

(2) *Faecal borne*—gastro-intestinal infections
  Typhoid and paratyphoid fever
  Food poisoning
  Dysentery
  Infantile gastro-enteritis
  Poliomyelitis
  Infective hepatitis

(3) *Direct spread by contact*
  (a) From animals—*anthrax*
    From milk—*undulant fever*—*brucellosis*
    From rats—*leptospirosis*
    From rabid dogs and other infected animals—*rabies*
  (b) From humans—Venereal disease—*syphilis* and *gonorrhoea*.

As will have been seen from the previous chapter (Chapter 6) immunization plays an important rôle in preventing many airborne and faecal borne diseases. No further discussion will be given in this chapter on immunization.

Epidemiological investigation is the second method by which communicable diseases are prevented and their spread controlled. *Epidemiology* is the study of all factors which affect disease—the cause of the illness and all the conditions associated with its incidence. A full investigation is undertaken in all cases so that, as far as possible, the exact method of spread of the disease in the patient can be traced. If this is possible, it will often prevent further cases, for some person may be infectious without showing any symptoms at all—he may be a *carrier*.

Before any investigation can be started, it is, of course, essential to know where all cases have occurred. For this reason, the majority of infectious diseases are compulsorily *notifiable*—they must be reported immediately on diagnosis to the Specialist in Community Medicine (Environmental Health) in metropolitan districts, single London districts and single district Area Health Authorities and in other places to the appropriate District Community Physician, so that he may arrange investigations. A small fee is paid to the doctor for each notification.

Venereal diseases have not been made notifiable in this country because it is feared that, if they were made so, it would result in much concealment of infections and inadequate treatment. Certainly those countries which have insisted upon notification have a higher level of venereal disease than the United Kingdom.

The complete list of notifiable diseases is:

Acute meningitis
Anthrax
Cholera
Diphtheria
Dysentery (amoebic or bacillary)
Encephalitis (acute)
Food poisoning
Infective jaundice
Lassa fever
Leprosy
Leptospirosis
Malaria
Measles

Ophthalmia neonatorum
Plague
Poliomyelitis (acute)
Rabies
Relapsing fever
Scarlet fever
Smallpox
Tetanus
Tuberculosis
Typhoid or paratyphoid
Typhus
Whooping cough
Yellow fever

The following communicable diseases are NOT notifiable:

Common cold
Chickenpox
Rubella (german measles)
Mumps

Influenza
Pheumonia
Venereal diseases

Method of investigation

A very careful *history* is always taken from the patient and his close contacts. Any link between the patient and other cases of the disease is carefully investigated. If the disease is one not normally present in this country, such as smallpox, malaria or typhoid, any link with someone who has recently travelled abroad is followed up. In a gastro-intestinal infection such as food poisoning or typhoid, which is usually the result of a food contamination, a complete history is taken of the food eaten.

In any infectious disease, there is a latent period between infection and the first symptoms and signs of the disease, called *the incubation period.* Thus a person infected with typhoid today will show no abnormal signs until fourteen days later when the early signs of illness first appear. In this example, the incubation period is fourteen days.

A knowledge of the likely incubation period is most important for it allows the questioning in collecting the history to be concentrated where it is most likely to be helpful—at the start of the incubation period (when the patient became infected). In a case of typhoid who first shows symptoms today, it is necessary to go very carefully over the movements of the patient fourteen days ago to find out how he has been infected—what food or drink he may have then consumed.

Incubation periods are never easy to remember and can vary in the same disease. They can be conveniently divided into three groups:

(1) *Very short incubation periods:* 2 hours—18 hours
Staphylococcal toxin food poisoning
Salmonella food poisoning
Clostridium perfringens toxin food poisoning

(2) *Short incubation periods:* 2 to 7 days

Streptococcal infections, scarlet fever, puerperal infection, erysipelas, Tonsillitis, staphylococcal airborne infections—pemphigus neonatorum

Pneumonia

Diphtheria

Influenza

Meningitis

Dysentery

Infantile gastro-enteritis

Paratyphoid

Anthrax

Gonorrhoea

(3) *Long incubation periods:* 12 to 21 days

Smallpox	(usually 12 days)
Chickenpox	(usually 17–21 days)
Rubella	(usually 17–20 days)
Measles	(usually 12 days)
Whooping cough	(usually 14 days)
Mumps	(usually 17–20 days)
Typhoid	(usually 14 days)
Poliomyelitis	(usually 11–14 days)
Syphilis	(usually 18–21 days)
Infective hepatitis	(usually 18–45 days)
Rabies	(usually 10–42 days but occasionally up to 4 months)

Bacteriological or *virological* investigations are most important in all communicable diseases. They aim at:

(i) confirming the diagnosis

(ii) discovering which close contacts are also infected (carriers).

In *airborne bacterial diseases, nose and throat swabs* are taken in most cases.
In tuberculosis, sputum tests, both by direct examination and culture are
always carried out on patients.

In the *faecal borne diseases, specimens of faeces or rectal swabs of patients
and contacts should always be examined.* In most outbreaks, it is usual to find
some contacts who are infected without symptoms (carriers). In many cases
the carrier state may only last a short time but, if the carrier works with foodstuffs, he may easily cause further infections.

Blood examinations are also carried out. In the early stages of typhoid fever
a *positive blood culture* will be found, allowing a certain diagnosis to be made
earlier than by any other method.

In virus diseases, virus isolations may be possible—i.e. influenza and
poliomyelitis. Another method is to examine the blood very early in the illness
and then about six weeks later when a significant rise will be noted in
antibodies. This test can be used for a retrospective diagnosis in such cases.
Because of the longer time taken with virus isolations and these blood examinations, they are less helpful in investigations than with the bacterial diseases.

In smallpox the electron microscope is used to identify virus particles and, in
this way, helps to confirm diagnosis.

Carriers

A carrier is a person who is infected with a disease and is excreting the bacteria

...sing the disease without suffering from any symptoms. Carriers are or two kinds:

(1) **Convalescent carriers.** Persons who have had the disease but who, in their convalescence, still excrete the bacteria. An example is a patient who has had typhoid, is now better, but who still has typhoid bacteria in his faeces. Such carriers are usually temporary and only carriers for a few weeks, but a few become permanent, and intermittently carry bacteria in their faeces all their life (chronic typhoid carrier).

(2) **Symptomless carriers.** This is a person who has never had any illness or symptom but who is a carrier. In such cases, infection produces a sub-clinical attack with no symptoms, and the carrier state follows. An example is given by typhoid, which shows all types of carriers, or poliomyelitis. Symptomless carriers can also be either temporary or permanent.

Types of carriers

Anatomically carriers can be divided into:

(a) Nasal carriers
Streptococci. Diphtheria. Staphylococci.
(b) Throat carriers
Diphtheria. Meningococci. Streptococci.
(c) Faecal carriers
Typhoid. Poliomyelitis. Dysentery.
(d) Urinary Carriers
Typhoid.

A chronic typhoid faecal carrier excretes typhoid bacilli in the faeces *intermittently*. Usually the faeces are positive for two weeks then negative for three to five weeks and then positive again. Because of this, repeated faecal examinations in typhoid are necessary otherwise a chronic carrier could be missed by examining him during a period when he was not excreting bacilli.

Special screening tests

X-rays form an important part of the investigation in an outbreak of tuberculosis.

DETAILED METHODS OF PREVENTING COMMUNICABLE DISEASES

AIRBORNE INFECTIONS

Streptococcal infections

These include such varied diseases as scarlet fever, erysipelas, puerperal pelvic infection, tonsillitis, cellulitis and septicaemia. The usual method of infection is from either a case or unsuspected case, or from a nasal or throat carrier. It is also important to realize that the same type of streptococcus may cause scarlet fever in one patient, tonsillitis in another and even puerperal pelvic infection if a woman recently confined is infected. A careful search should always be made to discover any infections, and among very close contacts a search for nasal carriers by examining bacteriologically nasal swabs is always worth while. Throat swabs are less useful.

In special problems such as the avoidance of puerperal infections, very great care must be taken to ensure aseptic conditions are always maintained during and after confinement. *No midwife with a nasal or throat infection should ever be allowed to attend a mother in her confinement.* The midwife in such circumstances must remain off duty until better and until bacteriological examinations of her nose and throat are normal. If an unexpected streptococcal puerperal infection occurs, the nasal and throat swabs of all who attended the birth must be examined to make certain that none of them are carriers.

Some of the most dangerous infections that can follow surgical operations are certain streptococcal ones. The stringent preventive measures taken in all surgical theatres to ensure aseptic conditions, including preparation of patient's skin, and theatre aseptic techniques, are all examples of preventive measures to reduce the chance of streptococcal infections.

In certain instances, such as a serious accident, it may be impossible to prevent infection gaining access into a patient's tissues. In such cases, prophylactic treatment with chemotherapy and antibiotics is started as a further preventive measure.

Staphylococcal infections

Some of the most dangerous neo-natal cross infections in the nursery units of maternity hospitals are caused by penicillin-resistant staphylococci (pemphigus neonatorum).

Preventive measures include:

(a) early recognition to enable the case to be promptly removed from the unit,

(b) strict barrier nursing techniques after the first case has been diagnosed,

(c) early discharge of mothers and babies so that time for cross infection is kept as short as possible,

(d) in those outbreaks which are not immediately controlled, the stopping of new admissions so that the chain of infection is closed.

Diphtheria

Immediately a case of diphtheria is diagnosed and removed to hospital, an investigation is started to discover the source of the infection. Nasal and throat swabs of close contacts (members of family and class mates) should be taken. Other members of the family are excluded from school until bacteriological tests are completed and also other members of the family are excluded from work if there is a risk of spread, i.e., a food handler.

Daily visits should be paid to the family by a health visitor or environmental health officer to check that no one has developed an illness as it is not only important to prevent the disease but to diagnose it early, as treatment is so much more effective then. Other children in the family and close contacts should be given a booster immunization and those who have never been immunized should be given their first immunizing dose.

If any of the contacts are found to be carriers, *a virulence test* must be carried out on diphtheria bacteria isolated. A minority of them are avirulent—incapable of producing diphtheria. No carrier should be implicated as a possible source of infection until it has been confirmed that he is a carrier of virulent diphtheria bacteria.

Any contacts who develop early suspicious signs should be given immediately a protecting dose of diphtheria antitoxin. An early small dose of such antitoxin is of great importance in reducing the severity of attack. The main method of *preventing diphtheria* is to see that *as many young children as possible are fully immunized* against the disease. Although it is hoped that the percentage of young children immunized will exceed 90 per cent, it is essential to see it never falls below 70 per cent for, below this figure, there is always a risk of an outbreak of diphtheria.

Smallpox

The level of smallpox is at present falling very dramatically and by early 1977 was only present in Somalia and Kenya. The following account of the principles of prevention of smallpox is still given in detail as isolated cases could still occur although the risk is becoming very remote.

The prevention of smallpox depends on:

(a) prevention of importation of smallpox;

(b) the control of the spread of the disease by contact tracing and surveillance.

(a) A careful international control is maintained by the World Health Organization so that every member country has an up-to-date record of those parts of the world where an outbreak of the disease is occurring. Stringent precautions are then taken to make certain that all travellers from such countries are fully vaccinated and medically examined on arrival (this international control is discussed in greater detail in Chapter 10).

(b) Once a case of smallpox has occurred, the spread of the disease is controlled by:

(i) immediate revaccination and vaccination of all contacts;

(ii) treatment of close contacts with the drug, β-thiosemicarbazone (Marboran);

(iii) very close surveillance of all contacts for 18 to 21 days.

(i) If a person is successfully revaccinated within four days of contact with a case of smallpox, the successful vaccination will boost his immunity sufficiently to prevent him developing smallpox even if he has been infected. Successful primary vaccination will usually protect the patient in the same way.

(ii) Very encouraging results have been reported by treating close contacts of a case of smallpox with the drug β-thiosemicarbazone (Marboran). Each contact should be given two doses of 3 g by mouth after meals within a period of 12 hours. The tablets are very large and need to be chewed by the contact.

To be of value, this *drug must be given in the incubation period*—before the development of any symptoms.

(iii) Every contact must be traced, medically examined and vaccinated. Arrangements are then made to visit each contact daily when an examination is made to ascertain that he is well and has not developed any symptoms or rash. After the eighth day of contact it is important also to examine the throat to see if there are any signs of lesions there. This visit, called *surveillance,* is repeated daily until 18 to 21 days after the last contact. If, on visiting the patient, he has developed any symptoms or signs, such as a raised temperature with headache and backache, he is immediately isolated. This method will succeed in preventing spread of infection because no patient developing smallpox becomes infectious until at least two to three days after his first symptom. Therefore, if he is immediately isolated and admitted to a smallpox hospital when he first shows symptoms, he is being isolated many hours before he becomes infectious. The accompanying diagram shows this clearly.

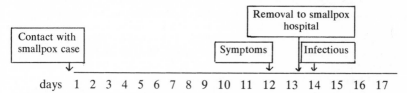

FIG. 7.1 To illustrate how daily surveillance in a contact who develops smallpox leads to isolation one to two days before he becomes infectious.

During this period of surveillance, there is no need for the patient's movements to be restricted. If he is travelling, he must tell the Specialist in Community Medicine (Environmental Health) or District Community Physician exactly where he is going so that arrangements can be made to continue his surveillance in his new area. If he leaves that area, once again he tells the Specialist in Community Medicine (Environmental Health) or District Community Physician of that area where he is going and arrangements are made for the surveillance to be continued in the same way. This surveillance must continue for at least *sixteen days* but it is safer to continue it for twenty-one days.

By conscientiously tracing all contacts in this way, sometimes called ring tracing, it is possible to control quite rapidly any imported infection of smallpox.

Widespread immediate vaccination of the general public would never control infection as it is never possible to immunize all persons in any community. Nor is it desirable to attempt to undertake widespread generalized vaccination. Even if staff and materials allow such a programme, if very large numbers of vaccinations are carried out, there is an increased risk of an isolated serious complication of vaccination, such as encephalitis.

Tuberculosis

Although there has been a dramatic fall in the number of persons developing pulmonary tuberculosis, 8208 people developed pulmonary tuberculosis in England and Wales in 1975 (5324 men and 2884 women). This shows that tuberculosis is still a major problem in this country.

Tuberculosis is usually diagnosed and treated by the chest physician at the chest clinic and chest hospital. The chest clinic is a specialized outpatient department for chest cases. In some areas specially trained health visitors called tuberculosis visitors carry out the preventive health work on the patients in conjunction with the chest physician. The majority of this work is carried out in home visiting of the patients.

The majority of cases of tuberculosis today are caused by direct infection from one human being to another by droplet (airborne) infection. The control and prevention of tuberculosis is concerned with:

(a) Tracing of infection

Tuberculosis does not spread like measles from chance, short-lived contact, but follows fairly long and continued repetitive contact such as that which occurs among the members of the same household or classroom or office. When any new case occurs, it is essential to search *for the cause of the infection* among such close contacts.

Arrangements are made to examine all members of the same family and household or members of the same office or classroom. In all instances, 'examination' must include a chest X-ray of all adults over the age of 15 years and, for children under this age, a tuberculin skin test and an X-ray for any found to be positive. It is most important that every effort is made to make certain that *every close contact* is examined. This is because the cause of the infection could be in someone who may have slight symptoms but may be afraid to have an X-ray. Because of the great preponderance of tuberculosis infection today in men over the age of 45, particular attention must always be paid to X-raying them. It is important to realize that a person may have a heavily infected sputum and be a most likely cause of infection and yet be able to carry on a normal life. Therefore, the *absence of any symptoms should never be used as an excuse to dispense with an X-ray*.

(b) Steps to reduce the chance of infection

(i) Sputum disposal

Every patient must be taught how to dispose safely of any sputum. Although it is hoped that every patient will be rendered quiescent, it is just possible that they may develop a transitory positive sputum from time to time and it is most important that, if this does occur, disposal of sputum is carried out carefully.

Expectoration of sputum should always be into a plastic sputum bottle containing a small amount of sterilizing fluid. This sterilizes the sputum after twenty minutes and also reduces the viscous and sticky nature of the sputum, making disposal easier. The contents of each sputum bottle should be washed down a water closet *and never brought into the kitchen*. Each sputum bottle should have a plastic screw top (not metal as the solution reacts on metal).

(ii) Housing

Overcrowded housing and sleeping accommodation produces conditions favouring the spread of this disease. No patient should ever sleep in the same room as another member of the family. The one exception is where the patient is a married person; in this case the couple can share the same room but should have twin beds. It is most important that *no parent who has had tuberculosis should ever sleep in the same room as a child*. Equally, no child with tuberculosis should share a room with other children.

If the house of the patient is not large enough to allow the patient to have a separate bedroom, *immediate rehousing is essential* to avoid infection spreading through the family.

Most local authorities have special priority housing schemes which enable such patients to be rapidly rehoused before further infection occurs.

(iii) Occupation

No person who has had tuberculosis should be employed in an occupation in which he may be likely to spread the disease if he has a relapse. This means he should not work in the food trade or work in close association with young children under the age of 12 years, such as a teacher or nursery nurse. Because of this factor, no person is allowed to enter training to be a teacher unless they have a clear chest X-ray. Periodic check-ups for teachers are also encouraged. Likewise all staff employed in childrens' homes or nurseries should always be X-rayed before commencing their employment.

It is illegal for a person with open tuberculosis to be employed in the food trade.

(iv) *Follow-up*

Careful follow-up of all patients must be carried out for five years after infection. This follow-up should be both at a chest clinic and by home visits to ensure that social factors at home have not deteriorated. If this occurs, a relapse in health is more likely.

In follow-ups, careful note is made of the importance of nutrition for it is known that a defective level of nutrition is more likely to lead to a relapse. Patients are also advised to be careful to rest properly and not to become over-tired.

It is wise for home visits to be paid at least *once in six months* even when the patient is quiescent. In women patients, this will ensure that any pregnancy will be known to the tuberculosis visitor before full term.

Pregnancy in a patient whose tuberculosis is controlled is likely to do no harm but it is essential that everything is done to help the mother meet this extra challenge. Delivery should take place in hospital and arrangements should be made for her to have a prolonged convalescence after delivery. The baby must be vaccinated immediately with BCG. If the problem is known early in pregnancy, before six months, it is usually possible to make satisfactory arrangements for the care of the baby and family. But if the problem is only discovered in the puerperium, the mother will be likely to ignore the convalescent period to look after her family and baby, and in this way, risks permanent damage to her health and, perhaps, spread of infection in her family.

With modern drug therapy, it is becoming increasingly popular for the chest physician to treat many early cases at home on chemotherapy. However, recent research has shown that in some cases treated at home, the patient fails to take his drugs regularly. This means that he will not get full benefit from his treatment and also runs a great risk of drug resistance developing.

(c) Immunization of those at risk

The ingestion of live virulent tubercle bacilli by any patient may, or may not, result in a recognizable clinical infection of tuberculosis. In many instances, the patient has sufficient resistance to prevent a clinical infection occurring. In all cases, however, a skin sensitivity develops.

If later a minute quantity of old tuberculin is injected into the skin of such a patient, a sharp reaction or flare occurs. This is called a *Mantoux positive skin test* or tuberculin positive test. It means that, at some time in the past, the person has been in contact with live tubercle bacilli. All such persons should be X-rayed, as occasionally a latent infection will be found. If no disease is discovered it can be assumed that there is enough immunity to resist infection. In this way, the tuberculin tests, although tests of hypersensitivity, can be used as indicators of immunity.

A negative tuberculin test occurs in persons with no special sensitivity. All newborn babies are tuberculin negative, and the change to positive only occurs by subsequent infection.

As mentioned on page 75 immunization using BCG vaccination should be offered to all negative reactors in the following groups:
(1) all family contacts of cases
(2) all medical students and nurses
(3) all schoolchildren aged 10–13 years
(4) children of immigrants in whose communities there is a high incidence of tuberculosis irrespective of their age.

(d) Detection of unknown infections by mass X-ray
There is no doubt that the main danger of spreading tuberculosis comes *from undetected cases who are sputum positive* but as yet undiagnosed. In some cases, the disease can become so chronic that such a patient may be infectious for many years without anyone discovering this fact. Such a case can infect numerous other persons with whom he comes into contact and he is a serious menace.

Once diagnosed and discovered, the danger can quickly be minimized both by treatment and the other preventive measures mentioned. *Mass radiography* plays an important part in discovering these unknown cases. Each year about 27 per cent of the new cases of tuberculosis are discovered by mass radiography.

Mass radiography consists of taking an X-ray photograph of the chest using a small film, either 35 mm, 70 mm, or 100 mm. This film is projected on to a screen and about 95 per cent of those X-rayed in this way can be cleared on this small film, while 5 per cent are recalled for a large film on which final diagnosis is made. Recall may be for technical reasons, such as a bad film, as well as any doubts about diagnosis.

Mass radiography can be used either:
(a) to screen contacts in the investigation of a local outbreak;
(b) in special industrial surveys;
(c) in wide community surveys;
(d) to allow general practitioners to refer doubtful cases;
(e) in special age surveys.

All are valuable but the widespread community survey has to be very carefully organized to be of any real use, and with the smaller amount of tuberculosis present today the mass survey is no longer worthwhile.

In the past, very successful surveys were carried out in Glasgow, Edinburgh and Liverpool in 1957–9 when 76–80 per cent of the population over the age of 15 years were X-rayed. The results of all surveys were similar and large numbers of unsuspected active pulmonary tuberculosis cases were found. These results are very interesting and are now given below because they demonstrate the marked variation between the incidence of tuberculosis in both sexes at different age groups which are still present today. The Liverpool figures are typical:

Table 7.1 1959 Mass X-Ray Campaign, Liverpool
Acute cases per 1000 X-rayed

	15–24 years	25–34 years	35–44 years	45–59 years	60+ years
Males	0.9	2.5	2.6	4.4	5.5
Females	2.0	2.7	2.5	1.3	0.8

Total acute cases: 2.41 cases/1000 X-rayed. These figures emphasize that the main problem of infection at present is in the middle-aged and elderly men. In an attempt to overcome this, special age mass X-ray surveys have been carried out in which men over 45 years of age are X-rayed.

Measles, whooping cough, mumps and german measles

The prevention of most of these diseases depends more on postponing infection by active immunization in cases of whooping cough, measles and german measles in girls and occasionally in measles or german measles by passive immunization when an attack would be more dangerous than usual (either a young child under 1 year of age or a pregnant woman during the first three months of pregnancy in rubella). See Chapter 6 for immunization details.

There is no certain way to prevent infection of these airborne infections by isolation as they all are infectious in their earliest stages often before the diagnosis has been made.

FAECAL BORNE INFECTIONS

Typhoid and paratyphoid fever

Typhoid fever can be spread by:
(a) water
(b) food
Paratyphoid fever is spread by food.

Prevention

The prevention of typhoid and paratyphoid depends on:
(a) full immediate investigation of cases to discover the cause
(b) control of chronic carriers
(c) food control including sampling at docks, pasteurization of milk supplies and ice cream, prohibition of infected shell-fish
(d) environmental hygiene
(e) immunization of holiday visitors to Italy, Yugoslavia, Portugal, Spain and Africa.

In both diseases, infection is introduced into water or food by another human being who is either suffering from the disease or is a carrier.

Most infections result from carriers. The majority of cases traced in England are contracted abroad. In 1974, 132 infections were traced and of these 98 were contracted abroad. Any person who is a carrier and who handles food of any description or who is employed by water supply departments can be most dangerous.

For this reason, whenever a case of typhoid fever occurs, a complete investigation must immediately be carried out to find the cause of infection. A careful history is taken to find out what food was eaten by the victim and close contacts at the time of infection. This means inquiry at the start of the incubation period, fourteen days before the first symptoms in typhoid and seven days in paratyphoid fever.

Immediate stool examinations must be carried out on all close contacts and especially on all the kitchen personnel. If a carrier is discovered, the typhoid bacteria must be identified and typed by *phage typing*. In this way, it is possible to divide typhoid and paratyphoid bacilli into a *number of different types*. These are then compared with the type causing the outbreak. If the types are dissimilar, then the carrier could *not* have caused the outbreak. If the type is the same, the carrier *could* have been responsible. The discovery of a carrier of the same type does not prove the cause and further investigations must be undertaken.

The large typhoid outbreaks of the past were mainly water borne due to water supplies being infected. In this country, the Croydon outbreak of 1937 involving 290 persons was the last large water-borne outbreak. This outbreak was caused by a urinary carrier among the workmen carelessly contaminating a deep well which formed part of Croydon's water supplies.

Careful methods of sewage disposal and purification and sterilization of water supplies which are universal in this country have reduced the likelihood of any further water-borne outbreaks in this country.

But every case must be carefully investigated to ensure that the cause is found. Omitting to do this can lead to a serious spread as was seen in the disastrous Zermatt water-borne outbreak of typhoid fever in 1963 resulting in 434 cases.

Food supplies may be infected from carriers. For this reason every known case of *typhoid or paratyphoid is very carefully followed up* with fortnightly stool examinations *for at least six months or longer to make certain that they do not become chronic carriers*. About 5 per cent of all typhoid cases become chronic carriers and intermittently excrete typhoid bacilli usually in their stools but occasionally in their urine. Animals are not a source of typhoid although in paratyphoid cases have been traced to infection in cows.

Once a chronic carrier is diagnosed, a careful check is kept on his occupation and family. No chronic typhoid or paratyphoid carrier is allowed to be employed in the food trade or to work in a kitchen or place where he may pass on the infection. Members of the family of a carrier must be protected periodically by immunization with TAB vaccine.

In 1945 a serious outbreak of typhoid fever was caused in Aberystwyth by home-made ice cream being infected by a chronic carrier. Now, by law, all ice cream must be pasteurized, a heat process which kills any typhoid bacilli present.

In 1964 an extensive outbreak of typhoid fever occurred in Aberdeen. Over 400 cases occurred with 5 deaths. The most probable cause was a can of corned beef which contained typhoid bacillus. It is thought that the typhoid bacillus gained entry to the can after it had been sterilized. This probably occurred by the tin being cooled by impure unchlorinated river water.

To prevent any possible recurrences, it is essential that all water used for cooling in any canning process should be pure chlorinated water.

Food poisoning

The main causes of food poisoning are:
(a) Chemical causes: Tin, antimony
(b) Bacterial toxin food poisoning

(i) *Staphylococcal* toxin
(ii) *Clostridium perfringens* toxin
(c) *Salmonellosis*

Incidence

In England in 1974, 7295 cases of all types of food poisoning were traced. 131 were caused by staphylococcal toxin, 945 by *Clostridium welchii* toxins and the remainder by various *Salmonella* bacteria.

All cases of food poisoning must be immediately and fully investigated, to discover, if possible, the cause. This investigation, if successful, will normally suggest ways and means to avoid a recurrence.

Chemical food poisoning is only likely to occur when completely unsuitable containers (such as those made from galvanized iron) are used in which to cook foods.

(i) *Staphylococcal toxin food poisoning* results in foodstuffs being infected with certain strains of staphylococcus aureus which, on multiplication within the foodstuff produce an *enterotoxin,* a poison acting upon the stomach. An interval of at least 12 hours must occur between infection of the foodstuff and its being eaten to allow sufficient toxin to be produced to lead to food poisoning.

Staphylococci usually contaminate foodstuffs from either a skin or nasal lesion in a food handler. They do, however, also attack the skin of animals and, in the cow, may lead to a staphylococcal infection of the udder with subsequent contamination of the milk.

Once staphylococcal food poisoning toxin has been produced in any foodstuff, it is *very difficult to destroy by heat as it is heat stabile.* This means that even boiling a foodstuff already contaminated with toxin would only destroy a very small and insignificant amount of that toxin.

As staphylococci are usually present in the noses of 10 per cent of people, this food poisoning can best be avoided by ensuring that all foods are:

(a) either eaten within an hour or two of preparation;

(b) if kept are always stored in cool, refrigerated conditions which are too cold for bacterial multiplication and thus no toxin is produced (toxins are produced only by bacterial multiplication);

(c) prepared under the cleanest conditions possible. This means that a high degree of personal hygiene is important. Hands must be frequently washed and habits avoided which would encourage transfer of staphylococci from the nose and mouth of the food handler to foodstuffs.

Great care must be taken to prevent any food handler who has an acute or chronic skin infection, infected cut, boil or paronychia from handling food. Legal regulations recommend *all infected cuts must be covered with waterproof dressings* to avoid contaminating foodstuffs. It is even more satisfactory to exclude from food handling any person so infected.

(ii) *Clostridium perfringens (Cl. welchii) toxin food poisoning* is less severe than staphylococcal toxin poisoning.

The toxin, which is also heat stabile, is produced by multiplication of *Clostridium perfringens,* a spore-bearing anaerobic bacterium which also can cause gas gangrene. The spores of this bacteria are widespread—in soil and often in faeces. However, being an anaerobic bacterium, it will only multiply in the absence of oxygen. For this reason, it mainly produces food poisoning in meats or in stews and soups made by long standing low temperature simmering.

Prevention

Spores of *Clostridium perfringens* are found in many meats and therefore inevitably will gain access to kitchens. Infections with this type of food poisoning will only be avoided if the following rules are strictly observed:

(a) avoid precooking of meats

(b) avoid storing any food between 49°C and 10°C for more than 3 hours

(c) if meats have to be precooked, it is essential that they are rapidly cooled and maintained below 10°C in a domestic refrigerator.

(d) care must always be taken when gutting animals such as rabbits to avoid contamination of the flesh with faeces from the intestine (which will contain large quantities of spores of *Clostridium perfringens*).

Salmonellosis

Salmonellosis is usually the commonest type of food poisoning, and is an infective gastro-enteritis in which the small intestine is attacked by one of the salmonella bacteria producing an acute inflammation. There are over 1000 serotypes but the commonest is Salmonella typhimurium which is responsible for 40 per cent of cases. Salmonella enteritis and agona are the next commonest types found in the United Kingdom.

Method of spread

There are 5 main sources of salmonellosis:

(1) human cases and carriers

(2) domestic animals and rodents

(3) eggs of ducks and hens

(4) pigs

(5) chickens

Any one of these sources may lead to contamination of food but fortunately a very heavy infection is necessary to lead to a salmonella food poisoning and this means that, if foods such as duck eggs are avoided, there is nearly always a history of incorrect method of storage of the food, i.e., the foodstuff has been stored for more than 12 hours at normal room temperatures and *not refrigerated temperature*—this allows rapid bacterial multiplication which will not occur at cold refrigerated temperatures.

Whenever an outbreak of salmonella food poisoning occurs, a complete investigation must take place to find if possible the cause of the infection.

A particular *search for faecal carriers* should always be made among all kitchen personnel and all should have their stools bacteriologically examined. If any carrier is found, it must not be assumed that he or she is necessarily the cause, for such a carrier may also have been infected in the outbreak. All carriers must immediately stop handling food until clear. It is most unusual for carriers of salmonella organisms to become chronic carriers and the carrier state usually only lasts a few weeks.

Any foodstuff, which is precooked and then stored for a lengthy period before consumption, such as cooked and prepared meats, may be dangerous if storage has been faulty and the food has become infected. Recently serious outbreaks followed heavily contaminated egg and coconut products imported from abroad and used by the baking trade. Fortunately a method of heat treatment was devised which has reduced the danger.

Prevention

It will be seen that all salmonella food poisoning can be avoided if:

(*a*) extreme care is taken in preparation of food, and with personal hygiene among food handlers. This reduces the chances of a carrier accidentally contaminating any food.

(*b*) all food prepared is eaten immediately. Any left over should be thrown away. In this respect, it is most undesirable to prepare a sweet today for lunch tomorrow, unless stored in a refrigerator.

(*c*) where food, such as meat pies, is stored for a lengthy time, it must be stored at low temperature, below 4°C—preferably in a refrigerator.

(*d*) gamma radiation from a cobalt-60 source can be used to destroy salmonellae in frozen whole egg, coconut, imported meats and animal feeding stuffs.

(*e*) pasteurization of liquid milk as raw milk has been traced as the infecting agent in about two to three per cent of cases.

Dysentery

The bacterial dysentery caused by *Shigella sonnei* (often called sonne dysentery) is the commonest form of dysentery in this country. It is usually a mild, short-lived gastro-enteritis which is only serious in young babies or debilitated elderly persons.

Sonne dysentery is spread by direct contamination from person to person. In a closed community, such as a ward or nursery, it spreads slowly at first but, as soon as a proportion of persons are infected, it spreads more quickly.

The best method to avoid outbreaks of dysentery is:

(*a*) to diagnose it early,

(*b*) to isolate all cases and carriers.

This is especially important in day nurseries and hospital wards. All cases of diarrhoea must be *bacteriologically examined* (stool specimens) to make certain that any early cases are identified.

There is always a proportion of symptomless carriers among close contacts but usually they are carriers only for two to three weeks.

By careful investigation and isolation of cases and carriers, serious outbreaks will be avoided. If, however, a widespread outbreak has been allowed to develop, isolation will achieve little. The aim should, therefore, always be to diagnose the first cases and this can only be done if it is a rule to submit routinely for bacteriological examination stools of all patients who develop any diarrhoea however mild or transient.

Infantile gastro-enteritis

This is a general term used for any severe gastro-enteritis in young infants. The exact cause of some outbreaks is often uncertain but in others infection has been traced to certain pathogenic strains of *Escherichia coli* including 0 26, 0 55, 0 111, 0 125, 0 126, 0 127, 0 128 and 0 229. Many enteroviruses (ECHO and Coxsackie B viruses) have also been identified as causes.

Recently a virus responsible for many attacks of infantile gastro-enteritis has been identified by use of the electron microscope. Serologically the virus which unfortunately has been given many different names including reovirus-like agents, orbivirus, rotavirus and duovirus, is related to the virus of calf diarrhoea. As soon as the problems of culturing this virus in vitro are overcome it should be possible to develop a prophylactic vaccine.

Prevention

These attacks can best be prevented by complete investigation when they occur and by arranging for all young infants to spend as little time as possible in hospital units. There is no doubt that many attacks result from cross infection—infection spreading rapidly from infant to infant in the ward. It is, therefore most important that any infant with any diarrhoea *be immediately isolated* and that *no child with a history of diarrhoea is admitted to a clean infants'* ward but straight into the *isolation unit.*

Once infection has occurred, especially the serious type of gastro-enteritis that occasionally attacks a nursery unit of a maternity ward, new admissions should be stopped and the ward emptied as soon as possible by discharging mothers and babies home early. In this way, the chance of widespread infection is reduced.

All attempts to control the spread of infantile gastro-enteritis by strict barrier nursing nearly always fail, probably due to the intensity of infection and the rôle infected dusts play in spreading the disease.

Encouragement of breast feeding can do much to reduce the incidence of infantile gastro-enteritis and every effort should be made to keep breast feeding going if the infant develops an illness. If the baby must enter hospital his mother should also be admitted so that breast feeding may be maintained.

Poliomyelitis

Poliomyelitis has the most well-defined seasonal incidence of any known infectious disease, for outbreaks of the disease in this country always occur in late summer and early autumn, in August, September or October. For this reason, there is only a serious risk of epidemic spread in these months. Fortunately following widespread immunization with oral poliomyelitis vaccine, the disease in England has become very rare

Poliomyelitis is a faecal borne disease which is spread by direct personal contact from person to person usually after close and constant contact. Thus, infection spreads rapidly and usually completely among the members of the same household. Although infected, the majority of close contacts show no symptoms and only rarely does clinical poliomyelitis result.

When a case of poliomyelitis occurs, it is, therefore, important that, as far as possible, the members of the same household are segregated from the general population. Child contacts should certainly be kept away from school for at least three weeks. By isolating the family as far as possible, the chance of spread of infection is reduced.

In addition, as soon as any case occurs, immediate immunization using oral poliomyelitis vaccine should be given to:

(a) all contacts at home, work and school
(b) all persons living within an approximate radius of a quarter of a mile from the patient.
This not only serves to boost their immunity but also blocks the entrance of 'wild' or epidemic virus into their intestines and thus will help reduce the chance of further infection.

Household contacts should also be placed under daily surveillance for three weeks. They should be visited by a health visitor daily to check their temperature and whether they have any symptoms. If any abnormality is noted, then the contact should be put to bed immediately and kept as quiet as possible. This is important because *violent exercise in the patient showing the earliest signs of poliomyelitis can result in a very severe attack*. As a further precaution, no close contact of a case of poliomyelitis should be allowed to indulge in strenuous exercise for three weeks. Close family contacts should, therefore, not go on walking tours or any similar activities at this time.

Restrictions among the general population regarding swimming baths are probably useless in preventing spread of poliomyelitis. However, swimming is a fairly violent form of exercise and should be avoided for three weeks among close family contacts.

As already explained, the most valuable preventive measure against poliomyelitis is to make certain that as high a proportion as possible of persons under 40 years of age are completely immunized against the disease using oral Sabin vaccine.

Cholera

Although classic cholera last appeared in epidemic form in the United Kingdom in 1866, recently there have been a number of outbreaks in westernized countries from the new El Tor strains. In 1974 three cases of cholera occurred in the United Kingdom in visitors from Portugal and Pakistan. No secondary cases occurred. Modern rapid air travel facilitates the spread of this disease which has a short incubation period of 2–3 days.

Contamination of water supplies is the classic method of spread but flies can also be responsible if sewage disposal methods are crude. Direct spread from food handlers who are carriers is also a possibility.

El Tor cholera remains in the stools of cases for at least 14 days and occasionally for up to 3 months.

Prevention

This mainly depends on purification of water supplies and safe disposal of sewage. In epidemics, water and milk must be boiled (unless already pasteurized) and careful segregation of all patients arranged with terminal and concurrent disinfection.

Active immunization should be arranged for those at special risk (doctors and nurses) and for travellers to countries where the disease is epidemic. Immunization provides about 50 per cent protection for a short period and revaccination is advisable every 6 months. Results, however, have been disappointing against the El Tor type of vibrio.

Infective Hepatitis

This disease was made notifiable in 1968 and approximately 7000 cases are recorded annually in England. 60 per cent are children and in all outbreaks it is possible to trace a number of causes without clinical jaundice.

Prevention

There is no method of active immunization but recently success has been observed by using immunoglobulin as a passive immunity. This resulted in a reduction of cases and also in a modification in the severity of the subsequent disease.

DIRECT SPREAD—FROM ANIMALS

Anthrax

This is a rare disease usually caught by direct spread from the hide of an animal, from wool or from the bones of animals. For this reason, anthrax is only seen in persons whose occupations bring them into contact with animals and their products. The main occupations at risk include dockers handling hides who occasionally develop anthrax, and wool sorters.

The prevention of anthrax depends on:
(a) special treatment of wool imports to kill any anthrax spores at a number of centres close to the mills.
(b) protective clothing being worn by persons handling hides and bones.
(c) immunization against anthrax for all associated workers (see page 76).

As a further safeguard, the dangers of anthrax are explained to all those working in occupations in which there is a danger of contracting anthrax. Diagrams of early symptoms are prominently displayed so that if anyone develops the skin lesions of anthrax, it is more likely to be recognized and diagnosed early. All such workers also carry a special card to show to their general practitioners when attending so that the doctor knows of the special risk of contracting anthrax which their occupation carries.

The early diagnosis is most important as modern treatment can quickly cut short an attack of anthrax.

Leptospirosis

This disease is caused by *Leptospira icterohaemorrhagiae* and is primarily a disease of rats. Infections in man result from the skin being infected by water contaminated with rat urine and usually only occur among abattoir or sewage workers who are most likely to come into close contact with rats. All such workers should be warned of the dangers of infection and of the importance of a high standard of hygiene. It is especially important that they *avoid contaminating skin with water which may have been infected by rat's urine.* It is especially dangerous to walk barefoot in such places.

Brucellosis

In the UK *Brucella abortus* produces a disease in cattle which also can cause the illness of brucellosis in man.

Prevention depends on:

(*a*) eradication of the disease from animals

(*b*) pasteurization (heat treatment) of all milk supplies.

Since 1970 there has been a Brucellosis Incentive Scheme operated by the Ministry of Agriculture, Fisheries and Food. Testing is carried out by the Ministry and a national register of brucella-free herds is maintained. To qualify for entry a herd must show three clear blood tests at four-monthly intervals. Money incentives are then paid for each gallon of milk produced and for each breeding cow in a beef herd.

In any outbreak of brucellosis, the local authority can apply for a 'pasteurization order' under the Milk and Dairies (General) Regulations 1959 if a milk sample shows the presence of *Brucella abortus*. Milk from such a herd must then be sent for pasteurization.

Rabies (Hydrophobia)

At present in the United Kingdom considerable concern is being shown about the dangers and problems of rabies because of the increase of this disease on the continent. Many different wild animals can be infected (including foxes, otters and many rodents) but the vast majority of cases in wild animals have occurred in foxes (about 90–94 per cent in European countries). In fact an epizootic in foxes has spread during the last 10 years to France from Germany, Switzerland, Austria, Denmark and Belgium. About 73 per cent of all animal outbreaks on the continent have occurred among wild animals and 23 per cent among domestic animals. Dogs are most commonly affected in this group but cats and bovines are also infected.

Two imported cases of rabies occurred in the United Kingdom in 1975. Both cases had been bitten by rabid dogs before arrival in this country and although both received intensive treatment both died. Another case from abroad died early in 1977.

Prevention

The virus of rabies is in the saliva of rabid animals. After a bite from a rabid animal, the virus spreads in humans to the central nervous system producing the characteristic symptoms. The disease is very dangerous with a high mortality and anyone who has been bitten by a rabid animal must be immunized (see page 76). The incubation period is usually about 2–6 weeks but in a few cases may be much longer.

Rabies Act 1974

Under this Act, there is a compulsory six months quarantine period for all animals entering the country. Effective precautions must also be taken against the transmission of the disease within quarantine kennels. All dogs and cats entering quarantine must be vaccinated on entry with a proved potency-tested inactivated vaccine; they must also be revaccinated after one month in quarantine to extend immunity.

Dogs and cats will be allowed to enter Britain only at a limited number of ports. Animals landed illegally may be destroyed on landing and the Act provides severe penalties, including up to one year's imprisonment for offences against the orders under the Act.

Further orders provide for a wider range of measures to control any outbreak of rabies in Britain. These include destruction of foxes, controls on the movement of domestic pets and their vaccination, the seizure of strays and the banning of hunting, and cat and dog shows.

Prophylactic vaccination against rabies (see page 76) should be offered to all persons who in their work are at risk including:

(1) those employed at quarantine kennels
(2) those working in quarantine premises in zoos
(3) agents who are authorized to carry such animals
(4) those working in research and acclimatization centres where primates and other imported mammals are housed
(5) those working in ports regularly importing animals.

Booster immunization should be given every 2–3 years.

CONTACT INFECTION FROM HUMANS

Lassa fever

This serious communicable disease was first reported from Nigeria in 1969. Since then three confirmed cases have occurred in the U.K. in travellers from Nigeria.

The cause of Lassa fever is a virus which naturally is endemic in a species of rat found in Nigeria. The common rats and mice of the U.K. are not susceptible but white mice can be infected in laboratories.

Infection in men occurs in 2 main ways;

(1) by food or dusts contaminated by virus from the Nigerian rat (the usual method of primary infection in Nigeria);

(2) by person-to-person infection in hospitals and *this is the most likely method of infection* by which the disease could be spread in the U.K.

Special precautions are therefore now laid down;

(a) diagnose any imported cases early—any unsuspected fever in a traveller from Nigeria should be investigated to exclude Lassa fever, by blood culture and isolation of the virus and by evidence of antibody development. The incubation period of the disease is 3–17 days;

(b) immediate removal of any suspected cases to special isolation hospitals (similar to smallpox isolation) and by special ambulances;

(c) strict precautions for all staff nursing such patients;

(d) daily surveillance of all close contacts for 21 days. Temperatures should be taken daily and special note made of any signs of pharyngitis.

Special laboratories and hospitals have been designated for investigation of Lassa fever and the Local Medical Officer for Environmental Health has full details (Specialist in Community Medicine—Environmental Health) in all one district Area Health Authorities and in metropolitan districts and in other places the appropriate District Community Physician.

Sexually transmitted diseases (venereal diseases)

These are spread by direct contact in sexual intercourse—one partner infects the other.

In both syphilis, with its incubation period of about three weeks, and in gonorrhoea, with its incubation period of 2–5 days and in non-specific urethritis with its incubation period of 10–28 days the mechanism of infection is similar.

The prevention of sexually transmitted disease depends on:

(1) complete and efficient diagnosis and treatment of all cases
(2) the searching out of suspected cases
(3) avoidance of casual or promiscuous sexual intercourse.

(1) Diagnosis, especially of gonorrhoea, is not simple in the female, and an infected woman can remain so for a lengthy period without necessarily realizing she is infected. In doubtful cases, hospital outpatient attendance is desirable so that bacteriological smears may be taken and blood tests examined.

Inexpert treatment by inexperienced doctors is most dangerous for it may lead to incomplete cure and suppression of symptoms. The danger of double infection, gonorrhoea and syphilis in the same patient must be excluded. This can only be ensured if all cases of sexually transmitted disease are investigated and treated by the special hospital unit provided.

(2) Whenever a case of sexually transmitted disease is diagnosed, a careful history should be taken and arrangements made for the *cohabiting partner to be medically examined as soon as possible*. To carry out this contact tracing, specially trained nurses and social workers are attached to all sexually transmitted disease departments. Their task is to trace the cohabiting partner wherever possible and persuade him or her to come to the clinic for a full examination.

(3) Better education is needed, so that all persons realize that only by self control and avoidance of casual sexual intercourse will such disease be avoided. It is especially important to realize that, *without bacteriological tests, it is impossible even for a doctor to exclude the possibility of such disease in any person.* This should be explained to young men who may otherwise be misled by older men into believing they can tell when a contact is, or is not, infected.

As the incidence of gonorrhoea has steadily increased over the past five years it is most important that health education measures to ensure better understanding of the problems of this disease are stepped up.

8 PREVENTION OF NON-COMMUNICABLE DISEASES

To prevent successfully any disease, it is essential to understand fully the various factors which cause it. For this reason, until the bacteria and viruses which cause infectious diseases were discovered at the end of the nineteenth and beginning of the twentieth centuries, the prevention of communicable disease was haphazard. With the greater understanding of bacteria and viruses in the last sixty years, it has become possible to control infectious disease much more effectively.

With non-communicable disease, the greatest barrier to prevention is that so little is known about the causes of disease. Research into the causation is continually being carried on and the factors connected with the incidence of such diseases are slowly being unravelled. It is, however, a very complicated story as there is a multiplicity of factors involved. Even in diseases whose cause is as yet hardly understood, wide differences exist between the various social classes as shown on page 30, suggesting that the living conditions of the various social classes may increase or diminish the dangers of developing such diseases.

Sometimes important factors only come to light by a steady increase in a disease leading to greater and greater research which finally finds an important causative factor. An example of this is given by *cancer of the lung*, the enormous increase has now been shown to be *connected with increased cigarette smoking*. But as yet, research even in this instance has not discovered the exact chemical factor in cigarette smoke which produces this carcinogenic effect. Another example is bladder cancer. Epidemiological studies made in England in the 1950s indicated that there was a much higher incidence of bladder cancer among workers in the dyestuffs industry and indicated three aromatic amines, α-naphthylamine, β-naphthylamine and benzidine as potent carcinogens. Also it was found that antioxidants made from α- and β-naphthylamines were used frequently in rubber and cable industries. Since the use of α- and β-naphthylamines were banned in 1949 recent surveys have failed to show a continued excess of bladder cancers in men who entered the industries after 1949 although those employed before 1949 still show a marked excess.

Research has also been heightened by the large increase recently in ischaemic heart disease and it is hoped that all these inquiries will eventually unravel the cause of this condition.

Prevention of non-communicable diseases can always be considered from two aspects:

(*a*) complete prevention of the disease ever occurring in any individual (primary prevention).

(*b*) prevention of deterioration or of relapses from a disease already existing (secondary prevention). This includes early diagnosis and a full understanding of the various social and occupational factors which predispose to further attacks of the disease. It is also important to remember that unless the correct treatment is carried out continuously in a chronic disease such as diabetes, then the finest diagnostic and treatment facilities will be wasted. In many instances, *correct treatment depends on understanding many of the social factors which can negate success.*

ISCHAEMIC HEART DISEASE

The incidence of ischaemic heart disease has increased markedly in the last twenty years. Even allowing for better diagnosis and the greater proportion of more elderly people now within the community, in whom the incidence is greatest, there is no doubt that a real increase has occurred, especially in the middle-aged group. Ischaemic heart disease, the clotting of blood in the coronary arteries supplying the heart muscle with blood, is usually associated with an atheromatous condition of the linings of the arteries in which tiny plaques of fatty material are laid down in the linings of these arteries making clotting more likely. Much research has been carried out throughout the world to discover what causes this atheromatous condition. Much has yet to be discovered but it is already clear that enormous differences in incidence of ischaemic heart disease occur throughout the world. For instance, the death rate from this condition in America is nine times that of Japan. France too has low rates while her neighbours are high, including England, Wales and Scotland.

Table 8.1   Deaths from ischaemic heart disease per 100 000 population 1970 (both sexes)

Japan	37.7
France	80.9
Portugal	119.9
Italy	134.0
Germany (Fed. Republic)	172.5
Israel	201.8
Canada	230.1
Australia	270.4
England & Wales	284.4
Denmark	297.1
U.S.A.	331.7
Sweden	333.9
Scotland	337.8

The reasons for these differences are not completely known. The latest views are that a number of factors are probably important including:
(1) high blood lipid levels
(2) hypertension
(3) cigarette smoking
(4) genetic factors
(5) physical inactivity
(6) increase in body weight
(7) diabetes
(8) nervous stress
(9) cold weather in older patients
(10) the sex of the individual.

The short heavier person is more prone to an *early* attack than the tall thin person. Regular exercise seems to have a protective effect and farmers and others leading active lives have a lower incidence than sedentary workers. There is certainly an endocrine factor which is probably responsible for the higher rate in younger men than in young women (before the age of 50). After the menopause the rate in women increases until by the age of 70 it is equal to that of men.

Prevention

At present, there is no agreement about the exact steps which should be taken to avoid ischaemic heart disease. Some suggest that it would be wise to do a routine blood cholesterol test on all men aged 35 and that, in those in whom a raised level was found, a diet should be commenced in which animal fats are replaced by vegetable fats, and that care should be taken to avoid overweight. However, many physicians feel that to do this would only worry many patients unduly and, in the end, more harm could be caused.

Further research is necessary to try and find the most important causes. Until this has been achieved, there is no doubt that the following simple rules are most helpful and likely to reduce ischaemic heart disease:
(*a*) avoid overweight at all costs;
(*b*) constant exercise, such as walking should be encouraged—probably daily exercise is much more useful than sudden bursts of exercise;
(*c*) do not smoke cigarettes (there is evidence of a greater risk among heavy smokers).

For the patient who has already had an attack of ischaemic heart disease, these simple rules are even more important, as well as the avoidance of sudden cold such as a sea bathe in cold weather.

THE CANCERS

The true causative nature of cancers is, as yet, unknown. There are, however, many associated factors now recognized which are known to predispose to the development of cancers—most of these are connected with some chronic recurring form of irritation. It is known that various skin cancers can be caused by irritation from oils and sunlight and cancers of the tongue by the irritation of a clay pipe. It is likely that the association between cigarette smoking and lung cancer, and between atmospheric pollution and lung cancer, is of this nature. Recently a clear connection has been demonstrated between the development of liver cancers (hepatic angio-sarcoma) and exposure to monomeric vinyl chloride. The greatest dangers have been traced to men who open and clean the autoclave where vinyl chloride is polymerized.

It is not always appreciated how cancers vary in incidence between social classes. The following table indicates this very clearly:

Table 8.2   Standardized Mortality Ratio (SMR) for Cancers by Social Classes, England and Wales 1961

Site	I	II	III	IV	V
All sites (males)	73	80	104	102	139
Lung (males)	53	72	107	104	148
Stomach (males)	49	63	101	114	163
Breast (married women)	111	104	104	96	104
Cervix uteri (married women)	34	64	100	116	181

Most cancers show their highest incidence in social class V and their lowest incidence in social class I. It is not known why cancer of the breast differs in this respect.

Prevention in cases of irritation can best be achieved by removing or avoiding the predisposing factor.

In other cases, prevention is connected with recognizing a very early precancerous condition which, if then radically treated, can avoid subsequent cancer.

An indication of the survival rate is given by the percentage of patients who after treatment survive at least five years:

Table 8.3   Survival after Cancer, England and Wales

Cancer	Percentage of patients surviving five years
Skin (excluding melanoma)	59
Uterus (other than cervix)	56
Uterus cervix	44
Breast (female)	44
Bladder (male	28
Rectum	22
Ovary	20
Colon	20
Prostate	17
Stomach	5
Lung	5

Cancer of the Cervix Uteri

Cancer of the cervix uteri is responsible for the deaths of over 2300 women per year in England and Wales but this death rate has been falling. Table 8.2 shows the marked variation in the various social classes. Repetitive damage to the cervix uteri is a predisposing cause to this cancer and this is one of the reasons for a higher rate in social class V women who generally have larger families than women from social class I or II.

Prevention

There is now a widely used screening test (exfoliative cytology) which can detect a precancerous condition in the cervix. The technique of the test is simple. A vaginal speculum is passed and a direct smear is obtained from the cervix and examined histologically. Abnormal mitotic changes in the nuclei of the epithelial cells removed is suspicious and a complete gynaecological examination should be carried out and a cone biopsy undertaken to find whether a precancerous cancer *in situ* exists. If these investigations confirm a precancerous condition, it is then usual to operate and remove the cervix (or complete uterus) before a dangerous invasive cancer develops.

The collection of such smears is undertaken by general practitioners or at a special clinic. Regular testing in this way should be carried out on all women once every three years.

Cancer of the Lung

The increase in cancer of the lung recently has been most dramatic. The disease has become commoner since the early part of this century, but the greatest increase has been in the last thirty years.

It is always difficult when comparing the incidence of any disease over a number of years to assess how much better diagnosis may be responsible—in other words, how much of the increase is apparent and not real. However, if the incidence of cancer of the lung is examined in England and Wales over the last twenty-eight years, 1947 to 1975, it is possible to ignore this diagnostic factor, as by 1947, wide spread use of radiology and bronchoscopy was taking place in the diagnosis of lung lesions, and it is safe to assume the degree of diagnosis was similar. In this period of twenty-eight years, the number of deaths from cancer of the lung has more than doubled from 9204 in 1947 to 33 000 in 1975 (Table 8.4).

This increase is serious especially as cancer of the lung is difficult to treat effectively and usually results in the patient's death within 1½ to 2 years of diagnosis in all but 5 per cent of cases. Prevention of lung cancer is one of the most serious problems facing medicine today. This is because cancer of the lung is easily the commonest cancer and it is unique, as it alone is the cancer which is increasing.The 1975 figures showed a small reduction for the first time.

Much research in various parts of the world has been carried out to investigate the factors associated with this great increase in cancer of the lung. All the various surveys in different countries have shown that more lung cancer patients are smokers of cigarettes than are the controls in the experiments. It has also been shown clearly that death rates from lung cancer increase steeply as consumption of cigarettes increases. Heavy cigarettes smokers have thirty times the death rate of non-smokers.

From 1962 to 1970 the Royal College of Physicians studied the problem and clearly stated that 'cigarette smoking is an important cause of lung cancer. If the habit ceased, the number of deaths caused by this disease should fall steeply in the course of time.'

Even more recently, research in America has shown that there are highly abnormal cells in the sputum of heavy smokers—cells which are showing many abnormal changes and may be precancerous. The interesting and encouraging factor is that, if smoking stops, then, within a short space of time, there is a diminution in the the the number of such cells in the sputum and finally they disappear altogether. This *suggests that to give up smoking is to reduce the chance of developing cancer of the lung*—a finding repeatedly reported from all surveys.

Table 8.4   Deaths from Cancer of the Lung, England and Wales

1947	9 204	1963	24 434
1951	13 247	1967	28 188
1955	17 272	1970	30 284
1959	21 063	1974	33 000 (26 400 men, 6 600 women)

As it is not possible to differentiate those persons who will develop cancer of the lung, if they continue to smoke, the only certain and practicable way to prevent cancer of the lung is to reduce the amount of cigarette smoking. It is most important to discourage young people from starting the habit which has no real advantages and, as well as damaging health, is most costly.

Careful examination of Table 8.4 shows a definite steady upward trend.

Women have not smoked for as long as men but today are rapidly becoming heavier smokers. Cancer of the lung used to be mainly a male disease but today the proportion of women who develop it, although smaller than men, is rising. *It is likely to continue to rise steeply* unless smoking is reduced.

No sensible person, who has studied the real facts could have any doubts about the connection between cigarette smoking and lung cancer. Yet, ever since the publication of the well known reports of the Royal College of Physicians in 1962 and 1970, cigarette consumption in this country has steadily increased and is now higher than ever before. As yet, although most adults have heard of the risks, they ignore them even to the extent of not discouraging their children from starting to smoke.

It is unusual to have defined an important causative factor of a serious disease such as cancer of the lung, often occurring in the later forties and early fifties, and for so many to choose to continue to run the risks. Doctors, however, have shown an alteration—compared with 75 per cent men who smoke, only 15 per cent male doctors smoke cigarettes and the proportion is still falling.

The problem is becoming increasingly important every year. Much more interest and encouragement is needed, especially by Central and Local Government to help teach people the dangers of smoking. Much more help should be given to those who wish to give up smoking by the setting up of anti-smoking clinics.

The Royal College of Physicians ended their reports by suggesting seven courses of action:

(i) more education of the public and especially schoolchildren concerning hazards of smoking.

(ii) more effective restrictions on the sale of tobacco to children;

(iii) restriction of tobacco advertizing;

(iv) wider restriction of smoking in public places;

(v) an increase of tax on cigarettes, perhaps with adjustment of the tax on pipe and cigar tobaccos;

(vi) informing purchasers of the tar and nicotine content of the smoke of cigarettes;

(vii) investigating the value of anti-smoking clinics to help those who find difficulty in giving up smoking.

Cancer of the Breast

Cancer of the breast is an important cause of death in women. Table 8.2 shows that there is not much difference between the mortality among the different social classes in the U.K. There is however a much wider range between the mortality in different countries as shown in Table 8.5.

Table 8.5 Cancer of the Breast death rate (females) per 100 000 population 1970

Japan	Australia	France	U.S.A.	Holland	England & Wales
4.7	23.9	27.4	27.9	34.7	42.2

Breast feeding is common in Japan and this fact may be partly responsible for the low death rate there. The high death rate in England and Wales emphasises the urgent need to prevent this disease as far as possible. The S.M.R. (1968 = 100) for 1975 for cancer of the breast was 109 showing that deaths from this cancer are increasing. The reduction in mortality from cancer of the breast is linked with early diagnosis. The type of cancer is also an important factor—the most rapidly spreading types being those which occur in pregnancy and lactation. Much cancer education today is directed to explain to women how important it is for them to palpate their breasts when taking a bath, and to report to their doctor at once if any form of lump is discovered, so that an investigation can be made immediately. Note that the survival rate 5 years after treatment is 44 per cent and there is ample evidence that the earlier the treatment is started, the better the results.

Cancer of the Bladder

There are many more cases of cancer of the bladder in men than in women. Reference has already been made (see page 102) to the incidence of cancer of the bladder in the rubber and cable industries due to exposure of workers to benzidine and naphthylamine-based derivatives.

There is also a marked difference in incidence in this cancer between different parts of the U.K. (see Table 8.6).

Table 8.6 Incidence of mortality from cancer of bladder U.K. 1971
(S.M.R. 1968 = 100)

	Females	Males
Northern Ireland	78	67
England and Wales	97	100
Scotland	136	105

BRONCHITIS

In England bronchitis was responsible for 24 380 deaths in 1975. In addition, it caused a great deal of invalidism in many sufferers and was responsible for much loss of working time in industry. Bronchitis has been called the 'English disease' as it is so common in this country compared with other countries of the world.

Our damp sunless winter climate may be connected with this increased incidence but the problem is made much worse by atmospheric pollution which turns fog into poisonous smogs as the smoke and sulphur fumes are trapped within the fog. It is obviously impossible to alter the climate but two important preventive measures are possible to reduce the incidence and severity of bronchitis:

(1) by reduction in cigarette smoking. There is no doubt that all smokers, but expecially cigarette smokers, are much more often affected than non-smokers.

Anyone with a tendency to *early bronchitis or asthma must immediately stop smoking.*
(2) by a reduction in atmospheric pollution. Much has already been achieved in this respect by the Clean Air Act 1956 whereby many areas in towns were converted into smoke control areas in which it is illegal to burn ordinary coal which produces so much pollution. Because of financial restrictions this conversion has had now to be deferred.

PEPTIC ULCERATION

Gastric ulceration shows a marked variation in mortality between the social classes. Duodenal ulceration however such a much more varied picture (see Table 8.7).

Table 8.7 S.M.R. for peptic ulceration in men aged 20–64, 1961

Social class	I	II	III	IV	V
Gastric ulcer	56	81	97	99	144
Duodenal ulcer	105	78	106	82	126

There are other marked epidemiological differences between gastric and duodenal ulceration. Gastric ulcers are four times commoner in men than in women. But duodenal ulceration is more commonly associated with mental stress. There is a particular increase in duodenal ulcer incidence in professional persons such as doctors and lawyers who accept a considerable degree of personal responsibility.

There is often a strong association with the occupational regime followed by patients suffering from peptic ulcers. Those whose occupations do not allow them to have regular meals, such as long-distance drivers, can often trace lapses in their ulcer history to periods when irregular meals were usual.

The prevention of recurrence of peptic ulcers depends as much on being able to regulate, as far as possible, the life of the patient so that irregular meals and worry are avoided, as on the medical treatment of the condition.

DIABETES

This is a disease commoner in women than in men. Over 200 000 cases of diabetes have been diagnosed in the U.K. but the incidence may be considerably higher as there are always many mild undiagnosed cases (in 1961 a survey in Bedford with a population then of 61 000 brought to light 356 such undiagnosed diabetics).

The disease is really of two types:
(1) The more serious diabetes seen in younger persons in which there is a strong heredity factor. In studies of such diabetes it has been shown that if one twin develops the disease the chance of the other also developing diabetes is five times greater in similar twins than in dissimilar twins.
(2) The 'adult' type of diabetes which is a much milder disease usually controllable by diet. There is a higher incidence of adult diabetes in overweight

persons. In the 1939–45 war less adult diabetes occurred and this was probably connected with less overnutrition due to food rationing. The avoidance of obesity is therefore an important preventive feature of adult diabetes (see below).

Another aspect of diabetes where prevention is possible, is *to ensure that treatment prescribed is properly carried out, by arranging for a health visitor to visit regularly all diabetic patients.* If the health visitor is attached to the diabetic clinic, she will be able to get to know the treatment prescribed for each patient. By visiting regularly, she can check whether the treatment is understood and is being followed and whether any early complications, such as peripheral skin lesions are present.

Adverse social conditions in the home can have a disastrous effect on the treatment of a chronic disease such as diabetes and this visiting can reduce the ill effects of difficulties at home. It also allows the physician treating the disease a means of discovering at an early stage any problems which the patient may have in treating the disease at home.

OBESITY

Marked overweight of any individual is associated with an increased tendency to develop the following illnesses:
(*a*) diabetes
(*b*) heart disease (especially ischaemic heart disease)
(*c*) osteoarthritis.

As the obesity increases, the expectation of life of the individual falls—it has been estimated that the expectation of life decreases by 1 per cent for every 1 lb. weight above normal.

Because of this clear association, much illness can be prevented by reducing the weight of persons who are excessively overweight. In particular, *it is most important that the tendency towards overweight is checked in the age group 35 to 50.* The aim should always be to keep the weight below average.

Recently the Medical Research Council has identified three distinct types of obesity:

(1) 'Hibernators' who are overweight persons who have adapted to low-energy diets so that dieting produces less and less effect. Such patients can now have their metabolic rate (and therefore their rate of weight loss) returned to normal under carefully controlled conditions in a metabolic ward.

(2) The 'compulsive eaters' who form a large and well-recognized group whose obesity is entirely due to their continuously ingesting much larger quantities than they need. Any method which reduces the food intake of such patients will reduce their weight. Various strictly controlled dieting methods can be used but often fail eventually because of the tendency of such people to over-eat later. A novel and simple method described by the M.R.C. team is to fit such patients with a dental splint which forces them to stick to a milk-based diet. This has proved a cheap and satisfactory method for it prevents any return to uncontrolled eating at the end of any dietary regime.

(3) The 'small' fat people whose energy requirements are very small because they have so little lean tissue. Such obese patients, who fortunately are a small group, are very difficult to treat and may prove intractable once the condition has become firmly established.

EPILEPSY

The problems created by epilepsy are:

(a) to find an effective treatment in the individual which will control the epilepsy

(b) to help the patient to overcome the social disadvantages which too often follow epilepsy

(c) treatment must be continuous and always calls for much care and patience to ensure that the best combination of drugs is found

(d) unfortunately many stigma are attached to the patient with epilepsy mainly due to ignorance on the part of the public who mistakenly associates epilepsy with dangerous behaviour. Many such patients find it essential to conceal their disease.

In many cases, much illness and many problems can be prevented by special care being taken in the rehabilitation of persons with epilepsy. The question of stigma must never be ignored. By the better understanding, which follows such social aftercare and preventive work, it is often possible to prevent someone who suffers from epilepsy from losing his job, and to add stability to his life. This alone can help him tremendously.

Much still requires to be done both individually with patients and collectively to educate the general public as to the true nature of this disease. Reference has already been made in Chapter 5 to the educational problems in epilepsy (see page 68).

NUTRITIONAL DISORDERS

It is necessary for minute quantities of vitamins to be taken continuously by man to maintain his health. A serious deficiency of vitamins (avitaminosis) will lead to the development of various deficiency diseases. A good sensible mixed diet will avoid any of the deficiency diseases in the adult. The following are the important vitamins:

Vitamin A (or its precursor). Found in liver, herring, eel, sardines, fish, liver oils, cheese, tomatoes, spinach and carrots. This vitamin is also introduced into most butters and margarines.

Vitamin B. Liver, lean meat, bacon and ham, wholemeal bread, oatmeal, nuts, peas and beans, rice-bran, yeast, marmite and bemax.

Vitamin C. Potatoes, hips and haws, brussels sprouts, tomatoes, oranges, lemons, grapefruit, watercress, asparagus tips, parsley, blackcurrants.

Vitamin D. Mackerel, herring, fish liver oils, salmon, eggs (yolk).

Deficiency diseases do not often occur in this country, although rickets was commonly seen 45–55 years ago.

Vitamin A deficiency

Vitamin A is essential for the proper health of epithelial surfaces and for the regeneration of visual purple in the retina.

A deficiency of vitamin A leads to:

(a) difficulties in night vision and eventually night blindness (an inability to see in very poor light);

(b) keratinization of the cornea and also to a hyperkeratosis of the skin.

Vitamin B deficiency

The vitamin B complex contains at least three important factors, *vitamin B₁*, *riboflavine,* and *nicotinic acid.*

Vitamin B₁ deficiency in an acute form is seen in tropical countries, as the disease *beri-beri.* In this country, vitamin B₁ deficiency is usually associated with chronic alcoholics who are taking a high carbohydrate diet with a very low intake of vitamin B₁. Symptoms which develop are those of a peripheral neuritis.

There is a slight risk of vitamin B₁ deficiency in patients on special diets for gastric ulcer, coeliac disease or obesity, but this risk is well known and vitamin B₁ is invariably given to such patients.

Riboflavine deficiency in man shows itself as a dermatitis of the seborrheic type affecting skin around the nose and mouth. Riboflavine should always be given to patients on long courses of wide spectrum antibiotics to prevent a possible subsequent deficiency.

Nicotinic acid deficiency is a major factor in the production of the disease pellagra seen in the maize-eating communities of eastern Europe and Asia.

Occasionally it is seen in this country in conjuction with chronic alcoholism with steatorrhoea.

Vitamin C deficiency

This leads to scurvy, a disease in which bleeding occurs in mucous membranes. Until 150 years ago scurvy was the disease which plagued all sailors whose long voyages using dried foods meant invariably a deficiency of vitamin C. However, Lind discovered that the disease could be avoided by a daily ration of 1 oz. of lime juice. This was an enormously important discovery and is said to have had the immediate effect of doubling the strength of the British Navy as it meant that no longer did ships have to return to port and release their crews every ten weeks. Although it was not then known why lime juice prevented scurvy, this is an excellent example of how a deficiency disease was prevented.

Today in this country there are two groups of people who are liable to suffer from vitamin C deficiency:

(1) *young infants.* All babies, being fed on either breast or dried milks, should always be given vitamin C additives. A convenient form is either orange juice or rose hip syrup;

(2) *old people living on their own* often neglect their diet and are commonly found to have a vitamin C deficiency on being admitted to hospital for some other cause. Occasionally signs of mild scurvy are found among old people living alone. This is most likely to be seen at the end of the winter. Preventive measures include arranging for the diet of the old person to be varied and to contain plenty of vegetables and fresh fruit. The simplest way to ensure this in old people neglecting their diet at home is to arrange for them to have 'Meals on Wheels' delivered to them at least three times a week or, if practicable, for them to attend a luncheon club (see page 205). In this way, it is possible to make certain that sufficient vitamin C is being supplied to them.

Vitamin D deficiency

Vitamin D deficiency leads to *rickets,* which is a disease of nutrition occurring in early childhood. Rickets is extremely rare today in this country. In 1970 an increase in rickets has been reported from Glasgow. This is a timely reminder that, if standards of nutrition fall in any area due, for instance, to increased unemployment, rickets may follow.

In rickets, there is an interference with the normal mechanism of ossification of the bones. Irregular ossification occurs and this leads to various deformities.

Rickets has been largely eliminated from this country by the introduction of vitamin D additives in margarines and by the practice of making certain that all babies have Cod-liver Oil extract, the importance of which is stressed by health visitors to mothers.

It is interesting to note that the rationing regime of the 1939–45 war, with its great emphasis on the importance of welfare foods such as orange juice and cod-liver oil, did much to educate the public of this country. The importance of a sound varied diet containing the necessary vitamins and also proper proportions of proteins, fats and carbohydrates was emphasized. Much health education work today in maternity and childhealth clinics concentrates on the importance of always making certain that the diet is well balanced. This lesson is constantly taught to all pregnant women as regards their own nutrition, as women are particularly receptive to health education in pregnancy, and to all mothers regarding their young children.

The lesson of good nutrition is continued in schools both by teaching and example, as shown by the school meals service.

Already the changes in nutrition are having a great effect on the new generation of children born in the last fifteen years and it is estimated that on an average the school child today is at least 2 inches taller than his counterpart 30 years ago—a change solely brought about by better nutrition.

Goitre

Goitre is an enlargement of the thyroid gland and is usually seen in certain areas of the world, especially Switzerland, parts of France, Derbyshire and Somerset.

The cause of this enlargement is still uncertain but it has been found that the addition of a very small amount of iodine to salt (1 part in 100 000) has greatly reduced goitre in these areas and this is now the normal practice.

Fluoridation of water supplies and dental caries

The association between the amount of natural fluoride in water supplies and the amount of dental caries in the population has led to much research into this question.

It is now clear that a level of 1 part of fluoride per million parts of water is sufficient to reduce significantly the amount of dental caries in children. Many countries of the world including America, Canada and New Zealand have now accepted this practice as a most useful preventive health procedure.

In this country, succesful field trials have been carried out in certain areas and the Department of Health and Social Security has strongly advised water authorities to introduce this important preventive health programme. By 1975, over 3 million of the 46 million population of England were receiving fluoridated water supplies. Unfortunately ill-informed persons have attempted to prevent this advance because of the mistaken viewpoint that there may be danger in the practice. The Secretary of State for Social Services has repeatedly advocated wider use of fluoridation of public water supplies to prevent future generations of children losing their teeth through repeated attacks of dental caries.

Iron Deficiency Anaemia

Infants. A mild degree of anaemia is commonly present in all infants but this normally disappears on the introduction of a mixed diet. However, it is important to realize that, unless some form of iron is introduced into the diet, it may get worse if weaning is delayed. For this reason, it is usual to give small additional doses of iron in the diet to avoid further anaemia.

Adults. In adults iron deficiency anaemia to some extent is commonly present in women between ages of 20 and 50. It is probably due to:

(a) insufficient intake of foodstuffs containing iron

(b) loss of iron in bleeding in menstruation.

The prevention of this anaemia is to encourage a well-balanced diet with adequate proteins and vitamins. Once a degree of anaemia has been confirmed, large doses of iron are given by mouth.

DISEASES CONNECTED WITH OCCUPATION

A number of diseases are caused by contact with various poisons, irritants and dusts. The prevention of such industrial disease is the responsibility of the occupational health services.

Strict standards are laid down regarding the uses of all dangerous chemicals, solvents and gases in industry which could lead to illness. These include the following:

(a) dangerous metals—lead, phosphorus, mercury, arsenic, manganese, antimony, cadmium, chromium, nickel, copper, aluminium

(b) oils, pitch and tar

(c) dangerous gases—ammonia, benzol, carbon dioxide, carbon monoxide, carbon tetrachloride, chlorine, nitrous fumes, petrol, phosgene, sulphur dioxide, sulphuretted hydrogen, trichlorethylene

(d) dangerous solvents

(e) radiation hazards in industry.

Safety measures in industry come under the H.M. Superintending Inspector of Factories to whom all poisoning accidents must be reported. A full investigation is always carried out and wide publicity given to any important preventive method recommended.

Illnesses from industrial poisons vary greatly, from blood disorders to cancers of the skin and to occupational dermatitis. In some instances, such as workers who are continuously working with lead, regular routine blood tests must be carried out to make certain that no hidden changes are occurring in the blood which is a sign of cumulative poisoning.

Some industrial dermatitis can be avoided by all workers having a medical examination *before* they work on hazardous jobs. In this way, it is possible to prevent certain susceptible people ever running these risks. This has been very useful in ensuring that persons with a previous or family history of dermatitis are never employed in a process in which dermatitis is a hazard.

Prevention of dust diseases

The chronic inhalation of certain dusts eventually leads to the development of pathological lesions in the lungs. The most dangerous dusts are those containing minute particles of *silica or asbestos dusts*.

The term *pneumoconiosis* is used to describe diseases caused by these dusts. The industries in which dusts are hazards include a section of the coal-mining industry where the mining of coal includes mining in areas where silica dust occurs. The South Wales hard anthracite mines are a good example.

The level of pneumoconiosis (especially silicosis) was very high among miners from such mines before preventive health measures were introduced in 1945. Silicosis is a fibrotic lung disease in which the lung tissue is slowly destroyed and replaced by fibrosis. Emphysema with loss of vital capacity follows, leading eventually to complete invalidism. Tuberculosis is also a common complication.

Strict preventive measures now include:

(*a*) Regular medical examination, including X-ray, of all men employed in any occupation in which pneumoconiosis is a risk.

(*b*) Immediate suspension from work of anyone found to be suffering from pneumoconiosis, including earliest radiological signs, or from tuberculosis, together with the payment of a special financial benefit if the worker is found to be suffering from pneumoconiosis

As well as these medical examinations, dust diseases may be prevented by:

(*a*) Replacement of a dangerous dust with a harmless one. An example is replacement of sandstone wheels for grinding metals with carborundum. Of course, this replacement is not possible in mining.

(*b*) Dust suppression by good general ventilation, by exhaust ventilation over the process, or by introducing a wet process by which dusts are kept to the minimum.

(*c*) Personal protection of workmen by wearing masks. This is usually only possible for short spells. General reliance should never be placed on workers wearing protective masks.

The inhalation of asbestos dust over a period of years leads to asbestosis. This disease is rather similar to silicosis, but tuberculosis is a rare complication. However, the *risk of cancer of the lung is greatly increased in asbestosis* and has been estimated to be at least ten times that of the general population.

The various preventive measures mentioned above have greatly reduced the risk of developing a pneumoconiosis. They also reduce the seriousness of the condition if it occurs, by removing the man from the dusty occupation as soon as the earliest abnormal signs are discovered on X-ray.

PREVENTION OF ACCIDENTS

Increased attention has been paid recently to all forms of accidents both at work, in the home and on the road.

Traffic accidents

Motor vehicle and other traffic accidents form a major cause of accidental deaths—about 5200 men and 2500 women are killed each year in accidents on the roads.

Industrial accidents

About 650 persons are killed every year at work—360 men and just under 200 women.

There are many contributory factors in occupational accidents, all of which are preventable. Accidents at work can be prevented by:

(a) Careful selection and training of personnel in the factory. Certain people are found to be 'accident prone'—that is, they are very liable to have accidents. Such people can sometimes be recognized early and steps taken to see they are not in positions of danger.

(b) Complete investigation of all accidents. This is undertaken by the Chief Inspector of Factories who publishes an illustrated booklet every quarter, where the causes of accidents are analysed so that the reasons for the accidents can be pointed out, and similar catastrophes avoided.

(c) Good working conditions—good lighting, intelligent use of colours in factories, proper guarding of all machinery.

(d) Good discipline among employees including the wearing of protective clothing. In this country, there has been a great resistance to protective clothing—for instance, the wearing of steel helmets among building operatives is still less common than in America. However, there are now signs that more protective clothing is being worn—certainly it can be decisive in preventing injury in the event of an accident.

Home accidents

Reference has already been made in Chapter 4, page 55, to the importance of preventing home accidents among young children.

The other age group that is particularly liable to home accidents is old people over the age of 65 years. Falls and falling objects are the main cause of accidents in old people. The extra dangers of accidents in the home for older people are shown clearly in Table 8.8 which gives details of such deaths by age and sex groups for England and Wales for 1972. It is important to note the larger numbers of deaths in old women compared with old men, a finding closely connected with the much larger numbers of older women in the community.

Table 8.8   Deaths from home accidents England and Wales 1972

Males aged				Females aged			
0–14	15–44	45–64	65+	0–14	15–44	45–64	65+
329	376	425	878	264	241	475	2371

These accidents can be prevented by:

(1) Good lighting, especially on staircases, landings and passages.

(2) Renewal of faulty equipment—worn carpets, broken stair rods, carpets not properly secured, trailing wires from electrical equipment, loose floor boards.

(3) Ensuring that visual defects in the elderly are corrected by suitable spectacles.

(4) Better understanding by old people of the dangers of home accidents—more effective health education in this respect would help.

PREVENTION OF MENTAL ILLNESS

The exact cause of most mental illness is not yet fully understood. However, a great deal is already known about some of the factors related to the development of mental illness.

These include:
(1) *Intrinsic* factors connected with the person himself and particularly associated with (*a*) heredity
(*b*) phases in his development.

(2) *Extrinsic* factors to do with his occupation, home and life surroundings.

(1) *Intrinsic* factors are complicated. Hereditary factors are more of an inherited predisposition to develop mental illness than being born with an illness. The predisposition may never result in illness and the likelihood of illness developing even in someone with a predisposition depends more on stages in his life and environmental (extrinsic) factors.

The most likely times for mental illness to develop in any individual are puberty, pregnancy, the menopause, late middle age and retirement. As seen in Table 2.7 (page 27) mental illness is the commonest cause of days lost *in women* but only the fifth commonest in man.

(2) *Extrinsic* or environmental factors are even more complicated as each person continuously selects from his environment different features which he perceives. The more unsatisfactory and insecure the surroundings of anyone, the more likely it is that he will develop mental illness, but each person will react differently if placed in the same surroundings.

Once a mental illness has started, the longer the illness has gone on, the more likely it is to be permanent, regardless of the detailed circumstances associated with its commencement. It is, therefore, important to try and diagnose even the very early signs of mental illness—in say a child—for early diagnosis will help treatment.

Many 'functional' disorders are due to bad social effects in the upbringing of the patient, or too rigid or ill-judged moral or cultural standards, or rejection by a parent. Such problems are met with by social workers, health visitors and school nurses in their ordinary work. More and more arrangements are being made to introduce preventive psychiatry into child care services, and many authorities have introduced psychiatrists into the routine work of the child health clinic and in work in community homes with disturbed deprived children.

It is important to realize that it is impossible to protect any person from mental or physical trauma in life—in fact, attempts to do this may very well encourage mental breakdown. It is, however, always possible to alter an environment in one way or another and this may help to avoid an impending illness.

The occupation and work which a person does has an important effect on his mental stability. Much illness can be averted by employment suitable for the person. Careful medical and psychological testing before people are placed in various occupations can help to avoid subsequent mental illness.

Training schemes, as described in Chapter 15, for mentally handicapped persons are invaluable in helping them to be rehabilitated. Great care must always be taken with the placement of maladjusted children in industry when they leave school.

Finally, it is most important that sensible, true and balanced advice is always given. Health education programmes should always be alive to the dangers of wrong advice which may be handed down from parents and grandparents. Many needless fears can be caused in this way and these, in a person predisposed to mental illness, may be the spark which starts off an illness.

9   HEALTH EDUCATION

This book describes some of the ways in which disease can be prevented or alleviated by widespread community services in both the health and social fields. But all these services can only succeed if they are widely accepted and used by the public. The process of persuading people to accept those measures which will improve their health and to avoid those which will have an adverse effect is called **health education.**

Although most people are interested in factors which affect health, the final decisions of each individual are influenced by many different factors making up that person's total environment. His home, the school he attends, the moral teaching, the prejudices and bias, his occupation, all influence decisions.

Much sickness today is the result of faulty personal or community habits including excessive eating and drinking or a lack of exercise or cigarette smoking. Most cases of cancer of the lung, chronic bronchitis and alcoholism come into this category and also a proportion of ischaemic heart disease attacks.

Because these factors are so varied, successful health education must influence the attitudes of individual people and, therefore, must permeate into the home, family life, school, work place and recreation. Health education, if it is to be successful, must therefore have access to as many people as possible—to parents, young children, adolescents, adults, elderly persons, to teachers, employees, employers and all sections of the community.

It is most important to realize that *health education is not the sole responsibility of any one professional health educator* but concerns doctors, health visitors, nurses, health education officers, teachers and social workers. It is the aim of these to ensure that many members of the public also play a rôle in health education—parents, employers, trades union officials, youth leaders, church leaders, politicians, etc. In this way, the educating rôle becomes spread out and the end effects will be equally widespread throughout the community. By these means, ordinary people will be most likely to learn the best ways to maintain positive health.

ORGANIZATION OF HEALTH EDUCATION

The Secretary of State for Social Services has overall responsibility for the policy and conduct and development of health education. Centrally many functions are delegated to the Health Education Council Ltd. Locally the Area Health Authority through its Area Medical Officer is responsible for health education. Local government still retains some health educational functions mainly in respect of the educational services and to a lesser extent in their environmental health and their social services.

Local

Health education is the responsibility of each Area Health Authority under section 28 of the National Health Service Act, 1946. The Area Medical Officer is locally in charge of the promotion of health education. Many of his health education problems are epidemiological; the Area Medical Officer must know what are the most important causes of morbidity or mortality in his area before he can effectively plan a local course of action to improve the health of that community. It is therefore important to measure local health problems carefully using various statistics (see Chapter 2).

Many different professionals play a vital part in this work:

(a) **Health education officers.** Just over half of all area health authorities employ such staff. Many of these officers have had training in a nursing, health visiting or teaching field. Their main function is the organization and promotion of health education by:

(i) training staff to carry out group or individual health education
(ii) collecting and distributing suitable material and information
(iii) assessing and evaluating the effect or impact of the health education undertaken.

(b) **Health visitors** (see Chapter 4) are probably more involved in detailed health education than any other health workers. Much of this work of the health visitor occurs when she is helping the young mother during her pregnancy or after her confinement by giving advice regarding the care of the baby. Any mother is very receptive to health education at such a time for she realizes that the health and proper development of her child rest mainly on the care she takes. She is, therefore, very anxious and keen to do all she can and listens carefully to the expert advice of the health visitor.

The health visitor is also very much concerned with giving health education advice to older children in school, to adolescents, to adults (especially those facing physical or mental handicaps) and also to the increasing number of elderly persons in the community.

The attachment of the health visitor to general practice increases her opportunities for health education.

(c) **General practitioners** have many opportunities for health education especially as the majority of patients have great faith in their doctor's advice. It is important that each doctor realizes his chance to carry out health education at all times during his practice.

(d) **Nursing staff** at all times should also realize the opportunities which they have to help people by educating them in the best ways to promote health and avoid disease.

(e) **Teachers** also have a widespread influence on the lives of their pupils. School life always plays an important part in health education, as any success with children moulds the attitudes of future generations. If children learn the best methods to avoid disease and maintain good health at school, they are most likely to ensure their own children benefit in the same way.

(f) **Social workers** are also involved especially when dealing with children, the handicapped and elderly persons.

It will be understood from this list that *health education is a multidisciplinary task* and that the rôle of the professional health education officer is mainly to help others to play a useful part.

National—*Health Education Council Ltd.*

The national body set up to organize health education is the *Health Education*

Council Ltd. This body has an annual budget of over 1 million pounds, the majority of which comes from a direct grant from the Department of Health and Social Security; and the Welsh Office and the Department of Health and Social Services, Northern Ireland.

The main functions of the Health Education Council include:

(1) To advise on priorities for health education.

(2) To advise and carry out national or local campaigns in cooperation with Area Health Authorities or local authorities.

(3) To produce information and publicity material and publish articles of interest to those engaged in health education.

(4) To sponsor and undertake research—this includes epidemiological and statistical research, cost benefit analysis and evaluation.

(5) To act as the national centre of expertise in health education.

(6) To encourage and promote training in health education work.

(7) To cooperate with local education authorities in schools, colleges and polytechnics.

(8) To maintain contact with and advise various national voluntary bodies engaged in specialized aspects of health education work.

Voluntary bodies and commercial organizations

Many different voluntary bodies are involved nationally in health education especially in the field of **accident prevention**—Royal Society for the Prevention of Accidents (RoSPA), and in cancer education. Commercial organizations mainly prepare visual aid material for use in health education—films, filmstrips, slides. Some of these have both a self-advertising and health educational content. However, much of this commercial advertising is discreetly carried out and such films can be most useful.

METHODS AND TECHNIQUES USED IN HEALTH EDUCATION

Much skill is needed in successful health education for it is never sufficient just to tell people about a special subject. If possible, those being taught should be involved themselves. This means successful health education must depend on first learning as much as possible about the audience. Discussion and argument are valuable and teaching sessions should never be too long. Visual aids of various kinds should be widely used as most people learn more quickly by their use.

There are four main methods of health education:

(*a*) individual health education

(*b*) group health education

(*c*) mass media health education

(*d*) special campaigns.

(*a*) Individual health education

This is always the most effective because most people learn quickly this way and the results are more lasting. Personal discussions between patients and doctors, nurses and health visitors and simple demonstrations in the person's own home are most effective. Much individual health education can most naturally be carried out in connection with ordinary medical, nursing or social work in the course of the day to day tasks. Probably the **general practitioner** is in the ideal position to carry out the most effective personal education as the patient and family have complete faith in him, which is always an important factor in all teaching. While treating patients, the general practitioner should notice conditions within the home and, where necessary, give advice to improve them. In this way accidents will be reduced and diet and food hygiene improved.

Much of the most valuable health education which the **health visitor** carries out is while visiting the patient's home rather than at a clinic. Health education given in this way is more personal and effective. It is invariably very practical because advice is being given in the surroundings in which the patient must carry it out—in his or her own home and environment.

(b) Group health education

This occurs when small groups of people (six to eight) are taught together in child health clinics, schools or factories. Wherever possible, group discussions should be promoted so that everyone plays an active part. Talks should be short (10–15 minutes) and various visual aids should be used—film strips, colour slides or 16 mm films.

Group health education can be particularly useful when the individual finds it difficult to follow the health advice being given as in the case of someone attempting to give up smoking or lose weight. The group itself helps to support the individual in these instances.

(c) Mass media health education

In this technique, the subject is presented to the whole community by means of radio, television, posters and other methods designed to keep certain topics in the public eye.

Many different types of subject can be taught by this means—examples include the prevention of accidents, immunization, nutrition, the dangers of smoking and of venereal disease. Much mass media health education is only effective if it is supported by other means, i.e., by individual and group discussions.

(d) Special health education campaigns

Examples of recent successful health education campaigns mounted by the Health Education Council include:
(1) Smoking in pregnancy emphasizing the dangers that can be created for the unborn child
(2) Alcoholism
(3) Safe handling of medicines.

Local campaigns are also mounted from time to time to encourage a certain topic, i.e., immunization or accident prevention. Excellent results can be obtained in this way by using a **'community mobilization technique'** whereby volunteers are recruited to visit 15–20 homes to persuade the occupants to co-operate. Spectacular results have been obtained in this way as seen in the most successful mass X-ray campaigns held in Glasgow and Liverpool (see page 90).

It is important to realize that health education campaigns have two limitations:

(1) all campaigns can only be effective for a short period of 3–4 weeks

(2) a very successful campaign may be followed by a dangerous lack of interest. This is seen particularly in campaigns held to boost immunization. Because of this feature, it is essential to combine the use of campaigns with other methods of health education so that the improvements will be more lasting.

Concentration on special problems

Occasionally it is necessary to concentrate health education on new problems that are developing within a community to prevent them becoming permanent. An example is *drug misuse* which is currently an increasing menace. In tackling any such problem, there will always be two main facets:

(1) *primary prevention* to reduce the likelihood of more victims becoming involved;

(2) *secondary prevention* to help those already misusing drugs and to prevent further deterioration of their condition.

In drug misuse one of the greatest difficulties to overcome is to build up an effective communication system with those already taking drugs. Special arrangements may have to be made and special social workers or volunteers have to be used in those taking drugs. This emphasises that health education if it is to be totally successful must use a wide range of staff.

Examples of health education

Most of the community health or social problems discussed in this book can be influenced by health education. *Much prevention of disease and of social problems depends on health education,* i.e., persuading people to act early enough to prevent a disease starting or a social problem from developing. Health education is important at all ages, but especially in *childhood, pregnancy and early motherhood* and in old age.

The list of health education topics is a long one and, to avoid duplication, the reader is referred to the appropriate chapter. The topics include:

(1) Ante-natal care (Chapter 3)

(2) All aspects of child health care (Chapter 4)

(3) Child care (Chapter 13)

(4) Prevention of disease by immunization (Chapter 6)

(5) Accident prevention in children (Chapter 4) and in old age (Chapter 16)

(6) Nutrition (Chapter 8)

(7) Prevention of communicable disease (Chapter 7)

(8) Smoking (Chapter 8)

(9) Venereal disease (Chapter 7)

(10) Cancer education (Chapter 8)

(11) Dental care (Chapter 5)

(12) Atmospheric pollution and other environmental health problems (Chapter 11).

10 INTERNATIONAL DISEASE CONTROL

The control of international health has become increasingly important in a world in which the rate of travel from one country to another is becoming progressively faster.

The international controlling body for health in the world is the World Health Organization (WHO) which was set up from the work of an expert committee of the Economic and Social Council of the United Nations in 1946.

By the end of 1976 there were 135 member states in WHO including all the major powers in the world, the headquarters of which are at Geneva but Regional Offices have now been set up in:

Africa	at Brazzaville
USA	at Washington DC
India	at New Delhi
Denmark	at Copenhagen
Egypt	at Alexandria
Philippines	at Manila.

Although WHO is concerned with all problems of health, it has always paid particular attention to the value of preventive medicine and has always played an important rôle in stimulating and assisting in developing the preventive medical services of the under-developed countries.

The principle that has been constantly followed by WHO is that 'health is now a world responsibility . . . for health, like peace, is one and indivisible'.

Reporting service run by World Health Organization on the world-wide incidence of serious infectious disease

The WHO publishes weekly a bulletin on the world-wide incidence of serious infectious diseases and particularly on:

Smallpox	Cholera
Plague	Typhus
Yellow Fever	Relapsing fever.

This bulletin contains exact details of numbers of such cases and the cities and ports in which they have occurred throughout the world. It also records brief details of other unusually large epidemics (such as influenza) which may be occurring in different parts of the world. It notes any changes made locally by a country in its immunization or vaccination requirements so that those advising travellers are kept informed.

These bulletins are invaluable as a reliable up-to-date record of the incidence of serious infection and are of the utmost importance to medical officers at all large ports and airports.

A daily epidemiological radio-telegraphic bulletin is broadcast by the World Health Organization from:

Geneva	Keelung
Saigon	Manila

and once or twice a week broadcasts from

Tokyo	Karachi
Hongkong	Madras
Singapore	Mauritius.

Control of smallpox in the United Kingdom

Smallpox is on the verge of becoming extinct. At the time this book goes to press, the last remaining focus of the disease in the world is in Somalia and Kenya. The World Health Organization is concentrating a great deal of effort into ensuring that the disease is totally eradicated from the world. This is very likely as there are no known reservoirs of infection in any living creature other than man.

A shortened account is now given (on page 86–87) of the well-proven methods used to prevent the importation and spread of smallpox in the United Kingdom.

Port and airport health control

New methods of health clearance at ports are currently being studied at South-ampton, Milford Haven and Immingham. The system being tried is similar to that used in the U.S.A. since 1973. Masters of ships must report by radio in advance of their arrival the occurrence of any illness in terms of signs and symptoms rather than specific diseases. Where necessary a doctor would visit and, in addition, a random sample of ships would be subjected to inspection. This is similar to the system which has operated satisfactorily at airports.

Control of imported foods likely to cause disease

Additional preventive medical work undertaken by the port health staff includes the examination of all imports of foodstuffs into this country to make certain that no unsound or diseased food stuffs are imported, which might later lead to disease. Stringent regulations are laid down concerning food imports. All meat, for instance, that is imported must be in a recognizable form and must bear *the official certificate* of the country of origin, stating that it has been properly inspected. In addition, food inspectors carefully examine the meat for signs of disease which, if found, results in the condemnation of that meat.

All tinned products are also tested to make certain that tins are sound. A small proportion are further examined by a bacteriologist to ensure that the tins have been properly processed and the contents sterilized.

Egg products that are imported are also carefully sampled and examined. In recent years investigations and sampling have shown that some egg imports were infected with salmonella bacteria which cause food poisoning. Much research work finally developed a satisfactory heat treatment process whereby such products can be rendered completely safe for human consumption without altering the nature of the egg albumen.

Dessicated coconut was another imported foodstuff shown to be infected with salmonella bacteria. These imports came from Sri Lanka and, as a result of the findings, the government of Sri Lanka has improved greatly the standard of production.

FURTHER PREVENTIVE MEDICAL WORK CARRIED OUT BY WHO

Each year there is a World Health Assembly arranged by WHO at which all important health problems are considered and special relevance topics are high-lighted.

The main concern of WHO is *to induce self help* in countries by sending small teams of experts to the under-developed countries to study their methods and suggest ways in which the preventive health services can be improved. This has been done very successfully in many places and, as a result of the improvements introduced, the infant mortality of some of the worst under-developed countries has already been dramatically reduced.

COMMUNICABLE DISEASE CONTROL

Some of the most successful preventive medical work of the World Health Organization has been in the control of widespread communicable diseases in many countries.

Malaria

The control of *malaria* has been one of the major aims of WHO since its formation.

This work has been so successful that the annual number of malaria deaths has dropped significantly. There are however still approximately 1100 million people in the world who are at risk of catching malaria. This number is steadily decreasing each year and malaria has already been completely eradicated from much of the world (i.e. the total North American continent north of Mexico). All countries still see imported cases. In England and Wales in 1974 these numbered 595 (with 2 deaths) although the risk of indigenous cases is minimal (about 1 cases annually in England and Wales).

The work of WHO in malaria control has always been concentrated:
(*a*) upon improving treatment facilities to reduce the effect of the attack and the chances of subsequent infection to others
(*b*) upon preventive measures which are specially planned
(i) to improve the environmental factors which, if faulty, encourage mosquito multiplication and aid the spread of malaria. These include the drainage of swamps, ditches and other stagnant water, and widespread spraying with insecticide. To assist in this work, a number of expert sanitary engineers are employed by WHO to visit countries and give advice:
(ii) to introduce medical preventive measures whereby populations at special risk receive drugs regularly as a prophylactic.

In addition, many research studies in the problems of malaria are encouraged and financed by WHO including:

(1) Susceptibility of mosquitoes to new insecticides;
(2) Researches using medicated salt to give populations prophylactic drugs;
(3) Studies in drug resistance;
(4) Studies on new anti-malarial drugs.

Cholera

WHO has been very active in planning programmes for the prevention of cholera especially in India and the East. During the past decade, the *El Tor* cholera vibrio has almost completely replaced the classic strain.

In 1971 there was a threat of a cholera pandemic when over 171 000 cases were traced in 38 countries. Since then numbers have fallen but the international surveillance of cholera has been one of the major tasks of WHO. It constantly receives, consolidates and disseminates epidemiological information about cholera incidence in its weekly bulletins. As many of the countries at greatest risk of cholera epidemics have limited health resources, much of the work of WHO has been to help research into finding suitable methods for cholera surveillance. Vaccination results against this type of cholera have been disappointing.

Tuberculosis

Tuberculosis has been the target for many preventive medical campaigns launched by the WHO. Work has included widespread immunization campaigns using BCG vaccine as well as the detailed planning of many national programmes for the proper treatment and control of this disease.

A widespread training programme for medical and nursing personnel has been arranged so that self help in the fight against tuberculosis can be encouraged in all countries.

The cost of certain anti-tuberculosis drugs such as PAS has been too prohibitive for some developing countries and research has been promoted by the World Health Organization to find cheaper alternative drugs.

One of the great problems in the eradication of tuberculosis which the World Health Organization has found, has been the *indifference of patients in the self-administration of anti-tuberculosis drugs.*

WHO has supported research into tuberculosis in:
(*a*) developing international quality control of BCG vaccine
(*b*) development of cheap and effective combination of drugs for treating the disease
(*c*) studies of drug resistance
(*d*) investigations into jet methods of injection of vaccines.

Sexually transmitted diseases

Many researches into the level of sexually transmitted diseases in many underdeveloped countries have been carried out by the World Health Organization.

At the World Health Assembly held in 1975 a resolution was passed requesting all Governments to consider the need;
(1) to make optimal use of existing services and health structures to strengthen the control of sexually transmitted diseases,

(2) to encourage the appropriate training, in this field, of medical personnel and other workers at all levels and the further training of existing personnel,

(3) to promote information and health education to all concerned in order to develop the sense of responsibility and respect for the integrity of all human beings.

Leprosy

The World Health Organization has been very active in developing services for the recognition and early treatment of leprosy.

In high endemic areas, special emphasis has been given to surveys of school-children. In one recent survey in Burma, the rate of leprosy in schoolchildren was found to be 36 per thousand. Early treatment of such cases prevents these children becoming open cases and developing disabilities, and will also reduce the contagiousness of the disease.

Special World Health Organization advisory teams are constantly visiting affected countries to carry out surveys, give advice on anti-leprosy program-mes and on the training of the countries' own medical workers.

The World Health Organization has also continued to support and carry out research into the transmission of human leprosy and into chemotherapeutic methods of treatment and into the epidemiology of leprosy.

Trachoma

This disease of the eye which so often leads to blindness has been one of the constant medical problems of many tropical countries. WHO has continuously helped in campaigns designed to prevent this disease. Widespread help has been given by the Organization in awarding fellowships for work on trachoma research.

Special teaching courses have been constantly arranged for ophthal-mologists, in laboratory, clinical and epidemiological techniques.

Consultant services are also provided to help countries develop their own trachoma control services.

Rabies

The WHO is playing an increasing rôle in providing up-to-date information on the spread of rabies in wild animals especially in Europe.

General work of WHO

In addition, the WHO has undertaken much international preventive work connected with the control of yaws, the parasitic diseases including bilhar-ziasis, trypanosomiasis, filarial infections, leishmaniasis and mycotic diseases.

The World Health Organization is also responsible for recommending changes in *international quarantine.*

Other preventive and research work assisted or supported by WHO includes:

(1) Many types of vaccine trials

(2) Promotion of maternity and child health services

 (3) Research into causation of accidents
 (4) Research into mental health
 (5) Studies in environmental health
 (6) Research into cardiovascular diseases
 (7) Studies into social and occupational health
 (8) Research into human genetics
 (9) Nutritional studies
(10) Promotion of dental health
(11) Health education
(12) Development of nursing services
(13) Prevention of radiation hazards
(14) Development of health laboratory services
(15) Drug addiction studies
(16) Standardization of pharmaceutical drugs and products

The World Health Organization also arranges for many travelling medical and nursing fellowships so that there is a high level of co-ordination in world health services.

11 ENVIRONMENTAL HEALTH CONTROL

Many of the everyday factors within our lives can have a marked effect upon our health. These include the area and house we live in, the atmosphere we breathe, the food we eat and the water we drink. Usually in a civilized well-developed country, most of these factors are well controlled and their effect upon health is often forgotten. In primitive communities, however, the connection between environment and health is more obvious as there is often much infectious disease spread in this way.

In this chapter, it is the intention to consider *environmental* health problems to show what effect on health defects of environment can produce.

HOUSING AND TOWN PLANNING

The house a person lives in has a very important influence upon that individual's life and wellbeing. It also has a significant effect upon his health.

A satisfactory house must reach certain physical standards, such as being free from dampness, being well lighted and ventilated, having a proper water system including hot water system and bath, an adequate internal water closet, sinks and proper drainage system, adequate means for preparing, storing and cooking food. These physical standards are invariably found in modern houses, but many of the old houses especially in industrial areas lack them.

The house must also be suitable for the family living there, and this means that not only must it be large enough, but it should be sited in an attractive way not being too close to other houses, and form an integral part of a group of houses or area.

No family living in an inadequate house will be able to enjoy life completely. But nor will all the families of a large area be able to live properly unless all the necessary community services—shops, churches, schools, doctors' houses, child health clinics, hospitals, community centres, cinemas, etc., are present. In communities such as a country town which has developed over many years—often centuries—all the facilities will usually be present for they have been added to the community gradually.

It is in the area which has developed quickly in which so many of these facilities are missing. Examples include:

(*a*) *'Slum' areas* in industrial towns which were built in the last century when the absence of transport led factory owners to crowd together too many houses in small areas. With the bad planning of these houses and their deterioration, they now provide overcrowded, unpleasant, damp and unhealthy homes.

(*b*) many new housing estates contain sound houses but all too often the necessary *community facilities* are ignored. So, hundreds of houses may be built without often even the barest essential community services, such as shops being considered.

It is now known that good town planning of a whole *neighbourhood unit* is essential in all urban development. Since 1948, new towns and housing areas have always attempted to follow the neighbourhood unit plan. No developments should be too large, and a neighbourhood unit for about 10 000 persons is considered ideal. Within this unit not only should the necessary houses be built but essential services such as shops, schools, community centre (library, police station, clinics), health centres etc. should be provided.

Effects of bad housing on health

Although slum clearance—the demolition of unsuitable houses—has been going on since the 1920s, there still remain many poor houses in the large cities and industrial towns. What effect does this poor housing have upon the health of those living in the slums?

It is not difficult to demonstrate that the health of the people living in slum areas is inferior to those living in good ones. There is a greater amount of communicable disease present, and the children developing the usual childhood infectious diseases have a higher incidence of complications. Overcrowding which is always present in slums leads to greater ease of infection of the airborne diseases and the best example is *pulmonary tuberculosis*. This disease is commoner in the slum population. *Acute rheumatic fever* is mainly seen today in children from slum areas.

The effect of the poor housing is often to make the individual *more liable* to disease than actually to produce the disease. Many a patient living in bad housing who develops tuberculosis, feels the bad house has caused the disease. This, of course, is not so, for the disease has been caused by an attack on the lung by the tubercle bacillus. But the poor housing and living conditions have made the accident of infection more likely.

The majority of poor houses are damp—either from defective roofs or gutters allowing rain water to enter the house, or by rising dampness percolating upwards from the ground, due to the absence of a damp-proof course. Damp living conditions lead to an exacerbation of various *rheumatic problems* so commonly found later in life, a *higher child mortality,* and a greater incidence of serious chest conditions such as *acute bronchitis.* Such conditions also aggravate *chronic bronchitis* in the elderly.

Dampness always has a most depressing effect on the occupants of the home who see their efforts at redecoration ruined and leads to much unhappiness and aggravation of minor mental and emotional disorders.

The overcrowding effect of poor housing has a stultifying effect upon the proper development of the family. It is obvious that no family can hope to reach its full potential in such conditions—children cannot work properly and their school development suffers—adults give up because the effort to overcome the difficulties becomes too great. The extra strain of looking after a mentally handicapped child in such conditions is tremendous and is often so difficult that the child has to be admitted to hospital when he could have stayed happily at home if only the house had been suitable.

Poor housing cannot be said to be a cause of mental illness but it certainly is a contributory factor and has a very bad and often disastrous effect on the mentally ill patient living in such a house. Even after the acute stage of the mental illness has passed, unsatisfactory home conditions can retard recovery.

The *level of accidents* both in children and old persons is much higher in those living in poor houses. This is due to bad lighting and very steep unsuitable stairs which predispose to falling accidents. Overcrowding often leads to an increased number of scalds and burns.

Poor housing conditions not only predispose the individual to attacks of some diseases but may also be a most important factor in the *correct management of illness*. A patient with angina of effort or a chronic cardiac condition must be able to avoid stairs. In a modern house, it is usually possible to arrange this by turning a downstairs room into a temporary bedroom and this works quite well, especially if there is a downstairs lavatory. But in the slum house, this would be impossible and the management of such a case is made difficult. Either the patient would have to climb steep stairs or stay permanently upstairs; there is also the complication that in the slum house there is not usually an inside lavatory.

The management of various forms of malignant disease is made very difficult in slum houses. A case with a colostomy, for instance, will produce many extra problems in the absence of a bathroom, internal lavatory and proper washing facilities.

Local authorities realize the importance of doing all they can to provide good houses. It is usual for the Housing Authority to give *special priority for urgent housing for really important medical reasons* so that the effect of poor housing on health can be minimized. Much tuberculosis infection is prevented in this way by the rapid rehousing of a patient's family if they are living in an overcrowded slum house.

Methods of dealing with unsatisfactory houses

Unsatisfactory houses can be dealt with in a number of ways:
(*a*) slight defects can be put right by using s. 93 of the Public Health Act 1936 and serving an abatement notice on the owner.
(*b*) individual unfit houses can be demolished or repaired (s. 16–17 Housing Act 1957).
(*c*) houses or parts of houses may be closed.
(*d*) large Clearance Areas can be defined under s. 42 Housing Act 1957. This is the usual method used for large scale slum clearance. The Department of the Environment holds a local inquiry where the council has to provide public evidence of unfitness of houses and where owners can bring their own evidence.
(*e*) houses in multiple occupation can be controlled (Part II Housing Act 1961).
(*f*) special measures can be used to improve houses.

All these methods are used by the environmental health inspectors who are responsible for this work.

Atmospheric pollution and health

Although atmospheric pollution has improved markedly in the last few years, many of our large cities and towns, especially those in industrial areas, have their atmosphere constantly polluted by smoke and other fumes in the air. It is known that the health of the people living in such areas is affected by this atmospheric contamination.

Atmospheric pollution is probably a small factor in the production of lung cancer, for it is known that the level of lung cancer is higher in industrial areas than in country areas. It is a minor problem compared with cigarette smoking, but is a factor.

However, the most serious danger to health occurs in those unfortunate people who have some degree of *chronic bronchitis*. Many of these are elderly and their respiratory and cardiac function is impaired. The climate of this country with its damp misty winter days always tends to make such patients worse but really serious medical problems arise when atmospheric pollution in the form of a smoky fog (smog) occurs. To such patients even minor pollution increases their symptoms while a major fog, lasting a few days, often brings them very near complete collapse. For instance, in the historic smog of London in December 1952, it is estimated that just under 4000 patients with chronic bronchitis died. The inhalation of smoky particles and/or sulphur gases commonly present in industrial areas both play a part in aggravating the chronic bronchitic.

Living in an atmosphere that is always dirty has a most depressing effect upon people and adds greatly to their daily problems. Since the Clean Air Act came into force in 1956, local authorities have progressed towards the ideal of clearing the atmosphere of all pollution. It is hoped to achieve this by:
(*a*) preventing the building of any new factory plant unless its means of producing heat or power are completely smokeless. *Prior approval* of all such plans must be given by local authorities before any building construction can start;
(*b*) introducing *smoke control areas* in which it is an offence to produce any smoke at all or to burn ordinary coal. Before any part of a town can be made such an area, all the houses must have cooking and heating methods which are smokeless. This may mean replacing old grates with modern ones capable of burning smokeless fuel. A more satisfactory method is to change to other forms of power such as oil, gas or electricity. To help the householder to meet the cost of these conversions, 70 per cent of the cost is paid by a grant from the local authority who in turn get 40 per cent from the central government. This means the householder has to pay 30 per cent of the cost. This grant is only given for conversions necessary to comply with the introduction of a new smoke control area.

Already in most industrial towns where smoke control areas have been widely introduced, there is a noticeable improvement in times of mist and fog. However due to the financial crisis much of this improvement has now ceased.

FOOD CONTROL

Many diseases that affect animals can also attack man. The prevention of such illnesses depends on the care and control of food production and on the various inspections taking place to avoid contaminated food ever being eaten by man.

Food inspection at ports

As much of our food is imported from abroad, a very careful inspection is made of all food imports at the port of importation. Each consignment is inspected and sampled and can only be imported if the *port health staff* are satisfied as to its high standard.

All meat imported has to have a special certificate of purity from the country of origin and, in addition, is carefully examined by *meat inspectors*. If any disease is found, the complete carcase is given a very careful further examination. If the disease is only local, and the diseased portion can be completely removed, this is done. But, if the disease is widespread, the whole carcase is condemned and either has to be re-exported or destroyed, or stained and sent for animal foodstuff after complete sterilization. Certain meats are *prohibited meats* and cannot be imported, including:

(*a*) scrap meat which cannot be identified

(*b*) meat comprising parts of the wall of the thorax or abdomen from which any part of pleura or peritoneum has been detached

(*c*) meat, except mutton and lamb, from which a lymphatic gland has been taken out

(*d*) the head of an animal without a submaxillary gland.

Tinned goods are sampled and examined and a small sample is sent to a bacteriologist for a full and complete bacteriological examination to check on the sterility of the product. If the results are unsatisfactory, the whole consignment is condemned and not allowed to be imported.

All types of foodstuffs are examined in the same careful way.

With many new independent countries developing, careful inspection and sampling of all imported foodstuffs is even more important than usual for, in the process of independence, there may be a temporary lowering of standards of cleanliness in food control. Sampling at the port is the great safeguard to ensure that no contaminated food can enter this country.

Meat inspection

Continuous meat inspection is undertaken on all meat and food produced and eaten in this country.

Meat is examined by specially trained inspectors immediately after slaughter in the abbatoir. A systematic, careful inspection is made of all carcases: if any disease is found, it is dealt with in the same way as already described in port meat inspection.

Tuberculosis was a disease which, thirty years ago, was common in cattle in this country. Today it is very rarely seen, but it is still important to take steps to avoid tuberculosis and other infected meat ever coming into a kitchen, for if this occurs, infection is very likely, as working surfaces, such as tables, will soon become contaminated. The pathogenic bacteria in the meat might be destroyed by heat in the cooking of the meat, but other foodstuffs would rapidly be infected via the contaminated working surfaces and disease spread in this way. The Aberdeen typhoid epidemic of 1964 was probably spread in this way—from a contaminated counter in a cooked meat department of a supermarket.

For this reason, contaminated meat can only be used for animal foodstuffs provided it is sterilized and thoroughly stained with a dye to make such meat easily recognizable.

Other diseases commonly found in animal carcases include various animal parasites and tapeworms such as *taenia solium, trichinella spiralis, hydatid cysts*.

There are also a number of infectious conditions in animals which lead to the condemnation of the meat including various forms of *salmonellosis, septicaemia, anthrax, pyaemia* and *actinomycosis*.

Prevention of disease by control of milk supplies

Milk is a very important and essential part of our food supplies and forms the basis of all infant feeding. Milk supplies have always been particularly liable to lead to the spread of infectious disease because:

(a) the cow suffers from two diseases which can be passed on to man via her milk—*tuberculosis* and *brucellosis*

(b) the ease with which milk supplies may be contaminated in the process of collecting and distributing milk. In the past, before modern clean methods of milk distribution were perfected, epidemics traced to such causes included *typhoid, paratyphoid, diphtheria, scarlet fever* and other *streptococcal* infections, *food poisoning, dysentery, gastroenteritis* and *brucellosis*.

The prevention of milk infection in this country is now complete and it is extremely rare for infection of any kind to be traced to milk and then only after very gross carelessness. It is, however, only relatively recently that such a satisfactory state has existed, for forty years ago much infectious disease was caused by milk.

The improvement has resulted from:

(a) a nationwide campaign by the Ministry of Agriculture, Fisheries and Food to eradicate tuberculosis from all dairy herds. This scheme, started modestly in the late 1930s, has rapidly been extended to include the majority of the country. This campaign, which was introduced with financial bonuses to encourage the farmer to keep a tuberculin free herd, has been so successful that today there is hardly any tuberculosis among cows.

The inspection of farms and equipment to ensure that good standards are maintained throughout the country, is undertaken by officials of the Ministry of Agriculture, Fisheries and Food.

(b) the large scale pasteurization of milk supplies. *Pasteurization of milk* means the subjection of the milk to heat treatment for a specified time so that any live pathogenic or disease-producing bacteria are killed. The usual process of pasteurization is the *High Temperature Short Time process* in which milk is retained at a temperature of not less than 71.5°C (161°F) for 15 seconds and then immediately cooled to a temperature of not more than 10°C (50°F).

Another but less popular method of pasteurization is by the *Holder* process in which the milk is maintained in a vat at a temperature of not less than 62.8°C (145°F) and not more than 65.5°C (150°F) for at least half an hour and then immediately cooled to a temperature of not more than 10°C (50°F). Both processes kill all pathogenic bacteria and so render the milk safe. No important food value is lost by pasteurization although the fat emulsion may be slightly affected and the cream does not rise as readily.

Immediately after pasteurization, the milk is bottled by machine and sealed so that no further chance of contamination can occur. In this way, the milk is delivered to the householder completely safe and free from infection.

Before the introduction of these preventive medical safeguards, many children and young persons developed attacks of tuberculous cervical adenitis and tuberculous peritonitis as well as tuberculous infection of the bones and joints, and meningitis. Raw milk has recently been shown to be the cause of a number of salmonella food poisoning outbreaks. Pasteurization is the only way to prevent such communicable diseases.

Sterilized milk is milk which has been filtered and homogenized and then maintained at a temperature of not less than 100°C (212°F) for such a period as to comply with the turbidity test. In practice the milk after filtering and homogenizing is poured into bottles and heated to 108°C (228°F) for 10–12 minutes.

Ultra-heat-treated milk has been retained at a temperature of not less than 132°C (270°F) for a period of not less than one second, and then immediately placed in sterile containers in which it is supplied to the consumer.

As a further precaution, any person working in a dairy shop who develops a communicable disease must notify the local 'proper officer' who is the Specialist in Community Medicine in a Metropolitan District and the District Community Physician in county areas. The 'proper officer' can prohibit the sale of milk if it is likely to cause disease, until it has been heat treated.

The 'proper officer' can also prohibit any person who is an open infectious case of tuberculosis from working in a dairy or milking cows on a farm.

There is no doubt that the widespread powers in this country to prevent disease from being spread by milk have been most successful. Today pasteurized milk in this country is a completely safe and reliable food supply and is completely free from possible pathogenic bacteria such as brucellosis or tuberculosisor salmonellosis.

Sampling to prevent adulteration of milk and food supplies

The adulteration of food supplies is very carefully guarded against by the continuous sampling of all foodstuffs. It is important that the public must be able to rely on any food they buy being unadulterated. At the beginning of the century, there was widespread adulteration of food in this country and this led to disease due both to dangerous additives to food and the lowering of nutritional value of some foods diluted in this way.

The adding of water to milk is fortunately easily detected by a test on the freezing point of milk—the *adulterated milk has a higher freezing point*. Sampling of milk supplies goes on all the time and very heavy penalties are given to the rare offenders. The dilution of milk by adding water is not only grossly dishonest but as milk is used for the basis of infant feeding, could lead to undernutrition in babies.

Only very limited preservatives are allowed to be added to certain foods. It is illegal to add preservatives to the majority of foods including all milk products. This is because preservatives could mask staleness of food and encourage incorrect food storage which would make food poisoning attack more likely. Examples of foods in which limited preservatives may be added are sausages, jams, and pickles.

Environmental health inspectors carry out sampling which, of course, is always without warning, on shops and stores selling food and drugs and drink. Samples are tested for purity and for any evidence of adulteration. This constant vigilance has resulted in a very high standard being maintained in all food products, and cases of adulteration are very rare.

SPECIAL PRECAUTIONS FOR SPECIAL FOODSTUFFS

Certain foodstuffs are particularly liable to contamination which may result in disease in man, and special precautions are necessary to avoid this. Good examples of such foods are shell-fish and ice cream.

Shell-fish

Many shell-fish are eaten raw. For this reason, special precautions must be taken to ensure that shell-fish do not become contaminated with pathogenic bacteria. Unfortunately shell-fish often contain *typhoid* and *paratyphoid bacilli* if they have been collected from a sea-shore or sea which is grossly contaminated with sewage. A number of outbreaks of typhoid fever have been caused in this way.

Many parts of our sea-shore are polluted, as crude sewage is often emptied into river mouths.

Special regulations are enforced preventing the collection of shell-fish from dangerously polluted beaches. Shell-fish can be purified by immersion in specially prepared tanks for two to three weeks, and this is carried out commercially in certain places to make certain that no danger of spreading typhoid exists.

Ice cream

Ice cream is particularly liable to spread infection because, although bacteria will not multiply at the low temperatures necessary for ice cream, the bacteria present in ice cream will be preserved at such temperatures. This means that a disease like *typhoid fever* which can easily be spread by a tiny infecting dose could be spread widely by ice cream which has become contaminated with typhoid bacilli. This is exactly what happened in the Aberystwyth ice cream typhoid outbreak in 1945 when over 100 cases of typhoid occurred.

To prevent any possible recurrence, all ice cream must now be pasteurized and then cooled and left at a temperature not above 9.3°C (45°F) until frozen. This compulsory pasteurization has prevented the danger of further epidemics of typhoid.

Special preventive measures relating to food handlers

Under Food Hygiene (General) Regulations 1970 special precautions must be taken by all food handlers in shops and stalls to avoid spreading disease. These include:

(*a*) All steps must be taken to avoid food becoming contaminated—food must be covered and protected from flies and contact with the public.

(*b*) No open food—that is food not in a tin or jar—must be placed lower than 18 inches (45cm) from the ground.

(*c*) Anybody handling food must keep his person and clothes clean.

(*d*) Any open cut or abrasion must be covered by a waterproof dressing. This is to avoid staphylococcal lesions in whitlows, boils, etc., from contaminating food and causing a food poisoning.

(*e*) All food handlers must refrain from spitting and smoking.

(*f*) All wrapping paper must be clean—newspapers are not allowed except for uncooked vegetables.

(*g*) Any food handler who becomes aware that he is suffering from *typhoid* or *paratyphoid fever, salmonella* infection, *dysentery* or *staphylococcal* infection, must notify the 'proper officer'—the Specialist in Community Medicine (Environmental Health) in Metropolitan Districts or District Community Physician in County Areas immediately.

In addition, there are widespread regulations about food premises all designed to reduce the chance of infection. These include regulations about the provisions of washing facilities with hot and cold water, working surfaces to prevent accumulation of bacteria in cracks on unsuitable surfaces. Also standards are laid down for the construction of premises and the temperature at which foods may be stored.

Further regulations concern many aspects of the transport and handling of foodstuffs. All are designed to prevent the spread of disease.

CONTROL OF WATER SUPPLIES

In this country, the control of water supplies, their purification and cleanliness has been so reliable that one hardly considers that this is an important health safeguard. The disastrous epidemic of typhoid in Zermatt, in Switzerland, in 1963 reminds one of the dangers which face any population which ignores stringent high safety standards.

There are two bacterial diseases spread by water—*typhoid fever* and *cholera*. Cholera is a disease seen mainly in the East which can spread mainly by grossly inadequate water and sewage systems. Its epidemic spread today in this country is virtually impossible.

But typhoid fever could quite easily be spread by water unless constant care is taken to ensure that the purification of water is complete. This entails:-
(*a*) storage of water in reservoirs;
(*b*) filtration of water;
(*c*) sterilization of water using chlorine to make certain that any bacteria not removed by filtration are killed.

In addition, great care is always needed to make certain that no employee in a water works contaminates the supply. In particular, *it is essential to make certain that no typhoid carriers are ever employed in a water works.* Careful medical tests including agglutination blood tests are carried out on all such employees to reduce the chance of a carrier not being detected among the staff of the water works. The last serious water-borne outbreak of typhoid fever in this country was in Croydon in 1937 when 290 cases of typhoid fever occurred. It was caused by a urinary carrier contaminating the water supply while he assisted in work on a deep well forming part of Croydon's water supply.

Very high standards are maintained in the water supplies in this country and further large scale outbreaks of water-borne typhoid are most unlikely to occur. The most vulnerable supplies are probably some country supplies especially during the crowded holiday months of July and August. Constant sampling, which goes on in all water supplies, is an extra safeguard for such sampling will immediately show if the purity of the water supply has suddenly deteriorated.

The freedom of infection from water supplies in this country is no guide to the hazards of many continental countries. *Many cases of typhoid occur each year in travellers from Italy, Spain and North Africa* especially when these travellers have stayed in remote country areas or on camping holidays. If such a holiday is planned, it is essential either:
(i) to *sterilize all water* with a simple camp sterilization outfit; or
(ii) to be *protected with a course of TAB inoculation* before starting. This protects against typhoid fever and paratyphoid fever (see page 77).

Fluoridation of water supplies

It is known that the variation in dental caries found in different areas is connected with the content of natural fluoride in the water consumed by the people of that area (see page 113).

In localities where the natural fluoride content of the water supply is low, fluoride can be added to the water supply to bring the level to about one part of fluoride per million parts of water. This has been done in many parts of the world and has always been followed by a substantial reduction in the amount of dental caries in the children in that area. After pilot trials, the Department of Health and Social Security has advised that all water supplies should have fluoride added to them where the natural supply of fluoride is deficient. It is known that if this is done, there should be a reduction of at least 60 per cent in the dental caries. A number of areas (about 7 per cent of England and Wales) have already introduced artificial fluoridation. Unfortunately ill-informed persons have campaigned very forcibly against fluoridation on the grounds that it is 'mass medication' and an intrusion into their individual liberty.

This attitude is very difficult to understand when it is realized that chlorine is added to all water supplies for safety. There is ample evidence that fluoridation would be a most valuable preventive medical factor and would undoubtedly result in far less pain and suffering in children from dental caries. It is to be hoped that this public reaction will not be allowed to interfere with what is a most valuable preventive dental service.

The 'social services' in the United Kingdom cover many different types of services but mainly fall into 3 well-defined groups:

(1) Social services provided by *local authority social services departments* which include a wide range of statutory, domiciliary and residential services for children, physically disabled, mentally disabled, homeless and elderly people. Since 1974, the hospital social work services are also provided by local authorities although such work is entirely undertaken within a hospital setting.

These types of social services are described in Chapters 13 to 16, each chapter dealing with one of the client groups listed above. Centrally these services are the responsibility of the Secretary of State for Social Services and the Department of Health and Social Security.

(2) The *probation and aftercare service* which is attached to the courts and works mainly with adult offenders who, as part of their sentence, are placed on probation. In addition, much of the aftercare work for discharged prisoners is undertaken by this service. Note that much of the court aftercare work of juvenile offenders (delinquent children) is carried out by local authority social services (see Chapter 13).

The probation service is quite separate from the above services and, like the Prison Service, is centrally the responsibility of the Home Secretary and the Home Office.

(3) *Voluntary Bodies.* There are many well established voluntary bodies providing social services of all kinds both on a national and local basis. They include specialist bodies working with children, such as N.S.P.C.C., Barnardos, National Children's Homes, the Family Welfare Association, and groups dealing with the elderly, such as Age Concern. The Women's Royal Voluntary Service covers a wide range of voluntary help while the Family Service Units provide assistance to problem families. There are many specialist voluntary bodies working in the field of the disabled including the Central Council for the Disabled and the British Council for the Rehabilitation of the Disabled. Locally Councils of Social Service and Rural Community Councils undertake a co-ordinating rôle in respect of many small voluntary bodies or local branches of the large national bodies.

Many of these voluntary bodies are providing services which could also be undertaken by Social Service Departments and it is therefore essential that very close working arrangements are made. In many instances, much of the finance necessary for their function is provided by the Social Services Committee of the Local Authority.

Nationally the government department which is mainly responsible for these voluntary bodies is the Department of Health and Social Security; in some instances this department encourages voluntary work in the social services by providing small grants to voluntary bodies especially in respect of experimental schemes. Examples of such grants recently made include financial help to reduce and prevent alcoholism.

A further example of voluntary work in the social services is the Citizens' Advice Bureaux. These were first developed in the 1939–45 war to help various queries about rationing, missing relatives, etc. Their rôle has been widened recently to include consumer protection, the provision of legal advice and the explanation of various pension rights. They are particularly valuable in helping families who may be unwilling to seek help from statutory services (such as a Social Service Department) because they may feel aggrieved for some reason—they may have been evicted for rent arrears or generally are resentful of the way they have been treated in the past by local authorities and other statutory services. For this reason many local authority Social Services Committees give financial grants to the Citizens' Advice Bureaux to enable them to help clients who otherwise would be unlikely to seek help. Centrally there is a National Association of Citizens' Advice Bureaux linked to local bureaux by a regional committee.

LOCAL AUTHORITY SOCIAL•SERVICES

Social services for children, physically disabled, mentally disabled, homeless and elderly people are provided by large authorities—by the metropolitan districts in the large conurbations (by the London boroughs in London), and by the county councils in the rest of England and Wales (see Figure 12.2, page 149).

Central Government Control of Local Authority Social Services

The main government department in England which is concerned with the administration of local authority social services is the Department of Health and Social Security. The Minister in charge is the Secretary of State for Social Services, a member of the Cabinet, and he is also responsible for both the health services (see page 2) and for social security (see Chapter 18), the system which supports those in need of financial help because of illness, disablement or old age.

The reason for having the same senior minister (Secretary of State for Social Services) and the same government department (Department of Health and Social Security) responsible for social services, health services and social security, is because all three are very closely related. Most families will need all three from time to time for social services provide the main supporting services in the community for children, the disabled (physically and mentally handicapped), the homeless and the aged. Social security provides various allowances or pensions for the family—family allowances, widows' pensions, sickness benefit claims, old age pensions and family income supplement (see Chapter 18). Medical services for the family are, of course, provided by the health services (see Chapter 1).

The rôle of the Department of Health and Social Security in social services is similar to that described for the health services (see page 3), for the Department is mainly concerned in assisting the development of social services in three main ways:

(a) Advisory

From time to time important advisory memoranda on various social services are issued by the Department of Health and Social Security. These deal with every aspect of the services including the planning of various residential establishments. Recent examples include advisory memoranda on home helps, community services for the elderly and mentally handicapped and methods of running a sample survey to find out the number of seriously handicapped persons in any area.

(b) Policy and planning

Policy and planning of the social services is an important function of the Department of Health and Social Security. This aspect is particularly essential as many of the plans for the health services depend on simultaneous development of community services. An excellent example is in the case of the services for mentally disordered persons who are cared for in mental hospitals. It is hoped to discharge from mental hospital many such persons during the next ten years, *but this will only be possible if a parallel increase is provided in all forms of community social services,* including a marked increase in the hostel provision by local authority social services departments.

Recently the central structure of the Department of Health and Social Security has been reorganized to improve the integration of planning between the social and health services. A central planning division has been set up alongside a central regional division so that in both the social and health services professional officers are closely working with their linked administrative officers. An interesting innovation in the planning of the social services by the Department of Health and Social Security is the 'Regional Plan' introduced for residential services for children under the Children and Young Persons Act 1969. In this, the country is divided into a number of regions and all local authorities within each region co-operate to form a Regional Planning Committee under the guidance of the Department of Health and Social Security to ensure that the accommodation planned within the region matches the likely need of the area, as closely as possible.

(c) Financial

This is another important indirect method of control of the social services. Special extra financial allocation is made by the government (acting on the advice of the Secretary of State for Social Services) in the rate support grant (paid by the government to local authorities) so that certain social services can be developed.

Revenue (or costs of running day-to-day services) is financed by

(a) the rate support grant from the government

(b) the local rates.

The *rate support grant* is the large block grant of money paid from the government to local authorities to assist them with their services (it represents approximately 61 per cent of all local government expenditure). It includes a 'population' element and a 'needs' element which reflect the social problems and social services provided by that authority. The actual division of the block grant is decided by each local authority (who therefore decides how much will be spent on social services, education, roads, environmental health etc.) However, the larger the rate support grant, the greater the likelihood of social services being developed locally.

Special investigations in the field of social services

The Department of Health and Social Security arranges for special research investigations to be undertaken in the field of social services. A recent example was the large scale national survey carried out by the Department's research staff into the incidence of handicapped persons living in the community. A full report was published; this forms the main basis for planning such services nationally and is a useful guide to local needs.

The Secretary of State for Social Security can, through Parliament, appoint special expert committees to look in detail into certain aspects and to report back.

Rôle of other government departments in social services

Although the main government department dealing with social services is the Department of Health and Social Security, other departments, particularly the *Home Office* and *Department of Employment and Productivity* do have certain powers.

The **Home Office** is the main department dealing with the problems of law and order in the country and has been active in the encouragement of *community development* in England. This attempts to improve the social conditions of people by encouraging them to participate more in the running of their own affairs. The Home Office has set up a number of interesting seven-year experimental *community development projects* in some cities including Liverpool and Coventry, which could have a very important effect on future social service development.

The **probation service**, run in conjunction with Clerks of the Magistrates, is controlled centrally by the Home Office and a very close link must be maintained between Probation and Social Services Departments especially in relation to the problems and care of delinquent children.

The Home Office also has an important function in social services in the **Urban Aid Programme.** This is a special form of financial aid (both capital and revenue) given to certain projects to encourage new developments, mainly in the large cities and urban areas where there is an urgent need to develop social services. Under Urban Aid the Home Office provides 75 per cent, and the local authority 25 per cent, of the cost. Urban aid covers projects by both local authorities and voluntary bodies, although in the latter instance the appropriate local authority has to pay 25 per cent of the cost of each project. This help usually !asts from 1–5 years. Examples in social services of urban aid projects approved in the last three years include many new day nurseries, day care centres for the elderly, residential units for children and various schemes for the physically and mentally handicapped.

The Department of Employment and Productivity is mainly concerned with the special employment problems of the handicapped (see page 171). Its officers include the Disablement Resettlement Officers (see page 171) and the Blind Placement Officers. Both work very closely with the social services.

THE STRUCTURE OF THE LOCAL AUTHORITY SOCIAL SERVICES

Following the Local Authority Social Services Act 1970, which was introduced on 1st April 1971, each major local authority must have a Social Services

Committee to control its social services (full list given below). Each local authority must appoint a **Director of Social Services** who is the chief officer in charge of the Department of Social Services which administers all the services.

Local authority social services are run by the new County Councils and within the Metropolitan areas (the large conurbations such as Greater Manchester, Merseyside, South Yorkshire, Tyneside, West Midlands, West Yorkshire), by the Metropolitan District Councils, and in London by the London Boroughs. In Scotland, the social services are controlled by the new Regional local authorities.

Types of social services provided by the Social Services Committees

The following is a summary of services provided by each Social Services Committee:

(1) *Care of the elderly*—this includes both field work services carried out within the community, and residential care (see Chapter 16).

(2) *Care of the physically handicapped*—blind, deaf and dumb, hard of hearing, spastic, epileptic, paraplegics and other disabled persons (see Chapter 14).

(3) *Care of the homeless* (see Chapter 17).

The main legislation covering these services includes the National Assistance Act 1948 and the Chronically Sick and Disabled Persons Act, 1970.

(4) *All child care services* including child care protection, child care supervision, acceptance of parental rights for children committed into the care of the Local Authority, control of various residential units for children—admission units, reception centres, residential nurseries, children's homes, control of community homes with education on the premises and classifying centres (formerly approved schools and remand homes), and certain services for adoption. Much of the preventive work in non-accidental injury cases is organized under the child care services (see page 158). The legislation for these services includes the Children's Act 1948, the Children and Young Persons Acts of 1963 and 1969 and the Children Act 1975.

(5) *Social work and family casework* dealing with the **mentally disordered** including the provision of social workers (formerly mental welfare officers), adult training centres, workshops and residential accommodation (hostels) for the mentally disordered.

(6) *Day care for children under five years of age* including provision of day nurseries and the supervision of private nurseries and child minders.

(7) *Provision of home helps.*

(8) *Care of unsupported mothers* including residential care.

(9) *Hospital social workers*—provision of social work services for hospital patients.

Organization of Social Services Departments

There are many different forms of organization in social services departments. However, most have independent Area (or District) teams of social workers (see below). Headquarters are divided into three main sections dealing with Residential Services, Field Work Services and Training.

The chief officer is the **Director of Social Services,** next is the Deputy Director of Social Services, and usually an Assistant Director is in charge of the sections. Each Area (or District is usually under the control of an Area (or District) social services officer. (A typical arrangement is shown in Figure 12.1)

It will be noted that there are four main parts to the headquarters of a social services department:
(1) that dealing with residential services
(2) that dealing with field work services
(3) that providing facilities for training
(4) that dealing with hospital social work.

Full details of the various types of residential services are given on the pages mentioned below. In detail these include the following services:
(1) **Residential services** for:
(*a*) elderly (see page 215)
(*b*) children (see page 156)
(*c*) physically handicapped (disabled) (see page 174)
(*d*) mentally disordered (see pages 189, 198)
(2) **Field work services** cover wide types of facilities dealing with:
(*a*) family and child care (see pages 153–163)
(*b*) disabled (see pages 171–5)
(*c*) mentally disordered (see pages 188–190)
(*d*) elderly (see pages 204–6)
(*e*) transport (see page 172)
(*f*) home helps (see pages 217–8)
(*g*) meals services—meals-on-wheels or luncheon clubs (see page 205)
(*h*) day nursery provision (see pages 151–2)
(*i*) homeless families (see pages 218–220)
(*j*) adoption services (see pages 163–4)
(3) **Training** is provided as follows:
(*a*) induction training for new entrants
(*b*) in-service training for existing staff
(*c*) professional training (field work—social work training), usually by release to two-year full-time courses
(*d*) practical training—receiving students from full-time courses who are doing practical field work placements
(*e*) training for residential staff (in both children's units and in old people's homes)
(*f*) senior post-graduate training for qualified staff including training in management

The standards of training of social workers is the responsibility of the *Central Council for Education and Training in Social Work* which was established in 1971. This Council is responsible for the promotion of training in all fields of social work. At present there are three main ways to train to become a social worker:
(1) by obtaining a relevant degree in Social Sciences and then taking a one year course;
(2) by obtaining any other type of degree and then taking a two year course;
(3) by taking a two year course.

Much of this training is carried out in co-operation with Universities, Polytechnics and Commercial Colleges run by local education authorities.

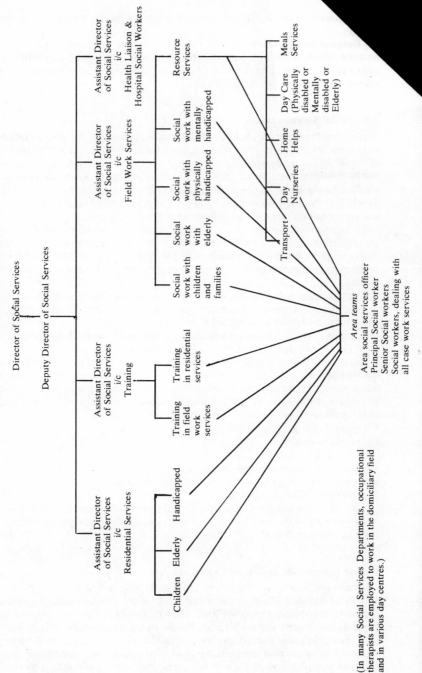

STRUCTURE OF THE SOCIAL SERVICES

TYPICAL SOCIAL SERVICES DEPARTMENT

Director of Social Services

Deputy Director of Social Services

Assistant Director of Social Services i/c Residential Services

Assistant Director of Social Services i/c Training

Assistant Director of Social Services i/c Field Work Services

Assistant Director of Social Services i/c Health Liaison & Hospital Social Workers

Children Elderly Handicapped

Training in field work services

Training in residential services

Social work with children and families

Social work with elderly

Social work with physically handicapped

Social work with mentally handicapped

Resource Services

Transport Day Nurseries Home Helps Day Care (Physically disabled or Mentally disabled or Elderly) Meals Services

Area teams
Area social services officer
Principal Social worker
Senior Social workers
Social workers, dealing with all case work services

(In many Social Services Departments, occupational therapists are employed to work in the domiciliary field and in various day centres.)

epartment should have a training unit plus training

147

rk deals with the various social problems of patients in
ework is undertaken to help the patient and family to
Other forms of help and assistance are given with con-
pages 220–221).

Area Social Services teams

A very important part of each social services department is the **area social services team**. By arranging for all the casework for family and clients to be under-taken by such co-ordinated teams of social workers, it is hoped that problems will be considered as a whole rather than in a fragmented way and that this will lead to a **family social service** dealing with all types of social problem in the family whether this presents as a problem in a child, a disabled person, an old person or a mentally disordered individual.

These teams of social workers are made up of social workers who formerly specialized in child care (with the former children's departments), in mental illness or subnormality (previously with the health departments) or with old people or the handicapped (formerly welfare officers of the welfare departments).

The size of areas varies from about 40 000 to 100 000 depending on the size of the district and its social problems. An ideal area will have from ten to thirty social workers mainly working in groups of five or six under the leadership of a senior social worker. Each team deals with the problems of **clients** (the term used for persons referred to the social services department).

Close co-ordination must be maintained with other workers—health visitors, home nurses, medical social workers, teachers, psychiatric social workers, educational welfare officers, community workers, youth leaders, general practitioners and the many voluntary bodies helping in the district. Usually each area social work team controls the allocation of:

(*a*) home helps
(*b*) meals-on-wheels
(*c*) day nursery places
(*d*) vacancies in old persons' homes
(*e*) places in residential accommodation for children
(*f*) allocation of telephones.

The key individual in each team is the **Area Social Services Officer** and any nurse working in the area who comes across a difficult social problem should refer the case to this officer.

Liaison between the health and social services

It is most important that the closest links are maintained between all medical and social services. Many of the social services in local authorities represent the main supporting services within the community for persons recovering from illness or suffering from some chronic disabling condition. Many of the necessary aids, gadgets or adaptations for the handicapped which are so essential for the successful rehabilitation of many disabling conditions (e.g., arthritis, paraplegia, multiple sclerosis, spasticity, etc.), are supplied by social services departments. The closest possible liaison between the two must therefore be developed.

Following the reorganization of the health services and local government 1974, both health and social services are generally organized over the same geographical areas. A map of the new Social Services Authorities in England is given in Figure 12.2. These represent generally the Area Health Authorities (see also page 8).

It is very important that liaison between the two services is good. On the health side a community physician is appointed with responsibility for liaison—the Area Specialist in Community Medicine (Social Services)—and

FIG. 12.2   Social Services Authorities, England, 1974

side a senior officer is appointed (usually an Assistant
rvices) to take charge of the hospital social work service
e for integration.

s should be made to assist day to day co-operation. Social
health centres and group practices from time to time so
ot only the general practitioners, but the health visitors,
hool nurses working from the centre.

There should be working links created between social workers and the
hospital services especially through the medical social workers at all hospitals
and particularly at geriatric and mental hospitals.

The Area Specialist in Community Medicine (Social Services) acts as medical adviser to the social services department and consequently becomes acquainted with all the medical problems of the department. It is particularly important that *health visitors work closely with social workers* for many of the problems they deal with are also important to the social services department and vice versa. Both health visitors and social workers find themselves working with 'problem families' dealing with different aspects—the health visitor from the preventive medical point of view and the social worker dealing with the social difficulties (this is particularly important in preventing non-accidental injury in children—see pages 158–163). The closer that the two groups of officers can work together, the better the results. **Case conferences** are arranged between such workers from time to time to consider difficult individual cases and other officers working with such families are also invited especially those from the education or housing departments. Although the social services department is responsible for the organization of social services within each local authority, co-operation with many different services is needed including those providing medical care, education, housing, probation, police and voluntary services. It is only by improving the arrangements between so many different services that the best possible result will be obtained for each family.

13   CARE OF CHILDREN IN NEED

Local authorities through their social services departments provide help and care to children for a variety of reasons and, under the Children Act 1975, have to provide an adoption service.

All Social Service Committees have very special responsibilities through their *child care services* in supervising and looking after children and young persons under the age of 18 years. In much of this work, the social services department is attempting to find *the best possible alternative arrangement for care of the child in the absence of the parents*—either because they have abandoned the child or the child is an orphan or because the parents have been found incapable of looking after the child properly. As will be seen later under 'Child Care Services' every attempt is made by trying to settle the child with suitable foster parents to provide the child with as normal a home as possible. For this reason, large institutional homes are no longer used.

Special help is given to the parent who, because of social reasons, cannot look after his/her child during the daytime. Most of this help is given in *day nurseries* or *day care centres, playgroups* or *with a child minder*.

DAY NURSERIES

Care of young children in day nurseries

Day nurseries are provided by the Social Service Departments of local authorities to help care for young children when this cannot be provided at home due to *social circumstances*. Such reasons would include sudden illness of the mother leading to her admission to hospital, or an unmarried mother who has to go out to work to support her family, or a widower or widow with a small child.

Day nurseries open five days a week from early in the morning, 7.30 a.m., to 5.30 p.m. The young child can be brought to the nursery by the parent on the way to work. He/she may have all his meals in the nursery and will be completely looked after during the day.

A small charge is made for this service but in priority cases the charge is usually in the region of 35 pence per day which is less than 1/10th of the economic cost. There is no doubt that a day nursery is most useful in helping to care for the children in a family which has to face social difficulties. It avoids having to arrange for the young child to be admitted to a residential home and thus break all contact with his home. Day nurseries look after children from a few weeks old up to the age of five years when they can go to school. In many cases, the need for care is temporary while an acute social crisis occurs in the family.

It is usual for about 50 children to be looked after in each nursery. 'Family groups' are set up in each nursery so that about 10–15 children are looked after together covering an age range from six months to five years. Babies under six months of age are looked after separately.

Each nursery has a trained matron and deputy matron plus a number of trained nursery nurses. The staff are responsible for all aspects of care of the children including their health which must be carefully supervised. Special attention is paid to ensure that:
(1) every child is fit when admitted
(2) every child is fully immunized
(3) any case of infectious disease is immediately investigated.

Dysentery or gastro-enteritis can be particularly serious if they spread in a day nursery (see page 95) and any child with diarrhoea must be sent home until all bacteriological tests are normal.

Day nurseries are being increasingly used for very young handicapped children (with various disabling conditions e.g. spina bifida) to help with their development. It is best if such children are looked after in ordinary day nurseries rather than being segregated in a special nursery. Where a day nursery has a number of handicapped children it will be necessary to employ larger numbers of staff. *Nursery Nurses* qualify after a two year course and by gaining the certificate of the Nursery Nurses Examination Board.

The main clients helped by day nurseries include:
(1) the unmarried mother
(2) widows or widowers with a young family
(3) mothers with a sudden illness
(4) parents with a handicapped child especially if the disability is of a type which has led to the child being isolated from the company of other children.

Private day nurseries, playgroups and child minders

Many private day nurseries, playgroups and child minders look after children and each Local Authority through its Social Services Committee is responsible for ensuring that proper standards of staff, fire precautions and accommodation are provided. This is done by insisting that each such unit must be registered with the Local Authority and inspected from time to time to check that the correct standards are being maintained.

Under the Nurseries and Child Minders Regulations 1948, all people caring for more than one child in their own home, whether for profit or not, must be registered with the local authority.

CHILD CARE SERVICES

These services primarily look after children who need care and protection because of the neglect, abandonment or inability of the parents to cope due to some sudden emergency (illness, separation, etc) or exposure to moral danger. Under the Children Act 1975, in all cases the first consideration is the *need to safeguard and promote the welfare of the child.*

Every social services department *must* investigate fully each case which comes to their knowledge and social workers undertake this inquiry.

In particular there are four main groups of children who need to be looked after:
(1) those who have to be cared for by the Social Services Department either because their parents are temporarily absent (such as an illness) or because they have no parents or guardians or because their parents have failed to look

after them properly or have abandoned them. The reason may be temporary or permanent and Social Service Departments can either

(a) receive the children into voluntary care—see below.

(b) through a court, have a statutory care order made which transfers the parental rights to the Social Services Department of the local authority.

(2) children and young persons who have been brought before a court for criminal proceedings;

(3) children placed by a court in the care of the local authority in connection with matrimonial proceedings;

(4) children who have been placed in foster homes or who have been placed privately for adoption.

CHILD CARE PROVISIONS

Any Local Authority may pass a resolution assuming parental rights over a child if there are no parents or guardians or if the Local Authority considers the parent or guardian unfit to care for that child. If the parents object the matter must be referred to a juvenile court. In practice, in all cases where a Local Authority claims that statutory care is needed (Section II, Children's Act 1948) the case is dealt with by a juvenile court.

The types of child care provided by Social Service Departments are either:

(1) Voluntary care (a) short-term (less than six months)
       (b) long-term (more than six months)

(2) Statutory care

(1) Voluntary care

This is in many ways similar to voluntary admissions to hospital and is *an informal arrangement* under section I of the Children's Act 1948. It is used for cases where the social worker is convinced that the circumstances bringing the child into the care of the authority are not serious, i.e. there has not been neglect of the child. Parents can later claim the child when the crisis is over.

There are two main methods of voluntary care:

(a) *short-term care* is used for a sudden family crisis such as an illness, confinement or other sudden emergency. The local authority looks after the child for a short period (never exceeding six months and usually only a few weeks) by the most appropriate method (boarding out, placement in a small home or group home, or even in an admission unit or residential nursery).

Children rarely suffer from much deprivation in such cases and it is usual for other members of the family (parent, brother and sisters) to visit the child.

(b) *long-term care* exceeds six months but is otherwise similar to short-term care. Because of the longer period of care, more permanent arrangements are made for the child which will depend upon the case (see pp. 155–61). Once any child has been in voluntary care for 6 months, under Section 56 of the Children Act 1975, any parent must give not less than 28 days notice of intention to remove the child from care. Such notice can be waived by the Local Authority in appropriate cases. Emphasis in long-term care is on *attempting to look after the child in circumstances* which are, as far as possible, *as near those in the child's own home.* For this reason, boarding out is ideal or, if this is not possible, placing the child in a family group home containing four to six children of varying ages (resembling a normal family).

(2) Statutory care

This is where a *Court commits the child,* whom it considers is in need of care and protection, *to the care of a local authority.* Such cases are the more serious ones involving serious neglect, abandonment or moral danger to the child. In all such cases the *parental rights are transferred to the local authority.* Once this has happened the only way that the natural parents can reclaim their child is by petitioning the same Court which made the original Order to revoke it. The Court must then decide whether the parents are now responsible enough to justify returning the child to their care. If the Court decides they are not, the child remains in the care of the authority; if the Court decides they are responsible enough, the parents will have the child returned to them.

All neglect, abandonment or moral danger cases are dealt with under the Children's Act, 1948.

Following the Children and Young Persons Act, 1969, a delinquent child found guilty of an offence can be committed to the statutory care of a local authority.

Note: In all cases where parental rights have been transferred to the local authority, these *cease when the young person reaches the age of 18 years.*

Transfer of a child from voluntary to statutory care

Occasionally a child is placed in voluntary care, but circumstances deteriorate and the social worker now considers that such an informal arrangement no longer provides sufficient safeguard for the child. In these circumstances it is possible for the *local authority to assume parental rights* under section II of the Children's Act, 1948. In all such cases, careful rules must be followed by the *local authority* who must always notify the natural parents. This decision by the local authority to assume parental rights can be challenged by the natural parents in the courts.

Children who are victims of divorce

Under the Matrimonial Cause Acts, the High Court can make the local authority *the guardian of the child in a divorce acting under the directions of the court.*

In practice the social services department will then look after the child in the same way as any other child in care (see below).

Child protection

A further safeguard is maintained by social services departments where there is a private agreement or contract between one private individual and another for the placement of a child. In all instances, the social services department of the local authority *must* be notified and it has a *duty* to check that this placement is satisfactory. It must also ensure by subsequent investigation that the child is well looked after.

Cessation of parental rights

In all cases where parental rights have been transferred to the Local Authority, these *cease when the young person reaches the age of 18 years.*

Under the Children and Young Persons Act 1933, a child is defined as a person under 14 years and a young person as one between 14 and 18 years.

Supervision of fostering

When any child is placed with foster parents, it is the duty of the Social Services Department to arrange *regular visiting which must be at not more than six week intervals* (Boarding-out Regulations).

PREVENTIVE SOCIAL AND REHABILITATION WORK WITH CHILDREN

Increasing emphasis is being laid on the importance of *preventive work in child care*. This depends upon the social services taking action early enough to enable them to prevent a child coming into care or appearing before a Court.

There is a great deal of evidence that everything must be done *to avoid family breakdown*. As this will be made more likely if the family gets into debt and is made homeless, there is power under the Children and Young Persons Act, 1963 for the Social Services Committee to make financial payments to prevent a child coming into care. These may even include the payment of rent arrears. Much of this financial help is concentrated on ways which are likely to prevent child delinquency—holiday adventure schemes or clubs, etc.

The social services department and its social workers should also do all in their power to try *to rehabilitate each child in its care* so that he/she may eventually return to his/her family.

TYPES AND METHODS OF CHILD CARE

The needs of every child should be carefully assessed on admission into care and each child should be placed according to that assessment.

The aim in child care is to look after every child in the way which is best suited to his/her needs. Supervision is always carried out by trained social workers and each *case must be reviewed every six months* (a duty imposed on all Social Service Departments by the Children and Young Persons Act 1969). The ideal is to care for each child in conditions and environment as near normal as possible.

It is usual for a child first to go to an **Admission Unit** where his/her special needs are carefully assessed. There are four main ways in which a child can be looked after:

(1) *Boarding out of the child with foster parents.* In this case the child lives with the family just as if the child was in his/her own home. This is an ideal arrangement and is always used wherever possible, particularly with long stay cases. A foster parent may look after one or a number of children and is always very carefully chosen to ensure the right type of person is always used as a foster parent.

All children in foster care must be visited regularly and at least once every six weeks by social workers of the social services department and the frequency of such visiting is very carefully controlled by the Department of Health and Social Security. Under the Children Act 1975, a new clause (to be introduced at a future date yet to be determined) will allow any foster parent who has looked after a child continuously for three or more years to insist that the child is only removed with the leave of the court.

(2) *Placement of the child in a family group home* containing four to six children of different ages. Wherever boarding out is not possible, this type of care is the next best. It aims to look after the child in small units where life can be very similar to that in any large family. These homes are scattered throughout the community and made inconspicuous so that the child's living conditions can be kept as near normal as possible.

(3) *Placement in a small children's home containing from twelve to eighteen children.* Some children do not seem suitable for either boarding out or life in a family group home and these are looked after in small children's homes. Many of the children living in these children's homes later progress to other forms of care described. A certain amount of assessment can be undertaken in such homes and an unstable child often settles well.

(4) Very occasionally a child can be placed *in its own home under supervision.* This arrangement is often used during the rehabilitation of a child and to see if he/she can settle back into a home from which he/she has had to be removed for some reason in the past.

(5) The child may be placed in a children's home run by a voluntary body (such as Barnardos, the National Childrens' Home, etc.).

Need for continuous review

In all instances it is most important *to review each child regularly* and to attempt *to rehabilitate that child* so that eventually it may be possible to return that child to his/her own home.

In the disturbed child with a difficult home background, this may mean many different stages have to be passed through. Such a child may go to a *reception centre, small children's home, boarding out, a short trial back at home* (which may or may not succeed) and much patience is always needed. The eventual success or failure will only be seen when that child becomes an adult; the constant aim is to help children to develop and mature so that they grow into responsible, mature and happy adults.

Community homes

All types of children's homes and the former remand homes and approved schools are now called *community homes.* Some of these have education provided on the premises (see below).

SPECIAL RESIDENTIAL UNITS

The larger local authorities social services departments usually provide five special residential units—an admission unit, a residential nursery, a reception centre, a community home with education on the premises—for children on remand or for assessment (former remand homes)—and a community home with education on the premises—for treatment (former approved schools).

Admission unit

The admission unit is the place into which all urgent cases are admitted. The number of children looked after varies, but many care for 45–50 children.

Children needing short-term care, especially if the emergency is likely to be short lived, are often looked after in admission units but others are carefully assessed in the admission unit to decide which type of care is best suited to the child. Once this has been decided the child goes on to the appropriate care which may be either *residential nursery, reception centre, boarding out* or *admission to a family group or small children's home.*

Residential nursery

Small children under the age of 5 years and babies are looked after in a *residential nursery* immediately following admission. Many of the short term-care cases will stay there while in care, but some of the older children may later leave for boarding out or other forms of child care.

Reception centre

Some children need a longer period of assessment or may have difficulty in settling down and these are looked after at a *reception centre.* Some of these children are maladjusted and the regime of the centre allows a longer and more expert assessment of the child to be undertaken.

Community homes with education on the premises (for children on remand or for assessment)

Separate community homes are run by the larger Social Services Departments for children on remand or for assessment. Originally their main function was to accommodate children on remand for some serious offence while full investigations (especially psychiatric) took place. Since the Children and Young Persons Act, 1969, *the assessment of each child* who is committed to the care of the local authority by a Court (because of conviction on some serious offence) is an important extra function.

Many children who pass through such community homes are maladjusted or disturbed having come from an unsatisfactory home. It is, therefore, important to have staff in charge who are trained in dealing with such children and each community home should make arrangements for a psychiatrist to be available to help.

Community homes with education on the premises (for treatment—formerly approved schools)

Entry into such a community home used to follow the decision of a juvenile court sentencing the child. Now the decision in such a case is made by social workers of a Social Services Department after assessment at a suitable assessment centre which indicates that a stay in such a community home could be beneficial for the child.

Education for children in care

In all community homes with education on the premises, including admission units and reception centres, the Local Education Authority may run one or two classes at each centre which the children can attend or the teachers may be employed by the Social Services Department.

Once the child is transferred to other types of care—boarding out, family group or small children's homes—the children attend normal schools in the community and, if this is still practicable, the same school that they attended before coming into care.

JUVENILE PROCEEDINGS

A care order under Section II of the Children's Act 1948 (which has the effect of transferring the parental rights from the natural parents to the local authority) may be granted by a juvenile court on the following grounds:

(1) that the child is being ill-treated and neglected;

(2) that he/she is exposed to moral dangers;

(3) that he/she is beyond the control of his/her parent or guardian;

(4) that he/she is of compulsory school age and is not receiving efficient full-time education;

(5) that he/she is guilty of any offence *excluding homicide* (homicide is dealt with separately by the Higher Courts).

A juvenile court can only commit a child to the care of the local authority if they are of the opinion that the child needs some extra parental training. The Social Services Department then assesses the child (a process that takes usually 6–8 weeks and may involve psychiatric and psychological examinations). After assessment the Social Services Department may decide to:

(1) send the child to a community home with education on the premises;

(2) send the child home under supervision;

(3) place the child with a foster parent;

(4) involve the child in some special type of training such as adventure training etc. (many of these special types of training are available under schemes of *intermediate treatment* provided by arrangement with Children's Regional Planning Committees).

Probation orders

Probation orders for young persons under 17 years have been replaced by *supervision orders* which may be made in both criminal and care proceedings. These supervision orders are now administered by Social Services Departments.

Borstals

The Borstal system of training was introduced in 1908. The aim is to provide training for offenders from 15–21 years of age and the sentence is in two parts: (1) a period of training in a Borstal establishment (run by the Home Office), minimum 6 months, maximum 2 years; (2) a period of supervision up to a further 2 years. Social Services Departments are not responsible for the Borstal system which comes under the Home Office and the Probation service.

NON-ACCIDENTAL INJURY TO CHILDREN

During the past seven years, much emphasis has been laid upon the problem of non-accidental injury to children. This used to be called 'battered baby syndrome' but the name has been changed as it is now known that older children may be involved (c.f. the Maria Colwell case).

Non-accidental injury is the deliberate injury of children, usually by parents, and is most frequently caused by many different factors. In some cases, criminal neglect by parents may be associated with other forms of anti-social behaviour—assaults or drunkenness, but in many instances, frustration, bad living conditions, unsympathetic neighbours or landladies complaining of babies who cry continuously, or psychiatric illness in a parent are the main factors. The problem can present itself in many forms but usually starts by one or both parents slapping, hitting, punching or severely shaking the child causing bruises and occasionally more serious injuries. Ill-treatment usually starts gradually but if it is unnoticed, it is quite possible for the child to be seriously injured and it is now estimated that approximately 700 deaths per year in children may be caused in this way.

Diagnosis and early recognition

The following may be the first signs of non-accidental injury:
(1) Minor bruises which show that the child has been gripped tightly or shaken.
(2) Minor injuries (such as facial bruises) probably caused by slapping or hitting the child. The type of injury is usually similar, 70 per cent being soft tissue injuries to the head and face. There may be 'finger bruising' in which the outlines of the fingers which slapped the child are clearly seen within the bruised area. Such bruising tends to pick out the bony prominences. In many cases, the lips are thick and bruised and there is a torn upper lip frenum. Ribs are frequently bruised or broken and X-rays often indicate that these injuries have been caused at different times. Occasionally small burns may be present.
(3) An unexplained failure of the child to thrive.
(4) Unusual behaviour by the parents. This may take many different forms—over-anxiety and frequent attendance with the child at clinics or surgeries, plausible explanation of an injury which does not fit the case, or unnatural lack of concern for the child's condition.

In many instances, the circumstances of parents involved in cases of non-accidental injury show many similar characteristics; stress of various kinds is common including poverty (in one survey 80 per cent were in receipt of social security), unemployment (many fathers batter their children when engaged on maternal tasks), overcrowding and unsatisfactory housing conditions and many have unstable marriages. Another interesting finding is that the parents are often very young (about four years below the national average). Studies have shown that teenage parents are less tolerant and have a low tolerance towards the baby's crying. A high proportion of the women involved are pregnant at the time.

A proportion of parents shown to be responsible for non-accidental injury are mentally disturbed or inadequate emotionally. It is interesting that the 'innocent' parent (usually the mother) does not do more to protect her child. The most likely explanation is that she has never learnt how to stick up for herself and for their children. Certainly many of the parents involved have never received any affection in their homes and consequently find it very difficult to relate as a normal parent does towards their child.

Any additional stress will tend to precipitate problems—moving house often results in much loneliness and resentment and battering is then more likely.

Early diagnosis of non-accidental injury to children depends upon the alertness of many professional staff including general practitioners, paediatricians, health visitors, district nurses, midwives, social workers and the staff of many voluntary organizations including the NSPCC. Because injury to the child is always a dominant feature, all those working in casualty or accident departments of hospitals should be especially vigilant.

Management and treatment

Once there is a reasonable degree of suspicion of non-accidental injury, the child should at once be admitted to a hospital (or very occasionally a children's home) for diagnosis and for his own safety. In many instances, a *place of safety order* will be obtained from a court (this can most easily be arranged by the Social Services Department) but the child may be admitted voluntarily.

In all cases an immediate *case conference* should be arranged which should include those concerned with the immediate case, the paediatrician, general practitioner, health visitor and social worker, as well as the NSPCC and a senior police officer. As the Social Services Department has the statutory duty to protect and care for all children, it is best if each case conference is arranged by the Social Services Department (within 24 hours).

In those instances in which the professional worker does not feel that the suspicions are firm enough to arrange immediate admission to a hospital, it is still adviseable to hold a case conference to decide on the next action. If suspicion is very slight, in every instance at least the doctor, health visitor or social worker should:

(1) consult the family doctor
(2) discuss the details of the case with a senior colleague
(3) make a record of such consultations and discussions.

Area review committee

There should be an Area review committee in each Area Health Authority or local Social Services area, to act as a policy forming body to ensure that the arrangements in that area for dealing with the problem of non-accidental injury are satisfactory. Each Area review committee should include representatives of the appropriate Local Authority (especially the Director of Social Services who usually acts as the Convenor and Secretary and the Director of Education), the Health Services (especially paediatric and other consultants, the Area Medical Officer, the Area Nursing Officer, the District Community Physician, the District Nursing Officer, plus the Area Specialists in Community Medicine for Social Services and Child Health) and a senior police officer, senior inspector of the NSPCC and the Chief Probation Officer.

Area Review Committees should meet regularly (three or four times per year) and should:

(1) Review local practice and procedure for dealing with such cases.
(2) Ensure that immediate hospital admission for children at risk is accepted.
(3) Approve written instructions defining the exact duties and responsibilities of professional staff in connection with non-accidental injury.
(4) Provide education and training programmes for staff in the health and social services.

(5) Review the work of case conferences.

(6) Inquire into the circumstances of cases which appear to have gone wrong and from which lessons could be learned.

(7) Ensure that procedures are in operation to safeguard continuity of care between neighbouring areas and in those instances when families move to another area.

(8) Agree arrangements for the operation of a total register of cases which have been dealt with by case conferences or other action.

Registers

A register of information is essential in each area to ensure there is good communication between the many services involved. Absolute confidentiality is most important and there should also be arrangements to share information between neighbouring authorities. Registers may be set up by voluntary bodies working in this field (e.g. the NSPCC) or by Social Services Departments or by Health Authorities. The most important feature of registers is that they should be accessible (at all times—on a 24 hour basis) to doctors, nurses and social workers, and that they should include accurate up-to-date information. The ability of a doctor in a casualty department or a health visitor or social worker in the community to seek information from such a register could be vital to early and effective diagnosis of non-accidental injury. Many past serious cases would probably have been prevented had an efficient register been operating in that area enabling early suspicions to be confirmed because a similar incident had occurred before.

Treatment and rehabilitation of known cases of non-accidental injury

Most cases will initially be in the care of the paediatrician who will be responsible for the assessment and treatment of the case in hospital. Assessment should include both physical and psychiatric investigations. Skeletal surveys should be undertaken in doubtful cases. A case conference will be held and should indicate the most likely methods of treatment. These will vary considerably in different cases and will include:

(1) Receiving the child into *statutory care* by the local authority (by Court Order). In the very worst cases there will also be prosecution of the parents.

(2) Accepting the child into *voluntary care*. (This may be risky in some cases because parents may suddenly remove the child from hospital or children's home. Therefore, in all cases received into voluntary care, the Social Services Department must always be prepared to seek an urgent *Place of Safety Order* if that need arises.)

(3) Arranging for the child to remain under supervision in the home by a Court Order.

(4) Returning the child home with planned help to the parents.

In all instances the aim is to ensure that the short and long-term interests of the child are met as far as possible. It is important to realize that, although there are a number of serious cases of intentional injury and neglect that can only be properly treated by permanent removal of the child from the parents, the majority of cases are quite different. In these the non-accidental injury has been caused by many other factors—bad living conditions, unemployment, poverty, threat of eviction especially if babies cry repeatedly and by minor psychiatric illnesses. These parents urgently require help and if this can be satisfactorily given they may be assisted to develop into perfectly satisfactory parents and families. However, the causative factors *must* be discovered. In many instances, the temporary provision of residential care (in a residential nursery or children's home) may be required to enable the parent to be treated.

Day care

Many mothers who have been found to ill-treat their children are very young and often very isolated and lonely. It is usual to find that the mother herself had an unhappy childhood or was brought up in a broken home.

A very useful method of helping is to admit the child to a day nursery or play group and then to arrange for the mother to help in the group. In this way, the mother is assisted to make new friends and to obtain the support she needs. Indirectly she will be taught to improve her relationship with her own child from the example of care she will see in the nursery or play group.

More and more Social Services Departments are now developing day care which can be extended to older children in the same family who come along to the unit after school.

Many girls' schools now arrange for senior girls to help periodically in play groups and day nurseries, and thus to learn more about the methods of care of young children. This is particularly important because more girls now marry before twenty and the incidence of non-accidental injury is highest in teenage mothers.

Some local authorities have arranged to deal with many cases in nurseries close to a paediatric department which makes the development of special working arrangements between the Health and Social Services Departments easier.

Periodic review of long-term cases

Some of the most difficult problems are found in long term cases. It is absolutely essential that *periodic reviews* of such cases are undertaken. These must involve the many professional workers who would normally be concerned with the care of that child and especially general practitioners, teachers, school nurses, health visitors, education welfare officers, social workers (including those working in child guidance) as well as those working with voluntary agencies in that area. In all older children (and some of the worst cases of non-accidental injury occur in older children) it is most important that the *levels of communication between teaching staff* and others concerned with the child in school and health visitors and social workers are always good.

The statutory duty to protect and care for all children who are in need is that of the Director of Social Services and his staff. But unless there is an effective network of information between all staff working in education, health and social services, action by the Social Services Department may be delayed until it is too late to prevent further injury. For this reason, long-term cases should never be written off until a case conference agrees that no further risk remains. Unless this multidisciplinary team approach is always used, mistakes of the past will be repeated.

In any serious case of doubt, a doctor or nurse should always arrange immediate hospital admission for the child to enable more detailed investigations to be undertaken. In cases of difficulty, the problem should always be reported by telephone to the Director of Social Services.

CHANGES INTRODUCED BY THE CHILDREN ACT 1975

The main purpose of this Act is to reform the existing law in relation to adoption, guardianship and fostering of children. Much of it gives effect to the main recommendations of the Houghton Report.

In addition, an important new principle was introduced by the Children Act, 1975 relating to children both for adoption and in care. In future *there is a duty* for Courts and Local Authorities when making *any decision* about such children:

(*a*) to have regard to all circumstances but that the first *consideration is the need to safeguard and promote the welfare of the child*;

(*b*) to find out as far as possible *the wishes and feelings of the child* and to give due consideration to them.

This means that the needs of the child must take pride of place over all other considerations, i.e. the child's needs are more important than the needs of the natural parents.

Adoption services

Every Social Service Authority (County Councils, Metropolitan Districts and London Boroughs) must establish and maintain *an adoption service*. It must do this in conjunction with its other social services for children and with the other approved societies in its area. In future therefore all Social Services Committees will be in charge of an adoption service.

The responsibility for approval and registration of adoption societies in England and Wales is transferred to the Secretary of State for Social Services. It is hoped that this will ensure uniformly good standards of adoption practice throughout the country.

The legal status of an adopted child will, in future, be exactly similar to a child born to the adopters.

Unless the child is related to the adopters or has been placed with them by a High Court order or an adoption agency, an adoption order cannot be made unless the child has had his home with the applicants for at least 12 months.

The following are some of the more important requirements for adoption:

(1) Legal adoption is by an *adoption order* granted by a Court of Law.

(2) Persons who may adopt must be at least 21 years of age.

(3) Adoption must be in the best interests of the child.

(4) Adopters must live within the U.K., the Channel Islands or the Isle of Man.

(5) A married person cannot apply on her own unless her husband

(*a*) cannot be found;

(*b*) is permanently separated from her; or

(*c*) is incapable of joining in the application because of mental or physical illness.

(6) A parent and step-parent will not normally be able to get an adoption order if the parent has been given custody of the child following divorce. The applic-

ants are directed back to the divorce court so that that court may consider the situation including that of the step-parent in the custody arrangements.

(7) A sole father or mother—the court cannot make an order in favour of a mother or father alone unless:

(a) the other natural parent is dead or cannot be found; or

(b) there is another reason justifying the exclusion of the other natural parent.

(8) Normally a male person cannot adopt a female child.

(9) Adoption must NOT be arranged for reward.

(10) During the adoption process, the court appoints a *Guardian ad litem* who is an officer appointed to safeguard the interests of the child on behalf of the Court. It is usual for certain social workers in the Social Services Department to act as *Guardian ad litem* officers.

Parental consent to adoption

Important new changes have been made in arrangements for parental consent by the Children Act 1975. In future parental consent to adoption (by the natural parent) will be given *before* the adoption order is made. A natural parent *will agree to free the child for adoption*. This will remove the present unsatisfactory uncertainty for all adopters and also will stop the natural mother from having to re-affirm her consent a number of times (this can be very harassing for any natural mother).

Ground for dispensing with parental consent. Parental consent can now be dispensed with if the parent or guardian has seriously ill-treated the child and, because of the ill-treatment, the rehabilitation of the child within the household of the parent or guardian is unlikely.

Religion

In future adoption agencies *as far as is practicable* must respect the parents' wishes in regard to the religious upbringing of the child. (This replaces the present system of parental consent to adoption subject to the condition that the child is brought up in a particular faith.)

Courts

At present adoption proceedings are held usually in Juvenile Courts. The Children Act 1975 enables *at some future date* adoption proceedings to be transferred from Juvenile Courts to domestic magistrates courts.

It is most important in all adoptions that:

(a) as far as possible, a careful matching process is carried out so that every effort is made to place the child with applicants who have similar intellectual, economic, cultural and religious backgrounds as the natural parents. Careful matching does much to ensure that the child is adopted by parents from a similar background and with similar educational attainments as the natural parents of the child.

(b) a careful medical history is taken of all children who are likely to be adopted and also of all prospective adopting parents.

The general health of the child should be good and every effort should be made to ensure the child has no serious defects of sight, hearing, speech, congenital abnormality. Mental handicap should be carefully tested for (as far as is practicable). Serological tests for syphilis should always be carried out.

The health of the prospective adopting parents should likewise always be carefully considered. They both should be in good general health, be suitable temperamentally and psychologically to care for a child. There should also be a good family history. In particular, the medical conditions which would cause doubt about the suitability of any person to be a prospective adoptor would include a history of mental illness, mental handicap, epilepsy, tuberculosis and any serious chronic illness.

Access to birth records

Adopted persons over *the age of 18 years have now a legal right to* information about their birth records. Section 26 of the Children Act 1975 lays this down and places upon local authority Social Services Departments and adoption agencies *a duty to provide counselling.* Those adopted after 12 November 1975 will be given an opportunity to see a counsellor *but need not do so.* Those adopted before 12 November 1975 *will be required to see a counsellor* before they are given the information they seek.

Custodianship

A new legal status called 'custodianship' was introduced by the Children Act 1975. This is meant to be an alternative to adoption and could be described as a half-way stage between adoption and fostering. Legal custody is transferred but the child keeps his name, and his family contacts are not cut off.

Custodianship can be granted by the Court on an application of a relative, step-parent or any other person who is not the father or mother of the child but who has the child in his/her care. Usually parental consent is necessary, and in addition
(1) the child must have had his home with the applicant for at least 3 months in the case of relatives and step-parents;
(2) and for all other applicants the child must have had his home there for at least 12 months.

Custodianship can be *granted without parental consent* in two circumstances:
(*a*) where there is no person having legal custody of the child, or
(*b*) when the child has had his home with the applicant for at least three years.

All applicants for custodianship must give notice to the local Social Services Department who then must investigate and report to the Court. However where applicants have looked after the child for at least three years or more (as in the case of long-term foster-parents) *that child* cannot be removed from their care without leave of the Court (section 41, Children Act, 1975). This is designed to prevent the 'tug-of-love' situations from developing where a foster parent who has had the child for three years or more wishes to keep the child although the Social Services Department who has parental rights wishes to remove the child for some reason. In future in such a case the foster-parent will be able to keep that child *while a Court decides on any custodianship application.*

14   CARE AND REHABILITATION
OF THE DISABLED

The Department of Health and Social Security is centrally responsible for the community social services for the disabled or physically handicapped.

Locally each major local authority (County Council, Metropolitan District Council and London Borough) is responsible through its Social Services Committee and the chief officer in charge of these services is the Director of Social Services (see page 145).

In addition, there are large numbers of national and local voluntary bodies working for the handicapped; examples include the Royal National Institute for the Blind, the Central Council for the Care of Cripples, the National Spastics Society, the National Multiple Sclerosis Society and various Deaf and Dumb Associations, etc. Many local authorities give monetary grants to help such voluntary bodies.

RELATIONSHIP BETWEEN MEDICAL AND NURSING SERVICES AND SOCIAL SERVICES

Medical, nursing and social services all attempt to help the handicapped in different ways. Doctors and nurses carry out the physical treatment of the handicapped in hospitals or in the community while the social services are more concerned with rehabilitation and with helping the handicapped to lead an active life and to overcome their social problems or difficulties. It will follow from this that doctors, nurses and social workers must work closely together if the best results are to be obtained. In the reorganization of the health service and of local authorities, the fact that the local areas of operation for each are the same geographical size should ensure that the closest working together can be reached—area health authorities and social services authorities (new counties, metropolitan districts or London Boroughs) are usually contiguous.

Generally social services concentrate upon *aids to normal life within the community*—upon *housing, adaptations to houses, employment, special workshops, transport, various aids and gadgets, handicraft centres, social centres* and *clubs* and *holidays*. For these reasons, most social services provided by local authorities are in the community while many medical and nursing services are in the hospital or outpatient departments. Home nurses, health visitors and general practitioners also are actively engaged in helping many handicapped in their own homes. It is *most important that the social worker links up with these medical and nursing services*; this is best done by social workers visiting hospitals and general practitioners to ensure that a continuous working arrangement is maintained at all times. The eventual success with any individual handicapped person is closely connected with the degree of such co-operation between doctors, nurses and social workers. Eventually it is hoped that social workers will work closely with primary health care teams and that they will be part-time members of such teams.

LEGISLATION

Disabled Persons (Employment) Acts, 1944 and 1958

These Acts are designed to help all disabled persons by maintaining a register of such persons and then insisting that all employers maintain a minimum percentage of disabled persons among their employees.

A '*disabled person*' is one 'who on account of injury, disease or congenital deformity, is substantially handicapped from obtaining or keeping employment'. Every employer who employs twenty or more persons must, under this Act, must employ a *minimum of 3 per cent of disabled persons* among his staff.

Although the wide definition of disabled persons has reduced the effectiveness of this Act, it has helped to increase the opportunities for employment of handicapped people.

Chronically Sick and Disabled Persons Act, 1970

The Chronically Sick and Disabled Persons Act, 1970 gives many special responsibilities to local authorities in respect of those who are substantially and permanently handicapped (including mentally handicapped). The main duties of local authorities are:

(1) *Information*

Local authorities must ensure (*a*) that they are adequately informed of the numbers and needs of the handicapped so that they can properly plan and develop their services, and (*b*) that the handicapped and their families know what help is available to them by general publicity and personal explanations.

(2) *Provision of services*

Local authorities, when satisfied that the following services are necessary to the handicapped person, can provide the following:
(*a*) Practical assistance in the home
(*b*) Wireless, television, library or similar recreational facilities in the home
(*c*) Recreational facilities outside the home and assistance in taking advantage of educational facilities
(*d*) Travelling facilities for handicapped persons
(*e*) Assistance in carrying out adaptations to the home
(*f*) Facilitating the taking of holidays
(*g*) Meals at home or elsewhere
(*h*) A telephone and any special equipment necessary for its use.

(3) *Housing*

Every local authority must have regard to the special needs of the disabled and any new houses planned must show special provision is made for the disabled. This clearly gives housing authorities a duty to plan and provide special housing accommodation for the handicapped.

(4) *Premises open to the public*

There are a series of requirements for public buildings. These deal specially with:

(*a*) Providing means of access to and within the buildings and in the parking facilities and sanitary conveniences for the disabled. Such provision must be considered before planning permission is given.

(*b*) Need for a local authority to provide public sanitary conveniences for the disabled.

(*c*) Need for anyone providing sanitary conveniences in premises open to the public for accommodation, refreshment or entertainment, to make provision, as far as is practicable, for the disabled.

(*d*) Adequate sign-posting for the above provisions from outside.

(*e*) Need to provide facilities for access, parking, sanitary conveniences suitable for the disabled as far as is practicable at school, university and other educational buildings.

In addition, there are special clauses about Advisory Committees for the handicapped either nationally or locally and these insist that members of such committees must include persons with experience of work for the disabled and persons who are themselves disabled.

Many local authorities have provided excellent new services (especially telephones) for the handicapped, but some have been slow to assist. As some of the more progressive local authorities provide these extra services free and others make charges, there is unfortunately a varying standard of service for the handicapped throughout the country.

National Assistance Act, 1948, Section 29

This gives the local authorities the responsibility of providing a further wide range of social services for the handicapped including home training, occupational therapy and many other domiciliary services.

GENERAL PRINCIPLES FOR HELPING THE DISABLED

In the rehabilitation of all these groups of handicapped persons, there are certain basic principles which are important. No social service can succeed if they are ignored, and it is essential to understand them, for they carry the secret of success and can quite simply be modified for every handicapped person. There are four main principles:

(1) The problems of every handicapped person are *highly individual* and *personal*;

(2) The best solution for any handicapped person is that *one which is as near normal as possible*;

(3) A large amount of *improvisation* will probably be necessary;

(4) *Great determination and singleness of purpose* is usually essential for success.

(1) The difficulties of any handicapped person vary with each individual. This is because the problems depend on:

(*a*) the age of the individual

(*b*) the nature and extent of the handicap

(*c*) the reaction of the handicapped person to the difficulties he faces.

Thus, many blind people are able to hold down an important job whilst others who are blind may be unable to carry out successfully quite a simple occupation. The handicap is the same—complete blindness—but the end result and size of the individual problem varies greatly. Age also is an important factor (see page 176).

The reaction of the handicapped person to his difficulties depends very much on the attitude of the persons who have tried to help him in the early and crucial stages of his handicap. A correct approach and attitude of mind here are essential. What is wanted is an understanding which very often means something quite different from ineffective and maybe sentimental sympathy. Very often the best approach is a fairly tough one which promises the handicapped person little but many hard struggles and disappointments.

For these reasons, *individual visiting* and *assessment* are always a most important first step in rehabilitation. As the social background of the handicapped person—his home and his family—will always play a most significant part in his efforts to overcome his handicap, it is important that assessment includes these.

(2) There is a very simple rule to follow in determining what any handicapped person should attempt to do. *The best solution is always the one which is as near normal as possible.*

This basic principle applies to all aspects of work with the handicapped including education and occupation. A normal person works in the industry or office with normal people—he is not in any way protected. This is also the best solution for any handicapped person.

If difficulties are found in suggesting the next stage in rehabilitation, a useful indicator is given by considering what occupation the person would be following if he was not handicapped.

The aim should always be for the rehabilitation process to progress towards this goal.

The constant hope given by successfully reaching various stages in rehabilitation will do much to counteract an attitude of self pity in the handicapped person which must be avoided.

(3) Just as the problems of each handicapped person differ, so will the solutions. Hence, an ability *to improvise* in overcoming the inevitable and unexpected difficulties is most important. No worker with the handicapped can ever afford to be narrow minded, too set in his ways or hidebound by convention. All the most successful social workers are resilient and often unconventional people to whom improvisation comes naturally.

(4) It is always easy to find an excuse for failure when dealing with the handicapped. Therefore, to succeed, it is important to *concentrate solely upon success* however remote this might seem to be. If possible, the handicapped person and those immediately around him, should be fired with an enthusiasm to succeed irrespective of the difficulties and inevitable disappointments ahead. A complete singleness of purpose should be encouraged and this often helps to overcome difficulties.

Main groups of disabled

The main groups of disablement for which local authorities provide social services include:

(1) Blindness and partial sightedness
(2) Total deafness from birth—including the deaf and dumb
(3) Hardness of hearing—acquired deafness, usually late in life
(4) Congenital disabilities—spina bifida or spastic diplegia
(5) Paraplegia and hemiplegia
(6) Various paralytic diseases—multiple sclerosis, muscular dystrophy, poliomyelitis
(7) Epilepsy
(8) Serious arthritic conditions—rheumatoid arthritis, spondylitis, severe osteoarthritis
(9) Accident cases.

SPECIAL FINANCIAL HELP AVAILABLE TO THE SERIOUSLY DISABLED

Attendance allowance

Attendance allowance is an allowance for adults and children aged 2 years and over who are severely disabled physically or mentally and have needed a lot of looking after for 6 months or more. There are two rates, the higher rate for those who require attendance both by day and night (£10.60 early in 1976) and a lower rate for those who need attendance either by day or night (£7.10). The allowance is NOT payable if the disabled person is living in accommodation provided by a local authority or is receiving free in-patient treatment in a National Health Service hospital.

Mobility allowance

A new *mobility allowance* for severely disabled adults under pensionable age (65 for men and 60 for women) was introduced in stages from 1 January 1976. In future such disabled persons will be able to choose between having a three-wheeled invalid car or a mobility allowance of £262 per year (£5 per week). Eventually the three-wheeled car will be withdrawn. The allowance is taxable and the special medical conditions which must be satisfied include:
(1) the person must be unable or virtually unable to walk because of physical disablement, *and*
(2) the inability to walk must be likely to persist for at least 12 months from the time the claim is made, *and*
(3) the person's condition must be such that he can benefit from time to time from increased facilities for mobility.

The disabled person must also reside in Great Britain. The first group to be eligible will be aged 15–25 years (from 1 January 1976), the 25–50 year age group from 1 April 1976. Children aged 5–15 and adults from 50–pensionable age will be introduced into the scheme at a date to be announced which will be before 1979.

The mobility allowance will be paid to more than one person who qualifies living in the same household. It is hoped that this financial allowance will enable either the disabled person to put the sum towards the purchase of a car or towards the cost of taxis in the case of a severely disabled person who cannot drive.

SOCIAL SERVICES AVAILABLE FOR THE DISABLED

The following are the social services provided by local authority social services departments and voluntary bodies working with them:

(1) Social worker support and assessment

Social workers are available to assess and advise the handicapped at home. Initially each handicapped person is **registered** and his/her needs carefully assessed and catalogued. Social workers are usually attached to area social work teams (see page 148) and include specialists trained to work with the blind who can teach Braille and with the deaf and dumb who can use sign and finger language.

Social workers work closely with other community workers such as health visitors, home nurses and general practitioners. Special services such as meals-on-wheels and home helps can be arranged by the social worker.

(2) Employment for the disabled

There are two main ways in which the disabled can be employed full time: (*a*) in ordinary or 'open' industry, (*b*) in special sheltered employment.

(*a*) *'Open' industry* refers to ordinary occupations where each handicapped person works with and under exactly the same conditions as a normal person. Full wages are paid without any subsidy.

This is always the best solution, but is unfortunately only possible for a proportion of the employable handicapped. The success of placing the handicapped in open industry will depend on the employment opportunities of the area and the efforts of the social services department and Disablement Resettlement Officers (DROs) of the Department of Employment and Productivity to find openings in local industries. It should be possible to place many intelligent well trained disabled persons in most industries. With the blind, *special Blind Persons Resettlement Officers* are employed to assist finding places in industry for the handicapped (see page 178).

(*b*) *Sheltered employment* is subsidized employment (full-time) arranged either in a special workshop or in a home workers scheme (details for the blind on page 179). The Employment Service Agency runs special Remploy workshops for the handicapped and some local authorities run their own workshops. There are also many voluntary bodies who run sheltered workshops usually with financial help from local authorities.

(3) Industrial therapy services

Many local authotrities run industrial therapy services and, in this way, assist the handicapped in their rehabilitation. Reference is made later to such services provided for the mentally handicapped (see page 198) and similar services are provided for the physically handicapped. The aim of these industrial therapy services is mainly to train and prepare the physically disabled for full-time work.

(4) Handicraft centres

Handicraft centres are also provided by local authorities for the disabled and are usually staffed by handicraft instructors. The main aim of such centres is to assist the disabled to enjoy recreational facilities although complete rehabilitation towards eventual full-time employment may not be possible.

(5) Occupational therapy services

Most local authority social services departments organize occupational therapy services. These may be on a *domiciliary basis* where the occupational therapist calls on each handicapped person at home from time to time, or the services may be provided at *special rehabilitation centres*. In such cases the handicapped are brought to the centre by special transport.

The concept of the work of occupational therapists has changed recently and much more *emphasis is now placed on teaching the disabled to live with their handicaps* rather than instruction in craft work. In this way the disabled are helped to overcome their muscular difficulties by the use of various aids or machines including knitting and fretsaw machines, various looms and treadle lathes. A number of crafts are also taught at such centres.

Occupational therapists train their women patients in *special training kitchens* and these are especially useful to the handicapped housewife to help her become more independent. Various aids and gadgets are tested out in these kitchens so that later the correct aid can be fitted for each handicapped person in their own kitchen.

Attendance at such centres may be on a full-time or part-time basis. As well as the training undertaken at each centre, the social value of the handicapped meeting each other and becoming less isolated is also important.

Much permanent invalidism can be caused by the disabled person becoming more and more withdrawn as he/she stays permanently at home meeting only close friends or family. If the handicapped person is brought to a rehabilitation or handicraft centre, his/her confidence is helped by meeting other people and further deterioration can be prevented. Occupational therapy services are also provided by many Area Health Authorities.

(6) Aids centres

Permanent aids centres containing a wide range of equipment suitable for the disabled have been established in London by the Disabled Living Foundation and by local authorities in Liverpool, Newcastle and Birmingham. These aids centres set out to enable the severely disabled and their families to see for themselves the range of equipment available. It is usual to staff such units with experienced occupational therapists and to run the centre on an appointment system as it usually takes 1½ to 2 hours to demonstrate all the equipment available.

The disabled and their families wishing to visit such centres should contact either the Disabled Living Foundation, 346 Kensington High Street, London W8, or the Directors of Social Services for Liverpool, Newcastle or Birmingham.

(7) Transport

Mobility for handicapped people is very important. Individual problems depend very much on the type of handicap. Various adaptations are possible to cars so that they can be safely driven by hand controls only.

Individual transport Special individual transport (motorized or non-motorized) can, in certain circumstances, be provided under the National Health Service at no cost to the patient. Only the more seriously disabled can be helped in this way. The procedure is for the appropriate hospital consultant (usually the orthopaedic surgeon or physical medical specialist) to complete a form and send it to the local appliance centre of the Department of Health and Social Security. If the application is accepted, it is usual for there to be a delay of three months before delivery of the vehicle. Four different types of motorized transport can be provided—motor car, motor-tricycle (invacars), electrically propelled tricycle and the electrically propelled indoor chair. In addition, a number of different types of wheelchairs can be provided. It is planned to withdraw the three-wheeled car after 1978.

The type of transport is decided by the type of disablement, i.e., motor cars can only be managed by persons who still have considerable hand power such as a paraplegic whose injury (spinal lesion) was mid-thoracic region.

Local authorities provide the run-in, drive and base for the garage which is erected by the Department of Health and Social Security.

Local authorities often provide *temporary* wheelchairs on loan to help those who have a transient need— less than six months. In permanent cases, after this period, the Department of Health and Social Security should provide the wheelchair.

Group transport Local authority social services departments provide various vehicles, *personnel carriers, mini-buses,* etc., to carry the handicapped from their homes to various centres. Many of the vehicles are fitted with *side hydraulic lifts* so that wheelchairs and their occupants can easily be loaded onto them while sitting in the wheelchair. At their destination, the chair and occupant can likewise be easily unloaded.

The success of many of the activities and services provided by local authorities (various centres and clubs, etc.,) depends to a large extent on the efficiency of transport services for the handicapped which must be adequate to meet the needs of the area.

(8) Holidays and outings

Many voluntary bodies and local authorities arrange special holiday schemes for the disabled. These have become more and more ambitious in recent years and include special holidays abroad.

Special staff go with the handicapped group which usually contains many quite severely handicapped people in wheel chairs. Special arrangements are made as regards transport and all holiday activities, and in this way, many handicapped people are able to enjoy a holiday who otherwise could not do so.

Some local authorities also help the handicapped by subsidizing ordinary holidays arranged by the disabled person himself/herself with a small monetary grant (in the region of £15). This enables the disabled person to arrange a more expensive type of holiday (e.g., to stay at a hotel with a lift rather than in more modest accommodation).

Emphasis today is on the *provision of normal holidays* in which the normal members of the family can share with the disabled. There are, however, a number of special holidays arranged for the handicapped and some local authorities have special seaside holiday homes for the disabled.

(9) Social centres and clubs

Many voluntary bodies run special social centres and clubs for the handicapped. Local authorities usually give financial support to many centres or provide a central club which voluntary bodies may use at no cost. Transport which is an important essential to the successful running of such clubs is provided by the local authority.

(10) Housing for the disabled

The *design of the home occupied by the individual disabled person is very important.*

Many adaptations are needed to enable a severely handicapped person to live normally—larger doors, no steps, large bathrooms and w.c.s, and special fitments in the kitchen.

It may be possible to *adapt the home* or to introduce special aids (see below). But with the most severely handicapped, e.g., the paraplegic, it may be easier and cheaper for the local housing authority to *build specially designed bungalows* into which these adaptations are already included. Under the Chronically Sick and Disabled Persons Act, 1970, local authorities are encouraged to provide such special housing for the handicapped (see page 167).

In the case of an individual who suffers a paraplegia following an accident and who is consequently admitted to a regional hospital spinal centre, *it is most important that the housing requirements are considered shortly after admission* and not left until just before the patient is discharged home. Most patients will remain in such hospitals for at least six months and it is essential to ensure that the local authority has all this time to solve the housing difficulties which often are very great. Considerable adaptations may be needed at the patient's home or even rehousing—either of which may take months to achieve.

(11) Minor adaptations, aids and gadgets

Under the Chronically Sick and Disabled Persons Act, 1970, local authorities help by providing (usually at no cost) minot adaptations including:

(1) *Ramps or handrails.*

(2) *Hoists* in bedrooms and bathrooms for those paralysed in the legs so that they can become more independent and mobile.

(3) *Modifications to table implements,* knives, forks, spoons, to make them more easily used by people whose grip is weak or whose hands are deformed.

(4) Various *kitchen fitments for the handicapped.* These include many gadgets for one-handed people or those who only have power in one hand, and other aids for those whose balance is poor (slings to be fitted to sinks to allow such people to stand supported by the sling);

(5) *Kitchen management and planning* is most important. The height of various working surfaces and the design of kitchen furniture are examples. Many rehabilitation centres are fitted with *model kitchens* for the handicapped so that the occupational therapist can see which equipment best suits the handi-

capped person before steps are taken to fit out the handicapped person's own kitchen. Various kinds of cooking stoves can be tried in such demonstration kitchens.

(6) Various *personal aids in dressing* are all important so that the independence of the handicapped person is improved. In all this work, the aim is always to make the handicapped person as normal as possible and, in this respect, anything that engenders independence is valuable.

Other social services which are available include meals-on-wheels (see page 205) and home helps (see page 217).

Telephones Under the Chronically Sick and Disabled Persons Act, 1970, most local authorities help by providing a telephone (and paying rent) for the most severely handicapped living alone. Standards vary but most local authorities give top priority to *the handicapped living alone who cannot go outside in normal weather*. Telephones are also provided for special medical cases. Any nurse coming across such a handicapped person who urgently requires a telephone should report the case to the local Director of Social Services.

REHABILITATION OF THE DISABLED

This is a joint enterprise involving the medical services (hospitals and general practitioners), Employment Service Agency and local authority social services departments and in children and young persons the education authority.

Rehabilitation usually starts in the hospital—in the rehabilitation or orthopaedic departments and then transfers to rehabilitation centres run by local authorities. Special transport is used to enable the patient to be brought to the centre and makes it possible to extend much more quickly the range of rehabilitation.

At the centre, there are many and various machines and aids such as knitting machines, fretsaw machines, looms, as well as a training kitchen. There are also opportunities to follow many crafts.

The rehabilitation centre is open all day and people can attend for half a day or a full day. It is usual for the kitchen to be used by the handicapped learning to cook, and in this way meals are prepared for themselves and others attending the centre. One of the most valuable parts of the centre's regime is the *social one*, of variously handicapped people meeting other people. In many long and chronic illnesses or disabilities, there is a strong tendency for the patient to become more and more withdrawn as he stays permanently at home meeting only his family and close friends who call. Even when this physical condition improves, very often he tends to stay at home and this factor can have the effect of making it difficult or impossible to rehabilitate the patient back to an occupation.

Attendance at the occupational therapy centre and travelling to it increases greatly his self-confidence and does much to prevent permanent invalidism. Once a week at the centre, a social evening is arranged so that those attending the centre can relax together playing games, table tennis and dancing.

Rehabilitation from centre to workshops and industry

The aim of the occupational therapist is to transfer eventually the handicapped person either directly into *open industry* or to a *special sheltered workshop.* These are run by various voluntary bodies supported by local authorities by financial grants and by the Employment Service Agency through the special Remploy factories. These are sited throughout the country and are designed to provide permanent work for the less severely disabled person.

Another very important link in the rehabilitation chain is the Employment Rehabilitation Centre run by the Training Services Agency. These are designed to teach a handicapped person a new trade skill and are of great importance to those people who have had to learn a new job because the one for which they are trained is now unsuitable for them. An example would be a skilled miner who develops tuberculosis. Even though he may only develop a minor degree of tuberculosis, it is obviously undesirable for him to return to work in a dusty atmosphere. Therefore, he is retrained at such a centre and is given a new industrial skill. This is most essential as it is the industrial skill of the handicapped person that usually determines whether he can be employed or not. The *highest unemployment rate is always in the unskilled workers.* If, therefore, in addition, there is a history of physical handicap, their chance of employment may be very slight. For this reason, *all handicapped people should be taught an industrial skilled occupation* suitable to their handicap, and the Training Services Agency Industrial Rehabilatation and Training Unit is provided to do this.

There must, at all times, be complete co-ordination between the occupational therapist and the Disablement Resettlement Officer of the Employment Service Agency.

DETAILED SOCIAL SERVICES FOR THE DISABLED

BLIND

Registration
Proper registration is essential. Each person who is thought to be blind is examined by a consultant ophthalmologist who carries out a complete visual examination and indicates, in his report, the degree of lack of sight and the prognosis.

Expert examination is most important to make certain that further active treatment is not possible, and to obtain an accurate knowledge of the number of blind persons present, their ages and requirements.

At present there are approximately 104 100 blind persons registered in England and Wales. Of these 85 per cent are aged 50 years and over. So, the problem of blindness is mainly in late middle-aged and elderly persons.

Just over 11 000 new cases of blindness are registered each year. There is a marked increased incidence of blindness in women compared with men. There is an even more marked tendency among the newly blinded to be elderly as only 8 per cent of the newly blinded are under 50 years of age and 81 per cent of them are aged 65 years and over.

Because of the close association between blindness and old age, it must always be remembered that many of the problems already discussed in Chapter 16 on the elderly may also present major difficulties in the blind.

Individual assessment

The problems facing any blind person vary greatly from individual to individual. The age at which blindness develops is a major factor. The child born blind has to learn to live the whole of his life as a blind person—he must be educated as a blind person, must be employed as a blind person and face the difficulties of retirement and old age with the same handicap. Many elderly persons going blind over the age of 70 have only the last years of their life to lead as blind people—education and employment never present any difficulties. In the intermediate group there obviously are different problems.

The *personality, past training, intelligence* and the *home conditions* will all have a marked effect on either reducing or increasing the difficulties facing the blind person.

Each blind person must be carefully and individually assessed by expert social workers (usually called *home teachers for the blind*) whose task it is to unravel each problem and arrange for social services to help.

As already explained, the attitude of the social worker can do a great deal to minimize the difficulties of each blind person.

With newly blinded adult people (rather than with aged newly blinded), assessment is never easy, for often the blindness has suddenly occurred leaving the person uncertain, full of self pity and maybe bitter. Such newly blinded people should always be sent to a *special assessment centre* such as the one at America Lodge, Torquay, which is run by the Royal National Institute for the Blind. Here, under expert guidance, the newly blinded person spends from four to six weeks while being assessed. He quickly loses any self pity and realizes that the horizon of his capabilities even as a blind person, is much wider than he had ever before realized. After a visit to America Lodge, most newly blinded people return home and approach the necessarily difficult period of industrial retraining with a new and essential spirit of hope.

Even when the blind person has settled down well, *periodic visits to his home should be paid by a trained social worker* to continue in an unobtrusive way the assessment of his current problem. Only in this way is it possible to ensure that the wide social services available to blind people are being properly used.

Education

At present about 2500 children in England are being educated as blind persons. Highly specialized education is always necessary. Apart from a few day schools in London, Birmingham, Liverpool and a few other large cities, all the remaining schools are residential as no one area has enough blind children to make up a school.

Because of the difficulty in training a young blind child at home, where it is almost impossible to avoid over-protection, blind children start their education, often between one and two years of age, in a Sunshine Home run by the Royal National Institute for the Blind. They later move to *special residential blind schools.*

All blind children are taught to read by using Braille and many reach sound academic levels. A few progress to Universities and train for professions, while many are given some kind of technical training and are then found a suitable job in industry.

Employment

About 16 per cent of the blind people in this country are between the ages of 16 and 60 years, and it is in this group that the problem of employment occurs.

Full time employment of blind people includes:

(1) Employment in 'open-industry'
(2) An occupation in sheltered employment:
(a) in workshops
(b) in home workers schemes.

(1) *Employment in 'open industry'*

The term 'open industry' is used to denote employment in an ordinary job (in industry or commerce) where the blind person works with sighted people. No special arrangements are made as regards his remuneration, for the blind person in open industry is exactly like his sighted work-fellows.

There are many different types of occupations in which the intelligent, highly trained blind person can make a success, including a number of industrial processes such as capstan lathe operatives, telephone operators, piano tuners, etc.

The placing of blind people successfully in open industry depends on:

(a) having a helpful and sympathetic employer who is prepared to try out one or two blind people in his factory
(b) being able to train the blind person not only before he starts his job but actually while he is carrying the task out.

In both these respects, the *Blind Persons Resettlement Officer* of the Employment Service Agency is invaluable. These officers include very highly trained blind persons who arrange for the placement of blind people in industry. They act as a liaison with the employers and find out what vacancies exist in the area, in open industry, which would be suitable for blind people. The Resettlement Officer then assesses the potential of the blind persons wishing to enter open industry and trains those whom he selects. The officer then introduces the blind person to his new post and stays with him helping and training him during the first two or three weeks in his job. In this way, this officer is able to guide the blind person through the most difficult part of the job—the beginning, and help him to settle down. Afterwards visits are paid to the factory from time to time to check how the blind person is doing. If any difficulties occur in the meantime, the employer can call upon the Blind Persons Resettlement Officer to help sort them out. There is no doubt that this service helps many blind people to find out and maintain employment in industry.

On the general principle already mentioned, *the aim should always be to try and place as many blind people as possible in 'open industry'*—an employment solution which is normal. It is encouraging to note, in many areas, a steady increase in the proportion of blind people in open industry. In some areas, the proportion of blind people in open industry is in excess of 60 per cent of the blind persons employed full-time.

(2) *Occupation in sheltered employment*

For those blind people who cannot for some reason manage to hold down a job in 'open industry', the next alternative is to try and place them in what is known as 'sheltered employment'. This is specially subsidized full-time occupation applicable to blind persons only.

(*a*) If possible, the blind person needing sheltered employment should be sent to a special workshop for the blind. Here the blind person, after a period of training in a suitable occupation, is employed in the workshop. There are many traditional trades for blind persons in workshops including basket making, rug making, brush making, chair caning, machine knitting.

Each blind person attends the workshop full time just as in an ordinary factory and is employed in his special craft. Specially trained sighted foremen assist them in the finishing off of articles, and arrange the marketing and sale of the products.

Each blind worker receives the usual wage for the occupation although because of his handicap he might not have been able to earn his wage 'on piece rates'. The difference between what he actually earns and is paid is called a grant paid by the local authority, which receives a large contribute from the Employment Service Agency to help meet this cost.

At present the annual grant payable by the Employment Service Agency to local authorities for each blind person employed in a workshop is a maximum of £700 a year.

Because of the extreme difficulties facing workshops, it is usual for an additional annual loss per worker to be incurred which the local authority has to subsidize.

Example

The employee would receive	39.67 per week
A blind person employed as a basket maker in a workshop could earn	14.25 per week
Therefore, grant would be	£25.42 per week

(*b*) Home workers schemes are mainly to be found in rural areas and smaller towns where it is never possible to collect enough blind people together to form a sheltered workshop.

In any home workers scheme, the blind worker is provided with materials at home and makes a certain quota of goods which are later collected and marketed. Provided the blind person averages a certain minimum output per week, he receives augmentation of wages as in the workshops.

An example would be a blind person employed at home as a machine knitter; the knitting machine is provided by the local authority together with materials and orders for socks. Each home worker so employed receives augmentation provided they maintain a certain agreed minimum.

Blind persons are employed in similar occupations in home workers schemes as in the workshops. Although many blind home workers schemes are excellent, they do not provide such a satisfactory solution as workshop schemes. In particular, it is often difficult to supervise the blind people as satisfactorily and the blind persons themselves miss the company that they meet in a workshop. It is also more difficult for the blind person to concentrate on a high level of production—most homes contain too many distractions.

General social services for blind persons

(a) Part-time occupations

Some elderly blind people are keen to fill in a portion of their time by doing some part-time occupation. This is usually arranged by the home teacher who helps with assistance to be given in marketing the articles. There are various arrangements to help with this problem and many towns have a *disabled persons shop* which markets the products made in this way by blind or other disabled people.

Augmentation is never given to blind people working part-time as it is only intended to help and encourage blind people engaged in full-time work.

(b) Learning to read

An important part of any social service for the blind is concerned with *home tuition in reading.*

There are two forms of embossed type:

(1) *Moon*—raised letters—easy to learn but a very slow and inefficient method of reading which, for this reason, is not often taught.

(2) *Braille*—this is the usual method of reading used by the blind. It is a complicated system of embossed dots arranged in a rectangular pattern. It is taught to all blind children and younger blinded adults and elderly persons who have both the ability and desire to learn. It takes an intelligent blind person at least six months fairly hard study to learn Braille and, for this reason, is beyond the ability of many elderly persons who go blind in later life.

A useful indicator of the likelihood of an elderly blind person, who has recently lost his sight, learning Braille is given by finding out how much and what type of reading he did when he had his sight. If he was an avid reader, it is always important for him to persevere with Braille. If, however, he was a most casual reader contenting himself with the simplest and widely illustrated newspapers, it is not likely that he will be able to learn Braille.

All persons recently blinded under the age of 50 years, and all young persons should always be taught Braille.

(c) Substitutes for reading

The Royal National Institute for the Blind have a large *library of recorded tapes of books read aloud.* They also lend a standard tape recorder to each blind person wishing to take advantage of this service. The blind person then borrows the tape recording of the book he wants to hear, plays the tape and, in this way, can have a continuous and changing supply of books read aloud to him.

Each local authority makes a contribution to the Royal National Institute for the Blind for each person in its area who is using this service.

(d) Wireless for the blind

The radio is a most useful service and greatly enjoyed by all blind people. There is a special voluntary society (Wireless for the Blind Fund) financed by the traditional appeal over the radio each Christmas Day, whose object is to ensure that every blind person is provided with a wireless. Maintenance is arranged by local authorities.

(e) Special aids

Special aids in the home are available for the blind. A good example is the special braille form of 'regulo' which can be fitted to gas stoves to help the blind person who is cooking.

(f) Provision of guide-dogs for the blind

A society exists which provides and trains *special guide dogs* which can be used by the blind. The selection and training of the dog and blind person is lengthy and costly and necessarily limits the number of blind people who can be helped in this way. Only a few breeds are suitable for training c.f. retrievers. In particular, it is a most valuable service for any active blind person living on his own. Local authorities meet the cost of training and provision of guide-dogs which is, today, usually in the region of £500.

(g) Holidays and hostels

The provision of *special holiday homes for the blind* is another general social function. Many of these are run by various voluntary bodies, and local authorities assist by contributing and paying for the blind people from their area who use them. The holiday homes are specially adapted and make it possible for a blind person to have a holiday. The difficulties and dangers of going alone to ordinary hotels and boarding houses usually meant that blind people living alone did not take any holidays.

There are a few specially designed permanent hostels for elderly blind people. But many more old people who are blind are looked after very satisfactorily in ordinary elderly persons hotels—perhaps two blind people in a hostel containing 40 sighted elderly persons—and in many ways the blind people seem to enjoy such hostels more.

(h) Financial help

Although local authorities cannot help blind people by direct money grants, there are *special pension facilities* available to blind people. It is the responsibility of the social workers employed by local authorities to make certain that the blind people understand what these are:

(a) All blind persons are eligible for the retirement pension at 40 years of age.
(b) Supplementary pensions may in certain circumstances be paid by Social Security.

(i) Voting

A blind person has a right to vote by post in parliamentary and local elections or to have his ballot paper marked with the help of a sighted person.

(j) Free postage
Free postage is allowed for a number of 'articles for the blind' including embossed literature, paper for embossing, and for recordings acting as an alternative to an embossed book.

(k) Television licence
There is a reduction of £1.25 in the cost of a black and white television licence and the blind person does not need a dog licence for a guide dog.

(l) Income tax allowance
There is a special £130 income tax allowance for blind persons—less any tax-free disability payments (no relief if such payments exceed £100).

SOCIAL SERVICES FOR OTHER GROUPS OF DISABLED
The social services described in detail above, provide a useful basis for a discussion of the services available to other handicapped persons.

In all groups, it is always important to arrange:
(1) as complete a system of *registration* as possible
(2) *individual assessment* by means of home visiting so that the difficulties and problems of the handicapped person can be assessed in the surroundings of his own home.

Compared with the other social services described for the blind, there are many differences for other handicapped groups and these will now be discussed separately.

DEAF AND DUMB
This general term describes persons *born completely deaf* and who, in the past, *never developed any speech,* not because of a defect of voice production, but because normal speech is only learnt by copying what is heard—a process impossible in the congenitally deaf. With very modern methods of teaching, it is now possible to teach some speech to most congenitally deaf children.

The problems of the group as a whole are mainly connected with the isolation from which they suffer.

The need of most deaf and dumb people is, therefore, connected with arranging:
(a) suitable *interpreter services* in obtaining a job or in sorting out any difficulty; (b) *clubs and recreational facilities* for the deaf and dumb. Many deaf and dumb people use a mixture of sign and finger language by which they converse with each other. Because of this, they enjoy mixing with other deaf and dumb people rather than normal persons with whom they often find it difficult to communicate.

Lip reading is also used to understand speech and many deaf and dumb people find television very enjoyable.

Finding and keeping a suitable occupation is not usually a difficult problem for the deaf and dumb, provided they receive help, especially in interpretation, from a trained social worker.

Most of the social services for the deaf and dumb are carried out by voluntary societies, many of whom are connected with church bodies. There is an historical reason for their welfare which was originally started in the nineteenth century by the church, with the object of providing special church services which the deaf and dumb could follow. Today services have developed widely to include all types of social services, but there are still special religious services held weekly for the deaf and dumb in many places.

HARD OF HEARING

People who develop deafness, having in the past enjoyed good hearing, are usually referred to as *'hard of hearing'*. This term indicates that although deaf, such handicapped persons have normal speech—listening (often assisted by a hearing aid) and lip reading.

The greatest proportion of hard of hearing are elderly persons, as deafness, like blindness, often develops seriously in old age.

The preventive medical aspects of hard of hearing are primarily to make certain that:

(*a*) *correct assessment of hearing* is undertaken from time to time
(*b*) that *hearing aids are provided* when needed and well maintained so that they are constantly helpful.

The assessment of hearing is usually carried out in an Ear, Nose and Throat department of a hospital, or in a special centre, such as those found in the school health service of large authorities. Hearing should always be tested by a *pure tone audiometer*. Coarse tests often used, such as listening to speech or the ticking of a watch, are of very limited value and of no use at all in assessing the degree of deafness to different frequencies of sound.

Probably there is no more neglected health aid than a hearing aid. The fitting of a hearing aid needs patience to ensure that it is fully understood by the deaf person, and is completely comfortable. Unless this is so and the deaf person understands its working, it will be bound to be a failure. Care is also needed to maintain the aid and it is always helpful if a home visitor—health visitor or social worker—can call periodically on the deaf person to check that the aid is being used.

PARALYTIC CONDITIONS

This contains both progressive conditions (multiple sclerosis, muscular dystrophies) and non-progressive states—poliomyelitis and the sequelae of accidents.

Many of these individuals need a variety of community services outlined on pages 171–175. Occupation should be possible for those whose mobility is maintained and especially for mild cases. Much of the social help this group needs is assistance with housing, transport and the fitting of various aids to enable them to live more normal lives within the community.

Paraplegia

Many of these cases result from accidents in which the spinal cord is permanently injured. The extent of the paralysis will depend upon the site of the injury—the lower the site the better the outlook and vice versa. All will be paralysed from the waist down, but if this is the main lesion (i.e., if the arms are unaffected) then up to 80 per cent of patients should be able to lead reasonably normal lives and be able to carry out an occupation. Such disabled can, with the aid of suitable mechanized transport, become quite mobile as each develops tremendous power in his/her arms to compensate and soon learns how to improvise.

Sporting facilities have always been an important part of social facilities provided for paraplegics. This is because the strengthening of compensatory muscles is an essential part of training the paraplegic to overcome his disability. Following the lead given by Stoke Mandeville Hospital both national and international sporting events are held each year culminating in the Paraplegic Olympics which are held in the same year as the Olympic Games. Many different sporting activities are suitable including archery, basket ball, etc. Many local authorities assist paraplegics by providing suitable premises and sports centres where this activity can be carried out.

Spastic diplegia

Many spastic handicapped persons need similar services to other paralytic or crippling diseases. Most of these conditions date from birth and, therefore, suitable education and training facilities for the young adolescent are important. Speech defects also pose special difficulties.

Recent work has emphasized that it is better to look after spastics in conjunction with other handicapped persons rather than attempt to provide suitable services solely for spastics. About 25 per cent of spastics also suffer from epilepsy and, therefore, for this group the services outlined below are important.

Persons with epilepsy

Persons with epilepsy present many problems not met with in other groups of handicapped people. This is not due to the unusual difficulties of treating epilepsy, but to the ill-informed and unfair attitude of the public generally.

Most epileptic patients suffer from minor degrees of the illness and are well controlled and can quite satisfactorily be employed in most professions and occupations. In fact, there are many examples of persons, who have epilepsy, succeeding in most occupations. But the public have an unreasonable fear of this disease because quite wrongly they believe that the epileptic may be dangerous. A number of people even think the disease is some form of mental illness.

All this adverse public reaction leads to many patients with epilepsy concealing the fact that they have had occasional epileptic seizures, because they fear if it is known they have epilepsy, they may lose their jobs or find it difficult to find employment. The strain of an epileptic concealing the fact he is one is considerable, especially as he must realize that a sudden unexpected attack of epilepsy at work would lead to discovery. For this reason, many patients in good posts live in constant fear of discovery and this often leads to the development of other difficulties including a minor anxiety state.

To help the person with epilepsy, it is important to realize this difficult background and to try and arrange for his employer or prospective employer to know the full facts and that his epilepsy, if properly controlled, may be no hazard. It is usual for the epileptic person to have some form of warning of an impending attack and, apart from avoiding a few dangerous occupations in which he will rarely want to work, there are a few jobs which are not suitable.

It is, however, essential that a constant and careful watch is kept on each epileptic person to make sure that the treatment he receives is controlling his disease.

The final success of any treatment depends on his complete rehabilitation. Because of this, it is most helpful to attach a specially trained health visitor or social worker to the hospital which treats most of the serious epileptic persons in the area, so that all the social aspects of the illness—home, occupation, etc.—can be carefully investigated. In this way, much preventive work can be done with the epileptic client and many social problems can be avoided or corrected before they can have a serious effect.

Occasionally, it is necessary to admit to an *epileptic colony* the severe epileptic patient whose illness cannot be controlled by treatment or whose home is quite unsuitable. Most epileptic colonies are run by voluntary bodies and local authorities meet the cost. Although most people in colonies have to stay there permanently, every effort is made to rehabilitate them back to community life if at all possible.

Special medical assessment and treatment centres for epilepsy

Important special centres for medical assessment of difficult cases of epilepsy have been set up for children at Oxford (based on the Park Hospital for Children) and for adults at York and Chalfont (Bucks.) Skilled assessment in difficult cases is essential and such units are just beginning to probe some of the complicated facets of some cases of epilepsy.

15 CARE OF THE MENTALLY DISORDERED

Rôle of local authorities

The social services departments of local authorities are responsible for developing widespread community social services for the mentally disordered (mentally ill and mentally handicapped). These mainly fall into three categories:

(1) Social work support provided by social workers (formerly called mental welfare officers).

(2) Day care facilities to help with the reintegration of anyone who has had mental illness. These include social rehabilitation, occupational therapy, industrial therapy and workshop provision.

(3) Residential facilities for those who have no satisfactory home to return to after their illness.

Law relating to the mentally disordered

The Mental Health Act, 1959, changed the entire law relating to all forms of mental illness and handicap. This followed the realization that a completely new approach was essential if progress was to be made in the prevention and care of mental illness and handicap.

There were 4 main aims in the new Mental Health Act of 1959:

(1) To remove wherever possible the stigma attached to mental illness.

(2) To bring mental illness and mental handicap under the same code of practice.

(3) To bring the medical treatment of mental illness and mental handicap on to the same basis as the treatment of physical illness.

(4) To develop as far as possible community social services for the mentally disordered.

(1) *The removal of stigma* attached to mental illness is not easy as it is necessary to change the attitude of public opinion to mental disability. Due to ignorance as to its cause, many people feel ashamed, or have feelings of guilt, when a member of their family develops some form of mental illness.

There is really no basis at all for such a reaction. Hardly any mental illness is hereditary. Mental illness is not uncommon—each year 439 per 100 000 of the population are admitted to mental hospitals in England and one third of these are admitted for the first time.

It has been estimated that one in twenty to twenty-five persons are admitted to a mental hospital at some time in their life while probably double that number seek advice from their family doctor for an illness whose basis is primarily mental not physical. This means that few, if any, families, do not contain some member who has had or will have some form of mental illness.

Probably one of the most effective ways to help reduce stigma would be for all large district general hospitals to have mental health departments to replace the isolated mental hospitals. This would mean that the reason for a patient's admission would not be so obvious—as it is when admitted to a mental hospital. It would also help to get better understanding between doctors and nurses treating physical and mental illnesses.

(2) Until 1959, *mental illness*, that is a disease whose main problem is some form of *emotional instability*, was treated quite separately, in the legal as well as medical sense, from *mental handicap*, which is primarily a defect of development of the intellect in which *the intelligence of the patient is seriously retarded*. From the pathological aspect, it is reasonable to consider them separately. However, in the individual case both factors often play a part. For example, in a moderate mental handicapped case (in which the intelligence of the person is retarded) the prognosis will depend, to some extent, on the emotional stability of the patient. If the emotional stabilty of a person is quite normal, there is much more chance of successfully training him/her to carry out some occupation and lead a reasonably normal life. However, if there is even a moderate degree of emotional instability, this may prove quite impossible.

The Mental Health Act, 1959, deals with both forms of mental handicap—*mental illness* and *mental handicap*.

(3) *Treatment of physical illness* is designed to carry out a full investigation, to correct various pathological processes discovered and, if possible, to restore the patient to full health. If this is not possible, the aim is to arrest development of the disease and to control problems. Treatment may take place at home by the family doctor, or the patient may be referred to hospital either as an outpatient or an inpatient for investigation and treatment. But once these are completed, the patient invariably returns home. Even in the case of a steadily developing disease with a fatal outlook, such as a malignant new growth, the patient is sent home and remains there as long as possible.

The *treatment of all forms of mental illness* has the following important differences:

(*a*) There is usually a question of protecting both the patient and the community from the effects of the mental illness—e.g., the danger of suicide (a special problem to watch is any insomnia in puerperal depression—immediately after birth—for such symptoms may be seen in women just before a serious suicide attempt). Occasionaly violent behavious is noted (even criminal behaviour) which means that special arrangements have to be made to admit a few patients compulsorily and to retain them by compulsion in a mental hospital (*custodial care*).

(*b*) Much mental illness and handicap is a long standing or chronic problem whereas the majority of physical hospital patients are acute or sub-acute patients who are being treated for a short time.

Because the cause of mental illness, compared with physical illness, was so little understood, few effective and dramatic treatments were available to the mentally ill patient, until recently.

Fifty years ago, mental hospitals were almost entirely asylums—places where the mentally ill could safely be cared for rather than treated. Because of this, many who entered them remained there as inpatients for many years, and often for the rest of their lives.

New treatments, electrical convulsion therapy, leucotomy, the introduction of many tranquillizer drugs, better rehabilitation facilities and social services have changed all this. The aim today is to use hospital admission in mental illness mainly for investigation and early treatment, and then to return the patient home for follow-up treatment and special social services after-care and rehabilitation. Occasionally it is still necessary to arrange an admission compulsorily, but it is hoped this will eventually only occur in rare cases. Wherever possible, the patient is encouraged to be admitted as a *voluntary patient* even if he is acutely mentally ill.

(4) *The development of widespread community social services* has made it possible for continuing treatment to be carried out while the person lives at home. If home conditions are not suitable, he may live in *a special hostel* provided by the social services department or by a voluntary organization. Such an arrangement is more normal and therefore to be preferred. Occasionally *boarding out* may be arranged with sympathetic persons who understand mental disability.

Successful community care will only be possible if a wide range of supporting social services are available—social workers skilled in after-care work, *hostels, adult training centres, special workshops, occupational therapy, clubs, job placement services* leading, if possible, to full-time employment being obtained in ordinary industry.

Such extended social services (provided by social services departments) must be supported by better training of general practitioners and home nurses in the medical care of the chronic mentally disordered individual. Both the community social services (provided by social workers) and the community health services (general practitioners, home nurses, health visitors) must work very closely together so that both complement each other.

THE MENTALLY ILL

It is convenient to discuss social services for the mentally ill first under the following headings:
(1) prevention
(2) housing
(3) hostels
(4) occupation
(5) general after-care
(6) hospital admissions

(1) Prevention of mental illness

Much preventive work in the mental health field is concerned *with the avoidance of further breakdown,* rather than with the initial mental illness.

In many instances, however, the extrinsic factors (see page 117) connected with the patient's environment especially at certain times of life, puberty, pregnancy, menopause, old age, are the precipitating cause of the start of the mental illness.

Because of the extreme importance of the early years of life on the subsequent development of any person, it is *most important to recognize early, if possible, unusual signs of insecurity in a child,* as this is likely to indicate unsatisfactory home conditions. Most maternity and child health services today have a close link with a child psychiatrist and psychiatric social worker so that health visitors may discuss such cases and get help in this way with their preventive work.

Social work support should be available to such a home at any time and the decision about who is best fitted to provide this should be made after joint discussion between doctors, health visitors and social workers in the case of a disturbed child and between social workers and the doctor in adults.

In the same way, close liaison should always be maintained between child guidance staff who are helping maladjusted schoolchildren and social workers who may have to provide after-care later.

(2) Housing

Home conditions which are unsatisfactory for the mental development of a child may be quite different from those precipitating physical illness. The home may be very well provided with the physical essentials of life, but the *important mental factor of stability, love and affection may be missing.* Some of the worst environments are those homes in which parental strife is continuous and unending, perhaps eventually leading to separation or divorce. For this reason, particular attention must always be paid by the social worker to any home with such a background.

Even when early recognition of mental health problems has been made, it is never easy to change that home so that it becomes quite satisfactory. But, it is always a great help to know the problem exists and it is usually possible to prevent the effects of the poor home conditions being very detrimental to the child.

The value of the right type of home is just as important for the person who has had a mental illness and has been successfully treated in hospital. It may be much better for him to go to a special hostel on discharge from hospital rather than return to an unsuitable home.

(3) Hostels (small homes)

Hostels can be of various types and are provided by either the social services department or by a voluntary body. The aim should always be to achieve maximum integration between those living in the hostels and the ordinary community. This is easier if the hostels are small, accommodating 6–8 persons and if they are scattered throughout the area rather than collected together. As far as possible hostels should be like ordinary houses; they can successfully be established in the older larger house or by modifying 2–3 adjacent terraced houses together in a modern council estate.

Boarding out can also be useful as an alternative to an unsuitable home provided sympathetic and understanding hosts can be found. Because of this difficulty few successful boarding out schemes have yet been introduced by local authorities although there is no doubt about their value.

(4) Occupation

A correctly chosen occupation can do much to prevent a person developing a mental illness or to avoid a relapse, and is always an important factor in rehabilitation.

Many large industrial firms and H.M. Forces carefully examine all new entrants to assess as far as possible the type of personality, intelligence, aptitude and emotional stability, so that the person can be fitted into the most suitable occupation. This is most valuable and forms an important part of any occupational health service, for correct selection of occupation can avoid many breakdowns.

Having fitted the new entrant into his job, it is equally important that a careful watch is kept on him in the early period of his employment so that any signs of undue strain are recognized. This is also a valuable part of all *student health services* at Universities for it is known that serious mental illness can be avoided in students by ensuring early recognition of signs of stress.

It is the duty of a specially trained employment officer of the Employment Service Agency, called a *Disablement Resettlement Officer* (DRO), to find employment for all handicapped people including those who are mentally disabled. It is often difficult to find employment for persons who have had a mental illness. They may have lost their original job and there is usually a resistance among employers to re-employ them for fear they will again break down and perhaps dislocate their staff.

Because of the problems in finding work it is most important that the unavoidable delay should not depress the person who has just left a mental hospital. *Occupational therapy at a special rehabilitation centre* or attendance at a day centre should always be provided as this will not only help in training him in physical skills, but what is probably more important, it will do much to restore his self-confidence and get him used to meeting other people at the centre and prepare him for normal working conditions.

Social workers assist the Disablement Resettlement Officer in trying to find suitable jobs for those recovering from mental illnesses. Some social services departments have found it useful to employ a full-time officer to do this task. Much of this work is slow, and in one year such an officer may only find employment for 35 to 45 patients. His efforts, however, not only in finding jobs for patients who otherwise probably would have been unemployed, but by meeting employers, are constantly helping to educate the public in the problems of mental illness. The successful placement of such a patient very often leads to another post being found in the same firm for another patient.

(5) General after-care

The follow-up after-care work is always most important as all who have had a mental illness will need long-term help. Much of this will be done by the person's own family doctor. However, much of this after-care is now carried out by *social workers* from the social services department working very closely with the family doctor.

All social aspects—home, family, occupation, etc., play an important part in after-care and the social worker must ensure that close co-operation exists so that the person who has recovered from a mental breakdown is given every opportunity to return to normal life as quickly as possible.

(6) Hospital admission

Most hospital admissions for mental illness today are arranged in the same way as in physical illness—by the family doctor arranging for the patient to go into hospital as a voluntary patient. In 1976 approximately 82 per cent of all admissions were informal or voluntary. The decision is made after discussion between the family doctor and the psychiatrist who will then treat the patient in hospital.

Occasionally it is necessary to arrange *compulsory admission* and detention in hospital of a mentally ill patient either for observation or as an urgent necessity.

In the admission for observation, application must be made by the patient's relative or the social worker of the local authority. This must be accompanied by written recommendations of two medical practitioners; one of these doctors must be specially approved under the Mental Health Act, 1959 Section 25. (This type of admission accounted for approximately 15 per cent of admissions.)

In an emergency, compulsory admission can be arranged by application of a patient's relative or the social worker of the local authority, plus one written recommendation of a doctor. In this case, detention only lasts 72 hours unless a second medical opinion is received (Section 29, Mental Health Act, 1959). (This type accounted for approximately 3 per cent of admissions in 1970.)

MENTAL HEALTH REVIEW TRIBUNALS

There are many safeguards to make certain that no patient is retained in hospital compulsorily unless it is essential. Special *Mental Health Review Tribunals* are set up in each area to deal with any requests from patients for discharge.

After hearing the application the tribunal may direct the patient's discharge. It must do so if it is satisfied:

(*a*) that he is no longer suffering from mental illness, psychopathic disorder, subnormality or severe subnormality
(*b*) that it is not in the interests of the patient's health or safety or for the protection of other persons, that the patient should continue to be detained
(*c*) in the case of a psychopathic or subnormal patient whose discharge at the age of 25 was barred or a patient whose discharge by his nearest relative was barred, that if released he would not be likely to act in a manner dangerous to others or himself.

In 1975 483 applications are determined by Mental Health Review Tribunals, discharge of the patient was ordered in 60 cases.

ALCOHOLISM

Alcoholism can be defined as dependence upon alcohol to such a degree that the person shows noticeable mental disturbance or an interference with bodily or mental health. Alcoholism is both a medical and social problem in its origins and manifestations—it interferes with interpersonal relations and with the normal economic and social functioning of the alcoholic and his family.

It is estimated that there are about 350 000 to 400 000 alcoholics in England and Wales. Recently there has been evidence that the incidence is increasing especially in women and young persons.

Causes of alcoholism

There are many causes of alcoholism. Social factors are very important and there is a higher incidence in people who are single, widowed or divorced. The average age for men who become alcoholics is the mid-forties while in women it is higher. Certain occupations are at high risk—commercial travellers, business executives, publicans, seamen and doctors. No particular personality is specially liable although both excessively shy people and gregarious extraverts have a higher incidence.

Types of alcoholism. There are 2 main types:
(1) *Alcohol addiction*—persons who cannot go for long without a drink of alcohol or who get withdrawal symptoms if they stop drinking.
(2) *Chronic alcoholism* in which serious physical and mental symptoms are important features. Loss of appetite and poor food intake encourage the development of cirrhosis of the liver and peripheral neuropathy. Severe memory loss is often present and dementia may occur. Withdrawal symptoms may also occur (including delirium tremens).

Treatment, rehabilitation and after-care

Early diagnosis is always very important. Increasing absenteeism, decline in job efficiency, increasing marital disharmony and self-neglect are always very suggestive. Memory loss, misinterpretations and feelings of guilt and low self-esteem should raise suspicions. Ill-effects in other members of the family, especially wives, may occur.

Treatment is aimed at reversing the damage to the physical, mental and social life of the alcoholic and *then* to deal with the underlying addiction. Eighteen special alcoholism units (including detoxification centres) have been set up and many mental hospitals also provide treatment.

Once successful treatment has ended, relapses are common unless a careful rehabilitation process is started. Doctors should work closely with social workers from either the Social Services Department or voluntary bodies in the follow-up. Special *hostels* and *day centres* may have to be used. As many alcoholics have lost their job the Disablement Resettlement Officer of the Employment Service Agency should assist.

Many voluntary bodies, such as various Councils for Alcoholism and Alcoholics Anonymous, can give useful support.

THE MENTALLY HANDICAPPED (SUBNORMAL)

Definitions

Although the Mental Health Act, 1959 refers to 'mentally subnormals', the usual convention today is to refer to this group as 'mentally handicapped'. Although there is no legal reference to the level of intelligence of any individual in determining whether he is mentally handicapped, in practice, the level of intelligence is the most important single factor. There is invariably a marked degree of mental retardation and this is shown by an abnormally low intelligence quotient. Reference has already been made to the meaning of the intelligence quotient on page 66.

The Mental Health Act, 1959 speaks of three categories of mental handicap:

(a) *Severe subnormality* means 'a state of arrested or incomplete development of mind, which includes subnormality of intelligence and is of such a nature or degree that the patient is incapable of living an independent life, or of guarding himself against severe exploitation, or will be so incapable when of an age to do so'.

(b) *Subnormality* means 'a state of arrested or incomplete development of mind (not amounting to severe subnormality) which includes subnormality of intelligence, and is of a nature or degree which requires, or is susceptible to, medical treatment or other special care or training of the patient'.

Persons who suffer from 'severe subnormality' are a small group of extremely retarded individuals who cannot even guard against common dangers. This group contains grossly retarded individuals formerly called idiots and imbeciles. They need to be looked after permanently in special units, usually attached to special mental hospitals, and training can be of little help to them. Mortality is often high among this group.

The majority of mentally handicapped people are in the second group as defined legally as suffering from 'subnormality'. This group includes a few low grade patients only a little better than the 'severe subnormals' and all types of grades up to the borderline subnormals many of whom are difficult to distinguish from normal persons with a somewhat limited intelligence.

The basis for determining whether anyone is mentally handicapped or not depends on:

(1) an estimate of their intelligence.

(2) a social test to judge the ability of the individual to make use of his intelligence (i.e. a test of performance). Generally children who are three years or more behind their average age group in school are probably mentally handicapped provided there is no other cause for this retardation (i.e. deafness or prolonged absence due to physical illness).

(3) the emotional stability of the person. The majority of those who need special educational or social services for the mentally handicapped have intelligence quotients between 45 and 65 although there are also a few whose intelligence quotient is higher, but in whom there is a degree of emotional instability.

(c) There is another category of mentally disordered person mentioned in the Mental Health Act, 1959—*psychopathic disorder* which is defined as 'a persistent disorder of the mind (whether or not including subnormality of intelligence) which results in abnormally aggressive or seriously irresponsible conduct of the patient and requires or is susceptible to medical treatment.

This category of mentally disordered person is a small proportion of all cases—approximately 2 per cent of all hospital admissions arranged for the mentally disordered come within this definition.

Incidence of mental handicap

Approximately 105 000 mentally handicapped persons of all ages are receiving services from local authority social services departments and these include 30 000 who are under the age of 16 years.

About 62 000 severely mentally handicapped are looked after in hospitals but this number is gradually diminishing as emphasis is laid on looking after as many as possible in the community. Many within hospitals are very severe cases and some have multiple handicaps.

Causes of mental handicap (subnormality)

The majority of mental handicap is present at birth and results from a mutation in which the individual is left with an incomplete development of the mind. Such mentally subnormal patients may belong to a recognized type such as 'Mongol' defectives (Down's syndrome) so called because of the characteristic facial development reminiscent of Mongol races and which is now known to be caused by a chromosome abnormality.

Occasionally mental handicap may follow severe birth injury—thus approximately 45 per cent of those with spastic diplegia have some degree of subnormality. Although there is a relationship between the degree of spasticity and intelligence quotient, it is important to realize that this is not invariable *for a few very severely spastic individuals have normal intelligence quotients.*

Reference has already been made to that rare metabolic disease—*phenylketonuria* (see page 51)—in which the child is born normal but soon his defective metabolism leads to a poisoning of the brain which results in producing, within a few months, a mentally subnormal condition. If phenylketonuria is diagnosed early—within six weeks of birth, and the child is fed on a special diet, there is every hope that the development of subsequent mental subnormality will be prevented. It is for this reason that it is usual to day for the blood of all babies to be tested by midwife and health visitor on the tenth day and between four and six weeks of life to make certain that every case is discovered (more details about this test on page 51).

Mental subnormality occasionally develops following a *severe infection of the brain or meninges.* For this reason, it is *essential that no delay ever occurs in diagnosing and treating such conditions.*

PREVENTION OF MENTAL HANDICAP (SUBNORMALITY)

At present the opportunity to prevent subnormality is very limited. However, the following is a list of likely ways to prevent this handicap:

(1) Genetic counselling

The aim in genetic counselling is to identify where there is a high risk of the transmission of hereditary disease leading to mental handicap. At present this is only possible after the birth of one affected child. In some cases it may be possible to estimate the risks of another handicapped child being born. If these are high because one parent is a carrier of an abnormality which is likely to show itself in other children, then the parents can seek family planning help to prevent conception of another child.

With the most modern techniques it is possible to predict the chances of parents who have already had one Mongol child having another. In the majority of instances the risks are small, but in a few cases the risk is high and these are the families in which genetic counselling can help.

(2) **Amniocentesis** (removal of a small quantity of amniotic fluid)
Mongol abnormality can be detected at 16 weeks, just in time to enable a termination of pregnancy to be carried out if investigations show that the fetus is abnormal.
(3) **Immunization of girls against rubella**
Immunization between the ages of 11–14 years will prevent the possibility of rubella infection in the first three months of pregnancy leading to a possible chance of mental handicap.
(4) **Use of anti-D-immunoglobulin** to prevent haemolytic disease of new born (see page 36).
(5) **Expert care in labour** to reduce the risk of asphyxia or brain damage to the infant.
(6) **Intensive care during neonatal period** for babies of low birth weight.
(7) **Screening to prevent phenylketonuria** (see page 51).
(8) **Earlier completion of families** will reduce the chance of a mentally handicapped child being born. The effect of this is shown by the chances of a mongoloid child being born to any normal woman. These vary with the age of the mother:

The chance of a mongoloid birth with mother aged 20 is 1 in 260
The chance of a mongoloid birth with mother aged 30 is 1 in 100
The chance of a mongoloid birth with mother aged 40 is 1 in 46.

SOCIAL SERVICES FOR MENTALLY HANDICAPPED (SUBNORMAL)

Importance of co-ordination and a multidisciplinary approach

Although this section mainly describes social services, it is essential to realize that the *medical, educational, psychological and social needs* should be considered together. No single profession can tackle successfully all the problems and the use of an *assessment team* is important.

In young children the paediatrician, psychiatrist, health visitor, social worker and educationalist will all be involved as well as the family doctor.

Older children will need educational, social and vocational assessment. Adults will require repeated assessments from psychiatrists, general practitioners and social workers. Much of this assessment will take place in hospitals, schools, training centres, workshops or in the individual's own home.

COMMUNITY SOCIAL SERVICES

Many of the main social services of local authorities aim to provide a supportive community service in which the mentally handicapped and his family are encouraged to live a more normal life. If possible such individuals should be trained to follow a full-time occupation.

Since the introduction of the Education (Handicapped Children) Act, 1970, the care of mentally handicapped children up to the age of 17 years has been transferred to the education services (see page 67).

Many varied types of assistance are provided by social services departments of local authorities including:
(1) Social work support or counselling
(2) Practical help—home help, day nurseries, laundry services, sitters-in, etc.
(3) Training centres for adults
(4) Occupational therapy centres
(5) Workshops for adults
(6) Employment in ordinary industry
(7) Small homes (hostels)
(8) Short-term care
(9) Holidays and recreational activities—clubs, etc.

(1) Social work support and counselling

Parents need much help to adjust to the problems of caring for a mentally handicapped child. Many professional workers are involved—doctors, health visitors, teachers and social workers. Much of the visiting in the community is undertaken by social workers especially after initial diagnosis and assessment has been made.

Although education authorities now train the mentally handicapped children in special schools, much of the social work for this group, e.g. visiting in the community, is undertaken by social workers from the social services department. This has the great advantage of improving co-ordination between the education and social services departments and enabling continuity of care to be maintained when the child reaches the age of 17, ends his education and then comes into the direct care of the social services department.

(2) Practical help

Many families facing the problems of caring for a mentally handicapped individual may need the assistance of *home helps* (see page 217), *day nurseries* (see page 151), *laundry services*. *Sitters-in* can be of great help to enable the parents to get a short break.

(3) Training centres for adults

Adult training centres are designed to carry on the training of mentally handicapped persons who have reached the age of 17 years. A few such centres are mixed but it is more usual to have separate male and female adult centres.

The main task of the adult centre is to concentrate on training the mentally handicapped to take their place in the adult sheltered workshops or in a few instances within ordinary employment. A few adult mentally handicapped may find it difficult to adjust themselves to workshop training, but with the modern workshop whose tasks are more diverse, these should be exceptions.

Social training should continue in the adult training centres and girls particularly concentrate on mastering the skills of helping run a home and the boys on becoming more skilled in carpentry, woodwork and model making. It is very often in these training sessions that the simple concept of numbers is finally understood.

It is most important to recognize *the importance of inducement and constant encouragement.* The mentally handicapped individual *must* be given targets to achieve and not just left to work at his own pace. The *potential of many mentally handicapped people is far higher than expected,* but full potential will only be reached by training which constantly pushes each individual to his fullest capacity.

The training given in the centre should always be linked with home life so that the girls can be encouraged to help in the house and the boys in simple tasks.

Problems occasionally arise as puberty develops in these mentally handicapped persons. It should always be carefully explained to parents that close supervision must be maintained on the activities of their child at home. In particular, it is most important that *every parent of a mentally handicapped girl realizes that her mental handicap will make her more vulnerable to the advances of unscrupulous men.* Too lax a control at home by parents only too often results in the female mentally handicapped becoming pregnant.

(4) Occupational therapy centres

Occupational therapy centres are also used to help the mentally handicapped. At such centres occupational therapists give the mentally handicapped an opportunity to become involved in many different activities. These include various handicrafts and also training in group activities. If possible evening clubs should be arranged and run in such a way that the mentally handicapped people themselves do much of the organization.

(5) Workshops

There has been widespread development during the last few years in the setting up of *sheltered workshops* by local authorities, in which mentally handicapped adults are employed.

The type of workshops varies greatly, but one of the most successful arranges for various simple tasks which can only be done by hand, to be contracted out to the workshops by industry and undertaken by the mentally handicapped. Such tasks vary but in one group of workshops include:
(*a*) fixing a pourer into the top of a salt container
(*b*) stamping tight the top of another container
(*c*) assembling packs of picnic cups
(*d*) assembling ball-point pens
(*e*) stamping the prescription pads of doctors with their names.

Because of the necessity to fit the regime into that of industry, the workshop remains open for the whole of the year. Although the workshop is, in effect, a place of employment for the mentally handicapped, the training processes still continue. This is often seen in the method of payment adopted. One successful scheme is to base weekly payment upon a 'points' system, by which points, which represent part of the maximum wage, are added for good steady work and rate and standard of production, and deducted for bad behaviour, lateness or non-attendance. In this way the mentally handicapped persons employed at the workshop quickly learn the importance of hard work and good behaviour.

Inducement is a very important part of workshop training and the method of financial remuneration used should encourage better productivity, hard work and better social behaviour.

It is usual to arrange that the maximum 'wage' be equal to the maximum amount each may earn without having any deduction made from his supplementary benefit. At present, this means each mentally subnormal person employed at the workshops may earn £4 per week without any deduction being made in his supplementary benefit.

One of the most encouraging and remarkable changes which has always been reported following the successful introduction of workshops for the mentally handicapped, has been the great improvement in the behaviour and outlook of the mentally handicapped persons employed in them. Almost without exception, they become better behaved, easier to control and seem to be very delighted to realize that at last they are 'earning'—they obviously feel they have made a great step forward by having shown they can do a useful occupation. There is little doubt that the introduction of such workshops has done much to improve the opportunities and facilities for the adult mentally handicapped person.

(6) Employment in open industry

Until very recently few opportunities occurred for the mentally handicapped person to move on from workshops to working in ordinary industry. Successful workshops report that it is possible to find work in ordinary industry for at least 10 per cent of the mentally handicapped who have been trained in the workshops. The success of this must depend to some extent on the employment opportunities in the district. It is, however, *most important that all those working with the mentally handicapped* realize their potential *which in a substantial minority includes successful employment in ordinary industry.*

(7) Small homes (hostels)

Most social services departments now provide special homes where the mentally handicapped person can live when for any reason he has to leave his family home.In some cases there is a need to provide a hostel (home) where the mentally handicapped person can live during his rehabilitation after discharge from hospital. It is most important that these people are not kept in hospitals any longer than is absolutely necessary, otherwise it always becomes increasingly difficult to arrange successful rehabilitation within the normal community.

The term 'home' is often used instead of 'hostel' because it is hoped that, by doing so, it will not give the impression of impermanence or of a certain austerity. All should provide a homely atmosphere and be friendly. The purpose of the home will be to provide a permanent substitute family home for its residents.

The size of each home varies, but it should not exceed 20 and many excellent ones are much smaller containing 8 to 12 individuals.

It is important that all the mentally handicapped persons living in the home partake of ordinary duties just as if they were living with their own family. These can include the cooking of breakfast and the preparation of a light evening snack.

Every effort should be made to integrate these homes completely within the community—children should attend normal special schools (i.e. not a school solely for the residents), adults should go out to work either in ordinary industry or in special workshops. The activities of the residents should be as nearly the same as those people in a normal home environment.

(8) Short-term care

Very many mentally handicapped children are looked after in their own homes by devoted parents. There is, however, a great deal of strain involved and many parents find the continuous caring process produces considerable problems for the family.

It is important that the devotion of such parents is not continued in such a way that matrimonial difficulties occur, and that other normal members of the family are not neglected.

One of the most useful aids in preventing this danger is for social services departments to provide 'short-term' care in which special temporary arrangements are made to look after the mentally handicapped child for a short period (2 to 3 weeks) to enable the parents and family to get a complete break. It has been found that such short-term care helps such parents considerably and enables them to return refreshed to the arduous task of looking after a severely handicapped child.

(9) Holidays, recreational activities (social centres, clubs, etc.)

Most social service departments provide social centres or clubs for the mentally handicapped person where they can carry out pastimes and form a *club*. Such activities are valuable in helping the person to gain confidence, to enjoy himself and to get used to meeting people. Social workers often attend such centres and, in this way, keep in touch with the mentally handicapped.

Holidays of various kinds are also arranged. Some of these are traditional type holidays but others are of a more ambitious type (i.e. adventure type of holidays, camping, etc.).

Services provided by hospitals for the mentally handicapped

A certain proportion of the low grade mentally handicapped children and adults are unable to settle at home and in a training centre, and it may be necessary to admit them to a special institution designed for the severely subnormal. Some will always have to remain in this special institution because of extreme low intelligence and inability to learn even simple social habits, or because of extreme mental instability. It is always the aim of the institution authorities to train subnormal patients to such a degree that they will be able to be discharged and attend training centres again. A close co-ordination is always maintained between the staff of the institution and the staff of the domiciliary mental health service.

SPECIAL LEGAL POWERS FOR MENTALLY DISORDERED PERSONS

Criminal proceedings

In criminal proceedings, courts have power to authorize the admission and detention of a mentally disordered person found guilty of offences by the Courts. A Hospital Order may be made if the Court is satisfied that, on the written or oral evidence of two doctors (one of whom must be specially approved), the offender is suffering from mental illness, severe subnormality, subnormality or psychopathic disorder warranting hospital treatment. This order authorizes the removal of a patient to hospital within 28 days. The Court may, if necessary, make an order for the detention of the patient in a place of safety, which includes residential accommodation provided by a Local Authority, a hospital or mental nursing home, a residential home for mentally disordered persons, a police station or any other suitable place where the occupier is willing to receive the patient.

Alternatively the Court may make a Guardianship Order instead of a Hospital Order if it is thought that the client should be cared for within the community. It is usual in such cases for local authorities to assume the office of Guardianship.

Protection and management of property and affairs

Once a person becomes mentally incapable of managing his/her own affairs, he cannot legally authorize anyone else to do this on his behalf. If power of attorney has been given to another person before the mental illness then such authority will probably become inoperable because of the illness. In such cases, the *Court of Protection* exists to protect and manage the affairs and property of any person who is mentally incapable of doing so himself. The Court of Protection usually appoints a receiver—usually a close relative (parent, brother or sister)—to administer the patient's affairs under the direction of the Court. This will continue until the Court of Protection is satisfied on medical evidence that the patient is now fit again.

Application to the Court of Protection (at 25 Store Street, London WC1) can be made by a close relative or by instructing a solicitor to make such an approach.

Proportion of elderly within the community

The proportion of old people in our community has been steadily rising during the last seventy years. At the start of the twentieth century, about 5 per cent of the population were of retirement age. Today, in the United Kingdom, 16 per cent are of retirement age (i.e., men aged 65 years and over and women aged 60 years and over) while it has been estimated that this figure is likely to rise to 16½ per cent during the next 15 years.

This remarkable change has resulted not because more and more people are now living to a very old age—80 years plus, but because more and more persons are living long enough to reach retirement age—60 years for women and 65 years for men.

The greatly increased proportion of old persons now within the community means that the problems of looking after them both economically and in terms of personal care, have likewise increased. A great deal of research has been carried out in the last 25 years to find out more about the medical and social problems of the elderly living within their own homes.

At present about 96 per cent of the elderly live in their own home—only 4 per cent of them live in hostels, hospitals and similar institutions. This means that the preventive services must concentrate on ensuring that everything is done *to reduce the likelihood of illness, accident, medical and social problems* in the elderly living at home.

There are many striking differences in the problems of elderly men and women. Men die at a much younger age than women, for the average expectation of life in men is at least six years less than in women (69 years for men and 75 years for women). Many reasons have been suggested for a possible cause of this striking difference. It certainly seems connected with the fact that the majority of women remain active looking after their homes, while many men find retirement very boring. Women also seem better able to resist the effects of chronic crippling illnesses, loneliness and boredom (which unfortunately often accompany old age) than the majority of men.

Approximately 65 per cent of all those registered as physically disabled are also elderly. About 11 per cent of all persons of retirement age and over suffer from some degree of mild mental confusion and this proportion rises to 16 per cent for those aged 75 years and over. In practice this results in many more very old women than very old men (in 1976 in England and Wales there were 349 900 women aged 85 years or more, but only 114 800 men in this group).

PREVENTION OF SOCIAL AND MEDICAL PROBLEMS IN OLD AGE

The avoidance of many problems in the elderly lies in various preventive steps including the earliest possible recognition of symptoms and social difficulties.

Advice to the elderly

Each local authority Social Services Department employs social workers and social work assistants who can help old people with advice and, if need be, visit them at home. This advisory work is carried out in very close association with many other persons working in the community and especially with those in the primary health care team—doctors, health visitors and home nurses. Links are also maintained with clergymen, voluntary workers, friendly visitors and community workers so that old people in need of special help can be found quickly. Any old person living alone (and in some cities these represent 25–30 per cent of all old people) is always at special risk. Special alarms can be fixed (see page 203) but neighbours must play their part. Any person living near such an old person should in some way ensure daily that the old person is all right. In country villages and small towns, such surveillance is natural and tragedies rarely occur; however in large cities old people living alone are at much greater risk.

Planning for retirement

Many of the difficulties can be eased by some degree of *planning for old age*. Most serious mistakes are made by people about to retire. All too often they move to some unknown seaside resort for their retirement and are disappointed and find it difficult to settle down. It must always be remembered that the older the person, the more difficult it is to readjust oneself on moving. Human friendships are often worth much more in old age than being in some more attractive place.

Housing in retirement

Not enough regard is given to the type of house needed in old age. Whatever its type—flat, house or bungalow—it should always:

(*a*) be sited on level ground. So many of the traditional seaside towns, full of retired persons, are too hilly

(*b*) have an entrance which can be directly approached by car—i.e., a car should be able to drive up to the front door

(*c*) have a downstairs room which is capable of being turned into a bedroom

(*d*) have a downstairs lavatory and washbasin (a downstairs bath is most helpful but often not possible)

(*e*) have an effective and simple system of heating.

    These five points are connected with the inevitable fact that physical limitations will eventually develop as the person gets older. The aim must always be *to help the old person to remain independent in his own home for as long as possible*.

    It is always important that, if the old person is living in a house which is obviously too large and unwieldly, he/she leaves it for a smaller home *early* in retirement or *preferably* before. No old person likes the disturbance of moving and it becomes more difficult as they increase in age. So he/she should, if possible, be settled in the last home by the age of 60.

    It is a help to ensure that in some way the house is heated automatically by oil, gas or electricity. Many old people feel the cold acutely and the constant stoking of coal fires is not without its hazards as regards falling. The inability of an elderly person to arrange proper heating of his/her accommodation will eventually lead to the dangerous chronic condition of hypothermia.

It is most important that *relatives do not take the old person permanently into their home unless this is clearly inevitable*. Many kindly relatives are tempted to do this as they feel the old person is barely capable of continuing to look after himself or herself. But independence is very precious, especially to old people and relatives such as children, who precipitately take their old parents into their homes, may soon find it is a great mistake as the old person is not happy and causes many difficulties in the house. It is far better to arrange a temporary stay with relatives for the old person—say for two to three weeks—and for the old person to retain his/her own home and independence.

Sheltered housing

This means a flatlet or flat for old people with a *resident warden in attendance* to ensure that help is readily available in an emergency. A bell or alarm is fitted to each flatlet. Old people living in such accommodation are usually fairly frail but can look after themselves. Occasionally a midday meal is provided for them in a luncheon club close by.

Sheltered housing is provided either by housing authorities or in accommodation built by housing trusts or voluntary bodies. The Social Services Committee usually pays a sum of £50–£130 per year per unit of sheltered accommodation to help pay the cost of the warden and other amenities (such as special alarms or telephones).

Interests, hobbies, part-time work

Once the old person has settled in his home, he should always be encouraged to cultivate some hobby, pastime or interest. This process should preferably have been started before retirement. It does not matter what type of extra activity is tackled provided that it gives a real sense of purpose.

It is always helpful to encourage an old person to do some voluntary work, such as helping other people (elderly, handicapped or children). Occasionally it may be possible to undertake some form of part-time job.

For those who are in some way handicapped, perhaps because of physical limitations, it is important to encourage the continuation of their usual activities for as long as possible. Thus, a woman should always be encouraged to look after the house even if she is unable to do all the work.

Financial help—pensions and allowances

Pensions and extra financial help are not provided directly by local authorities, but by the Department of Health and Social Security. However, many old people need help in claiming their pensions and other allowances (see Chapter 18) and the social worker is ready at all times to explain and assist. It is most important that maximum use is made of pensions and allowances and it is never safe to assume that every old person fully understands his/her entitlement. Many of the elderly only imperfectly understand the range of pensions available and it is essential for each nurse to realize this and therefore discuss the matter with elderly patients in hospital.

There are two special forms of financial help which are often over-looked—*rent rebates* and *rate rebates*.

Rent rebates

Under the Housing Finance Act, 1972, local authority tenants can obtain a rent rebate (reduction in rent) when their gross income is below a certain level. In the case of elderly pensioners this usually means that considerably lower rents are paid.

Rate rebates

There is also a national scheme of special rate rebates (reduction in rates payable) which are available to elderly persons over 65 years of age with low incomes. There is a special scale which enables old people on low incomes to be excused a substantial part of their rates.

Any social services department of a local authority will gladly explain and help an elderly person who may not understand his/her entitlement and assist him/her to claim this aid.

COMMUNITY SERVICES AVAILABLE TO ASSIST THE ELDERLY IN THEIR OWN HOMES

Numerous special services are supplied by the social services department to assist the elderly in their own homes. In all instances the constant aim is to ensure the old person remains as independent as possible. In most cases it is important to provide such services early enough so that they can prevent more serious difficulties from developing. Community services include:

(1) **Home Helps** (see page 217)

The main value of home helps is to assist old people within their own homes. It is usual for the home help, who is often a married woman, to do the housework, essential shopping and get the old person a meal. The home help should always help with those tasks that are beyond the old person's capacity—cleaning windows and some of the heaviest tasks within the home.

Home help service can be full-time or part-time but, apart from emergencies, most of the home helps visit two or three times per week spending four hours with the old person at each visit. Some Social Services Committees provide a free service but the majority make a charge for this service based on a sliding scale; the elderly person with a good income would pay the full charge, but for any elderly person whose sole source of income is his/her old age pension, the service is free.

The provision of home helps is a most valuable service to the elderly and enables many who would otherwise be too frail, to stay within their own home. An important part of any home help's duties is to observe the old person at home in a sensible but inconspicuous way so that adequate warning can be given if the individual is becoming too frail to manage on his/her own.

Applications for home helps should be made to the Director of Social Services.

(2) Good neighbour schemes

A number of local authorities have introduced 'good neighbour' schemes in which arrangements are made for someone living close by to call on an elderly person to help with many simple tasks—shopping, lighting the fire, simple cooking and light housework. Usually a small recompense of approximately £4 is paid to the good neighbour if she is helping regularly. Such services are usually given free to the old person, but are not provided by all local authorities.

(3) Home care programmes

Elderly persons living on their own are particularly susceptible to rapid deterioration when they are discharged home from hospital after an illness. New *home care* programmes have been devised to support old people at such times. A typical scheme provides a home help and meals service for 20 per cent of elderly patients discharged from hospital (selected from those at special risk) for 4 weeks following discharge. At the end of the 4 weeks, any further help is given through the normal home help service.

(4) Meals services

There are two types of meals services which social services departments provide:

(*a*) *Meals-on-wheels* provide a hot two course meal delivered to the home of the old person, usually three or six times per week depending on the need. A small charge (varying from 10p to 20p) is made for this service, which is heavily subsidized.

(*b*) *Luncheon clubs* are for less frail old people who attend at some local hall or club from three to six times a week and there obtain a hot meal. These luncheon clubs are especially useful as the old person is encouraged to meet others, gets exercise walking to the club and not only gets the benefit of a good hot meal, but has the opportunity to make friends. A similar charge is made for the meal at the luncheon clubs as for meals-on-wheels.

(5) Day care centres

These have been described as 'hostels without beds' as they are intended to look after frail elderly person requiring the kind of care and attention which is usually provided in hostels. Transport collects the old person from home and brings him/her to the centre to spend the day there and takes him/her home in the evening. Meals are provided as well as other services (laundry, hairdressing, etc.).

This type of care is of particular value where a frail old person is living with younger relatives who go out to work during the day. It is also useful for the elderly living alone and can prevent much loneliness as well as ensuring that the old person can remain satisfactorily at home without having to be admitted permanently to a hostel. It is usual for each old person to come to a day care centre two or three times per week. A small charge is usually made.

(6) Clubs and day centres

There are many types of clubs and day centres run by social services departments and by voluntary bodies (especially Age Concern). These provide a centre which the old person can visit at any time for company, a light meal, tea or coffee and, in many instances, carry out some handicraft. Many social services departments subsidize such clubs. Attendance is usually free, but charges are made for meals, etc.

(7) Holidays and outings

Most local authorities through their social services departments arrange special holidays and outings for old people and this is also widely supplemented by the work of voluntary bodies. Holidays are especially important to help those elderly living alone and also for those living with younger relatives for holidays enable each to have a break. In this way, a holiday can be of great value to both. the old person and the family with whom he/she is living.

Some local authorities own seaside holiday homes, but many rely on making block bookings at seaside resorts in the off-peak season—early in summer or in autumn.

(8) Bus passes

Facilties for unrestricted free travel on buses in off-peak times of the day (9.30 a.m. to 4.30 p.m.) can do much to maintain the independence of old people. Many local authorities have introduced special schemes in which elderly persons can obtain such a free pass while other local authorities provide a certain number of tokens which can be exchanged for bus tickets. Schemes vary in different parts of the country and are now mainly available to those aged 60 (women) and 65 (men) in receipt of a pension.

MEDICAL SERVICES FOR THE ELDERLY

All the community medical services provided by the general practitioner are available to the elderly person at no extra cost for *there is no charge for any prescription for any old person over 65 years of age.* In recognition of the extra medical work involved in providing medical services for the elderly, there is a special increased per capita fee paid to general practitioners for all patients on their lists aged 65 years and older. Social workers and health visitors usually work in very close association with general practitioners whether they are based on health centres or not. In this way, it is hoped that the supporting social services (described above) which are provided by local authority social services departments will be increasingly used.

Geriatric hospitals are widely available for investigation, treatment and rehabilitation of the elderly. The main differences between geriatric and ordinary acute hospitals are the special facilities the geriatric hospital has for:
(*a*) linking up with social services—this is because the social factors in the life of the old person often determine the seriousness of the illness and the outlook
(*b*) emphasizing the importance of **active rehabilitation** for all elderly persons treated. This is because there is a real danger that the bed rest necessitated in the treatment of the elderly will tend to prevent their full recovery unless very active steps are taken to assist the old person to become fully active during convalescence.

Day hospitals

Day hospitals have recently been developed to help with the rehabilitation of elderly patients. They act as a sort of half-way stage between hospitals and home. Patients are brought there by transport and returned home in the evening. Old people may attend daily or on a specified number of days per week; physiotherapy and occupational therapy services are provided at day hospitals.

The main value of day hospitals is:

(1) they allow the old person to be safely discharged home earlier—in this way they encourage independence;

(2) they assist with the active rehabilitation of the patient;

(3) they help to establish a better link between the geriatric unit and the community services for the elderly.

In country districts *community hospitals* have helped develop a day hospital approach for some of their patients. It is valuable if health visitors and social workers arrange to visit the day hospital periodically and in this way improve the co-ordination between the two services.

Chiropody

At present this is provided by area health authorities. In many instances the service is given at luncheon clubs, day care centres, clubs or any centre where old people congregate.

Foot defects can have a serious effect on the mobility of an old person (see page 211). Most people would benefit from this service, but the shortage of chiropodists makes it necessary for local authorities to provide this service only to those with obvious foot problems. There are two main ways of providing this service:

(*a*) special chiropody sessions are arranged in clinics and old people's clubs, where chiropody treatment is provided. Health authorities also carry out home treatment where this is essential. In most instances, however, it is much better to give chiropody treatment at a nearby centre for this encourages the elderly person to get out a little. However, initial treatment may have to be undertaken at home if the old person's feet are too painful to let him/her reach the clinic.

(*b*) chiropody treatment may be carried out at the private surgeries of chiropodists. In this case, the area health authority meets the total cost.

To obtain the maximum value, it is important that chiropody treatment is regularly arranged *once every six to eight weeks*, otherwise the condition of the old person's feet may very quickly deteriorate again. As many elderly people are living on small pensions and find it difficult to meet extra expenses, it is best if chiropody treatment for the aged is provided free of charge.

SPECIAL PROBLEMS SEEN IN THE ELDERLY LIVING AT HOME

Often an illness or accident is the starting point of rapid deterioration in any old person living at home. Because of this factor, *any illness in an old person* must be treated seriously even if it is trivial. Special steps must be taken to ensure that the old person is completely treated and rehabilitated.

Rehabilitation can be hastened by arranging for the old person, while recovering, to attend a rehabilitation unit run by a local authority or by a hospital.

Physiotherapy and occupational therapy are most valuable to old people whose rheumatism or arthritis has inevitably been aggravated by staying in bed during an illness. Both physiotherapy and occupational therapy will help the old person to get moving again during convalescence.

Convalescence on return home can be aided by arranging a full-time home help for a fortnight, and then reducing the help, as the old person takes over the routine tasks. In this way, it is often possible to nurse an old person through a serious illness without eventual loss of function and independence.

Prevention of mental deterioration

The mental state of the vast majority of elderly persons living at home is good. A recent survey showed that 82 per cent of the elderly at home were fully normal, with about 11 per cent showing minor problems, 4 per cent showing clear indication of mental breakdown and the remaining 3 per cent were classified as eccentrics.

There seems little doubt that an important factor in maintaining the *mental vigour of any old person* at home, is connected with living in the surroundings they have always been used to and of *having something useful to do.*

The memory of most people is good except for minor difficulties of remembering names. When mental impairment occurs, memory is one of the first factors to be affected.

Domestic anxieties, loneliness and physical defects resulting in limitation of movement seem to induce mental failure. Anxieties in old age often are due to the old person not properly understanding certain financial or legal problems. Careful, patient explanation *by the social worker* and the sorting out of pension and legal difficulties (rent, lease or will) can often do much to help. Some old people may worry excessively about financial problems and may increasingly stint themselves trying to save, when their financial circumstances are quite sound. This excessive anxiety about money often tends to get worse as age increases and is best prevented by ensuring that the old person fully understands how many of the financial worries are groundless. It is important to point out that today the same type of provision is made in all old people's homes whether the full cost is paid or whether the old person is living on a pension. *Much tact and patience are needed, however,* and it must always be remembered that the old people today, are a generation brought up before the concept of social security, and there is often a deep seated fear of 'living on charity'.

There seems to be a close association between the development of emotional disturbance in old people and either the death of a husband, or wife, or a severe fall. After either event, therefore, considerable help will be needed to assist the old person to overcome the effects.

When mental deterioration in the elderly living at home occurs, the symptoms often include:

(1) *Change in outlook of the old person*—either towards apathy or agitation.
(2) *Eating habits may change*—and often the old person becomes very fussy and will eat very little.
(3) *Depression* is commoner—as well as occasional outbreaks of verbal aggression making the old person much more difficult to live with.
(4) *Memory*—there is an early failure of memory noted.

(5) *Talk*—any tendency to talk a lot, a characteristic of many old people, soon disappears.
(6) *Worries* which may become morbidly increased.
(7) There is a marked loss in the ability of the old person to look after himself.

It is always valuable to recognize promptly impending early mental deterioration in the elderly at home, as it makes early treatment possible and may prevent, in this way, a serious and perhaps final mental breakdown.

Loneliness in the elderly

One of the most pathetic complications of old age is *loneliness*. It is not always connected with living alone, rather the very lonely old person seems to have cut himself or herself off from the world.

Many social and medical factors are connected with the problem. The most serious is the sudden loss of a beloved husband or wife. Men seem to suffer from extreme loneliness more than women. Extreme loneliness in widowers occurs even when they are not living alone—in other words, loneliness does not seem to result directly from their social circumstances.

Loneliness of some degree probably occurs in about 20 per cent of elderly persons. There are many causes—bereavement, departure of children, absence of hobbies, limitation of physical activity.

It is never easy to prevent loneliness developing. Increasing social contact may occasionally help. Another approach is in some way to make the old person understand he is of some value to others and especially to younger people. Loneliness so often is 'an attitude of mind' in which the old person loses interest in his position and isolates himself or herself.

Although not invariable, the old person who has varying interests and hobbies is less likely to suffer from extreme loneliness even if his circumstances may suddenly render him lonely. Thus the encouragement of widespread hobbies and interests among young and middle-aged men will do much to prevent extreme loneliness later in old age.

Home accidents

Old people living at home, either with a family or on their own, are *more liable to accidents*—particularly to falls. Recent surveys show that about 35 per cent of elderly people are liable to fall. In any elderly person, a fall is likely to be more serious than a similar accident in a younger person, both because (*a*) the fall is much more likely to result in serious injury, especially in the development of various fractures, and (*b*) it may also precipitate senile decay.

Women are more liable to falls than men and the tendency to fall increases with age. Sheldon in his classic survey in Wolverhampton classified home falls in old people in four ways:

(1) *Falls associated with attacks of vertigo*

A sudden attack of vertigo, dizziness, occurs in the course of movement and unless there is a solid object immediately at hand, the old person falls headlong.

(2) *Falls associated with an increased liability to trip*
Women seem particularly liable to trip over small objects. Many old people who, when younger never had a tendency to trip, find as they grow old, they are much more likely to do so. They trip more easily over small objects or if there is a trivial unevenness in the floor level.

(3) *Falls due to difficulty in recovering balance*
There seems no doubt that many old people find their power in recovering their balance after a trivial false movement is much impaired compared with their ability to do so when younger.

(4) *Falls due to sudden collapse, or to legs giving way*
This seems particularly to occur in very old people over the age of eighty. The old person suddenly collapses and often is unable to move for some time afterwards even if he or she has not been injured in the fall.

Many of these falls can be prevented and their effect diminished. The possibility—and in old people over eighty, probability—of a fall should always be considered by those looking after the old person.

The following steps should be taken to diminish the chance of falls:

(*a*) An old person increasingly depends on *sight* to maintain balance, as his labyrinthine function is often faulty. Thus, an old person who is quite steady in daylight may be very liable to fall in the dark. This should be explained to the old person who should always ensure that there is a good adequate light in any room or passage along which he is proposing to walk. It is particularly important to see that the lighting of passages or staircases is really good—in most homes it is quite inadequate.

(*b*) The likelihood of a tendency to increased tripping should always be remembered and care must be taken to ensure that floor fittings, carpets, linoleum, rugs, etc., are securely fastened. In families where old people live, children must not leave toys around on floors over which the old person is likely to walk. There should never be loose electric flex across a floor.

(*c*) Wherever possible, an old person should learn to walk with some support from a solid object—banister, handrail, chair, table, furniture, especially if it is known that there is a liability to fall. In such a case, an old person should carefully go from object to object so that, if he suddenly feels giddy, he can support himself.

Intelligent anticipation of the causes of a fall can do much to prevent one—the result of which could easily mean the death of the elderly person.

Rheumatism and arthritis

Many elderly people have some degree of *rheumatism* or *osteoarthritis*. It is difficult to ascertain the exact amount of these conditions, as the criteria of diagnosis varies with different observers. Surveys have reported that 50 per cent to 80 per cent of elderly people living at home complain of rheumatic symptoms of one kind and another.

It is interesting that many elderly persons, even with marked osteoarthritis, find that however painful initial movement may be, the more active they are around the house the less problem the arthritis is. For this reason, enforced activity in an elderly woman still looking after her home, often prevents her condition from deteriorating. With this in mind, all forms of activity—physiotherapy, the carrying out of some simple occupation, occupational therapy, are all useful in preventing further limitation.

The success of *hip replacement surgery* has been very marked and any elderly person who is seriously crippled with degenerative joint disease of the hips should always consider a hip replacement operation. In most cases such an operation will render them completely mobile for 10–15 years.

Some of the worst cases of osteoarthritis occur in fat persons. The prevention of obesity in younger persons will reduce the likelihood of severe osteoarthritis developing at a later age.

In all instances where there is a limitation in the range of movement of an old person, the various social services designed to help with their feeding problems—such as meals-on-wheels; with housework problems—home helps; and with shopping difficulties—visitors; are most important in avoiding the development of other medical problems.

Foot defects

Foot defects very often cause serious problems in old people. The types of abnormalities include ingrowing toe-nails, flat foot, hallux valgus, bunions and corns, and hammer toes.

At least half of the old people living at home suffer from some form of foot defect. In many of them, this leads to pain on walking and consequently usually produces some degree of limitation of movement. This can be of a serious degree and may result occasionally in the old person becoming more or less house bound.

Most of the foot conditions found in old people can be prevented at least from causing serious effects by either arranging radical treatment for the more disabling conditions, and for the minor conditions, regular chiropody (see page 207).

Hypothermia

This is a serious condition in which the body cannot maintain correct temperature control and consequently loses heat, especially in winter time. It is very important that the methods used in diagnosing this condition are fully understood by all people looking after the elderly. Hypothermia is a dangerous condition if not recognized early and is particularly likely to occur in old people living alone in houses that are inadequately heated.

Hypothermia is NOT only seen in old people living in cold homes (although such conditions will always make it more likely to occur). It may suddenly and dangerously occur in an elderly person who has been taken ill suddenly (as in pneumonia), even though he/she is seated in a chair in a room which is not unduly cold. It can also occur after strokes, or after a heart attack in which the old person may sit quietly in a chair for hours on end.

Whatever the cause, it is *most important* that the condition is *recognized early* and that all staff dealing with the elderly know the early signs of hypothermia. The old person *does not usually look cold* and certainly does not shiver. The hands and face often look warm and are red or reddish purple in colour. He /she is often drowsy and very inactive and his/her speech may become slow and slurred. The hands, feet and face feel cold and the body temperature (as measured on a specially low recording thermometer) is usually well below 35°C (95°F).

Once the condition is recognized, emergency treatment must be started; treatment is often difficult and unsatisfactory. Rapid warming *is very dangerous to old people with hypothermia* and therefore must be avoided at all costs. The aim should be to limit the warming up of the old person to approximately 0.6°C (1°F) per hour. The room temperature should be kept warm and a few extra blankets should be applied but no direct heat.

Prevention of hypothermia. The prevention of hypothermia involves more than anything else realizing that the condition can develop insidiously. All those looking after old people therefore should be on their guard. In particular three important factors should be stressed:

(1) ensuring that, by good housing, old people are accommodated in warm conditions;

(2) encouraging elderly people to move around and not allowing them to sit all day even if they are in relatively warm conditions;

(3) always realizing that *hypothermia is very likely to occur in any illness of an old person.* For this reason anyone nursing an old person, especially in their own home, should always be on the lookout.

Cardiovascular disease

Recent surveys show that about 18 per cent of elderly persons are limited in their activity on account of cardiovascular disease. Just under 5 per cent were limited to the house, while 13 per cent found some limitation in their activity out of doors. *Angina of effort* was the commonest single factor, with *pulmonary heart failure* and *cerebrovascular accidents* other reasons for limitation.

The outright prevention of many of these diseases is at present unknown, but some of them can be looked upon as accompaniments of an ageing process.

However, a great deal can be done to minimize the effect of many of these conditions by improving social conditions. The position of the home of an elderly person often has a marked effect upon the amount of limitation caused to any patient with even an early stage of heart failure and its effects. Any hill which has to be negotiated is likely to have a most limiting effect on the heart patient. Stairs in the house too are most undesirable. The best house for any aged person is on the flat, with direct access to the front door by car so that any elderly patient with heart disease can move from his house without having to go up an incline. A bungalow is much better than a house as it has no problems of stairs.

Hearing loss and vertigo

About 30 per cent of the elderly at home have some degree of hearing loss, but there is a much higher incidence of deafness in the oldest age groups—in those aged 80 and over the incidence of deafness approaches 60 per cent.

In many cases, it is impossible to prevent the deafness itself, but a great deal can be done to prevent the effect of the deafness by the provision and maintenance of a hearing aid. Many old people who are deaf have developed deafness over the years and have got used to a number of its great disadvantages.

However, *deafness* more than any other single cause, *leads to isolation of the old person*—isolation from the easy natural social contact of chatting to people. For the family living with a deaf old person, who can hear very little, the difficulty of communication greatly adds to the problems created by the elderly person. Mutual resentment soon follows with a general deterioration in the relationship between the family and the old person.

A properly fitted and maintained hearing aid can prevent such a situation developing and, in this way, avoid much unnecessary unhappiness to the old person. This needs patience, care and encouragement, otherwise the patient soon gets fed up with the minor difficulties of the aid and ceases to use it.

Reference has already been made to *vertigo, dizziness,* which is an important and distressing symptom of old age. It is more likely to occur in old women (Sheldon reported it present in 70 per cent of old women aged 85 and over) but, although found in men up to 79, is rarely seen in men over 80 years of age. In the extreme cases, there is little done to prevent its occurrence except to ensure that no old person, who is very liable to such attacks, lives alone. The extreme likelihood of falls makes great care necessary. In the less severe cases, a full investigation should always be carried out, as well as arranging for all the precautions already mentioned to prevent falls. In particular, it must always be remembered that old people with vertigo are likely to have *great difficulty in the dark*. It is, therefore, most important that they never get up from bed at night without turning on the light which should be a bright one. To ensure that the old person can easily find the switch on awaking, it is wise to have an additional dim bulb (15 watts) alight all night in the bedroom.

Visual defects

It is usual for old people to have to rely on spectacles to overcome visual defects. Well over 90 per cent of elderly men and women require spectacles for near vision and between 50 per cent and 60 per cent for distant vision.

Recent surveys have shown a different assessment regarding the incidence of unsatisfactory spectacles. It is, however, still clear that a considerable proportion of elderly persons are not obtaining the help they should from their spectacles because they are unsuitable and need changing.

Ignorance may still play a part, for some old people may not know how important it is to *retest the sight of any person regularly*. To avoid this problem, those visiting old people should try to ensure that their vision is tested every two to three years. It may not be enough just to advise retesting, it may be necessary for a social worker or health visitor to arrange an appointment and to take the old person by car to the optician.

Blindness or near blindness only occurs in 1 to 2 per cent of the elderly living at home. The individual problems of blindness are discussed in detail in Chapter 14.

Nutrition of the aged

Health is only possible provided there is an adequate and well-balanced diet. This is true of all ages and the maintenance of an adequate nutrition is important in all elderly persons.

A recent survey showed that, in the opinion of the investigators, 17 per cent of elderly men and 22 per cent of elderly women had a poor level of nutrition. Foods requiring some preparation are eaten less by old people living alone than when they are living in families or as a married couple.

Cases of extremely poor nutrition in old people are usually connected with an *elderly person living alone* who had lost interest in preparing meals, or who was not having any outside meals. Occasionally extreme difficulty of mobility (for any cause) may lead to inadequate shopping. With the very busy streets of many towns, old people may find it increasingly difficult to cross the road and if an essential food shop—say a greengrocer—is on the other side of the road, then the old person may unnecessarily restrict her diet just because shopping is such an ordeal. The realization that such a simple cause may start a chain of events, which could eventually lead to a severe state of malnutrition, should be sufficient to suggest a simple remedy—the arrangement with a friendly neighbour to help with the shopping of the old person.

All those who are, in any way, helping with old people whether as doctors, nurses, health visitors, social workers, voluntary workers or even just neighbours and friends, should always remember that, particularly in the case of an old person living alone, the monotony of preparing meals for oneself can soon lead to inadequate and quite unbalanced diet.

The remedy is to make immediate arrangements:
(1) for the old person to go, if able, to an old persons club for three or four good meals per week; (see page 205) or
(2) to arrange for *meals-on-wheels* service to be delivered three or more times a week; (see page 205) or
(3) to arrange a part-time home help service for the elderly person. Part of the duties of the home help would be to cook a hot meal for the old person when she visited him/her (see page 217).

Pulmonary disease in the elderly

Bronchitis and *emphysema* together with bronchial spasm are the chief causes of respiratory illness in the elderly.

About 40 per cent of elderly people have some degree of bronchitis with chronic cough; these figures are from industrial areas and are likely to be lower for rural ones. Men suffer more from this than women. About *4 per cent of the elderly are severely disabled by bronchitis.*

The prevention of bronchitis in the elderly is, of course, the same as prevention of the disease in adults. The bronchitis of the aged is only a later stage of the bronchitis in the middle aged.

Apart from the particular hazards of dust in certain occupations already discussed, there is no doubt that *persistent cigarette smoking* is the main cause of much of the irritation, chronic cough and expectoration. It cannot be too strongly stressed that any adult who is a smoker with a chronic cough and with winter attacks of bronchitis, *must give up smoking at once to prevent slowly deteriorating and progressive chronic bronchitis developing,* with all its crippling invalidism. Thus, the prevention of the problem of bronchitis in old age often rests with stopping smoking as an adult. If an old person stops smoking, it usually helps but if he has already developed a severe degree of chronic bronchitis, it may be impossible to halt the disease.

Prolapse and stress incontinence

About 12 to 15 per cent of married women over the age of 60 years probably suffer from some degree of prolapse with stress incontinence of urine. The highest incidence is seen in women who have had many pregnancies.

Enlarged prostate

About 25 per cent of men over the age of 65 years have symptoms of enlarged prostate. Symptoms in these cases usually include:
(a) frequency of micturition by day or night
(b) dribbling with overflow
(c) urinary incontinence both occasional and regular.

The prevention of both conditions consists of *early diagnosis and treatment.* It must be remembered that symptoms of prostatic enlargement can often be greatly helped by hormone therapy.

There is nothing worse than incontinence and it is also important to realize that radical operative treatment is nearly always worth while even with the very elderly, for the results are often excellent.

RESIDENTIAL SERVICES

Hostels for old people

Under the National Assistance Act, 1948, every local authority has to provide hostels for elderly persons. Most of the modern hostels are specially designed and newly built. A few have been converted from large houses.

The modern old person's hostel is usually designed for from 35 to 55 old people. Hostels larger than this are not built as it would be difficult to maintain the friendly personal atmosphere in larger places. Each hostel has a number of single and double bedrooms, and usually has lounges of varying size, situated on each floor. A lift is provided so that all the accommodation is of the 'ground floor type', in other words, can be reached without the old person having to climb stairs.

A resident matron and staff are in charge of the hostel, and minor illnesses are usually looked after by them, but in the case of more prolonged or serious illness, the old person is admitted to hospital and when fit again, returns to the hostel.

Each hostel provides a high standard of care for the old people living there and it is usual for all the needs of the old people to be provided, including clothing.

One very special arrangement in old persons' hostels is that *every old person contributes to their cost.* Each hostel has a standard charge—a usual present-day figure is approximately £58 per week which represents the economic cost of keeping an old person in the hostel. Each old person is asked if they can afford to pay this charge. If they can, they do. If not, then each old person must pay a portion of their old age pension of Social Security allowance. The statutory minimum charge is £12.25 per week. This portion is calculated so that the old person is always left with £3.05 a week pocket money for personal spending. The local authority is responsible for the additional cost.

Old people's homes today should be happy places. They, of necessity, take the frailer old people who cannot manage at home. This represents about 2 per cent of the old people in the country. This figure emphasizes the importance of developing domiciliary preventive services for the aged to help them stay happily at home, as well as continuing to build more hostels.

Hostels are also provided by many voluntary and church organizations. In many instances, local authorities will assist the voluntary body by paying a per-capita grant based on the weekly cost of keeping the elderly person.

Emergency compulsory removal of an old person from home

Occasionally it is necessary to consider removing compulsorily an old person from home because it is dangerous for him/her to stay at home and he/she refuses to enter a hospital or old person's hostel. Fortunately few elderly persons are removed in this way as most readily agree or can be persuaded. Cases that have to be moved are old people who have badly neglected themselves and include those suffering from late cancers and others who are afraid to go into hospital.

Action is taken under s.47 of the National Assistance Act, 1948 and the Amendment Act, 1951, which gives power for the compulsory removal of aged and certain other people to hospitals or other institutions. It is only possible to remove those who are:

(i) suffering from grave chronic disease or being aged, infirm or physically incapacitated, are living in insanitary conditions; *and*

(ii) are unable to devote to themselves, and are not receiving from other persons, proper care and attention.'

It is necessary for the Area Medical Officer, or the Community Physician who is designated to undertake this task, and another doctor to certify that it is in the interests of the person to remove him from his dwelling. The local authority then applies to a magistrate (or Court) for removal. If the magistrate (or Court) is satisfied, then the removal to hospital or hostel is made.

17 OTHER COMMUNITY SOCIAL SERVICES

HOME HELPS

Every Social Services authority (County Councils, Metropolitan District Councils and London Boroughs) has a duty to provide a home help service adequate for the needs of the area (s. 13 of the Health Services and Public Health Act, 1968). As already explained, the Local Authority Social Services Act, 1970, transferred the control of the home help services from the health department to the new social services department under the control of the Director of Social Services.

The majority of the work of the home help services is with the *care of elderly people* (see page 204) but other groups are also covered including *maternity cases, illness* (acute or chronic), and the younger physically handicapped. Home helps are also used to assist families with young children especially when sudden illness arises, or when either parent is away, perhaps in hospital, and when such help would enable the parent to rejoin the family more quickly.

In child care supervision, a home help is invaluable where parents are not competent to run a household and, in such cases, can help teach higher standards.

In looking after some handicapped children, home help care is most useful for it can allow a mother more time to spend teaching her child. This is especially important in a child who is born deaf, for a home help provided while the child is aged 1½ to 5 years can be of great assistance by allowing the mother to spend much more time teaching the child lip reading. While the mother spends say 4–5 hours solely with the child, the home help is assisting with housework and shopping.

In England during 1976 84 per cent of the work carried out by home helps was with the elderly. nearly 7 per cent with chronic sick and tuberculosis cases, 5 per cent other reasons, 3 per cent for maternity cases and the balance of 1 per cent with the mentally disordered. Approximately 650,000 persons receive home help assistance each year in England.

It is usual to make a charge for the service, but there is a sliding scale according to income; those on social security or those receiving the old age pension as their only income are given the service free.

Most of the 80 000 home helps at present working in England do so part-time. The duties of each home help vary with each case, but include many of the normal tasks carried out by the housewife—cleaning rooms, preparing food and meals, shopping, lighting fires and, in a family, looking after the children. Some social service authorities now provide free home helps for all clients.

Home help service can be provided full-time or part-time to the client depending on the circumstances. Apart from emergency work, most of the service by home helps is usually provided part-time, perhaps amounting to two or three sessions per week. This is particularly important when an elderly person is helped in this way over a long period for it is *essential to encourage the old person to continue to do as much housework as possible herself,* and, in this way, keep herself active as long as possible.

In emergency illness or maternity cases, a full-time help for a short period may enable a young family to be kept together and thus avoid the need to take children into short-term care. This type of support is particularly valuable where there are no relatives or family to help (apart from the father of the family who has to continue to go to work).

Links between home helps and a co-ordinated domiciliary team

The home help soon gets to know the client or family she is visiting very well and learns a great deal about their personal problems. It is, therefore, important that *all home helps form part of a balanced and co-ordinated domiciliary social work team* and, in particular, *work in close contact with social workers.*

Because of this, most social services departments have arranged for home help services to be organized within their area social services teams. In this way, any useful information the home help has learnt about her charges can easily be passed on to the social workers so that the fullest possible social support can be arranged.

For the same reasons, the local organizer of home helps must *co-ordinate closely with general practitioners, home nurses* and many others who need the assistance of home helps from time to time in their practices.

Occasionally the home help has to tackle a particularly difficult, dirty or heavy task to clean up a home which has become extremely dirty due to the neglect or illness of the occupant. Many social services departments arrange special teams or 'heavy squads' to do this special work and many provide special equipment. It is usual for those tackling such exceptionally difficult tasks to be given extra remuneration for such work.

'Good neighbour schemes'

Usually the demand for home helps outstrips the provision and some authorities have experimented with alternative methods of help such as 'good neighbour schemes'. In this local volunteers are sought, often from among fit older people, who will agree to carry out a number of light duties—shopping, cooking, light cleaning, etc. Most schemes rely on recruiting such volunteers from members of the public living close by so that no travelling is involved.

Most schemes arrange for the volunteer to be paid a small sum, say £4–5 per week as an honorarium, provided help is given on most or all days of the week.

CARE OF HOMELESS FAMILIES

Every large local authority (County Councils, Metropolitan Districts and London Boroughs) is responsible (under s. 21 (ii) (b)) of the National Assistance Act, 1948) for the care of families who are rendered homeless 'as a result of circumstances which could not have reasonably been foreseen'. This includes all sudden emergencies such as fire, flooding, or by dangerous collapse of buildings. Most social services departments extend their care of homeless families much wider than this definition to include evictions, famiy disputes, etc.

The best type of accommodation enables the whole family, man, wife and children, to be accommodated together, but a few units still only look after the wife and children.

Many families who require temporary accommodation have got into serious housing difficulties due to failure to pay rent or to keep up mortgage payments. Many of the parents of such families are immature and inadequate and drift easily into debt. Such families often have many problems and are often referred to as 'problem' families. For these reasons, such families need much support and help if they are to be prevented from drifting again into the danger of eviction.

Homelessness is growing especially in London and the large conurbations; it is now widely accepted that homelessness is a function for local government as a whole and can only be solved by a concerted effort by housing and social services departments. It is now no longer looked upon as a problem only for Social Services Departments to tackle. In many cities and other large urban areas, it is increasingly common to find housing authorities being made responsible for providing temporary and permanent accommodation for homeless families while Social Services Departments provide the social work support.

Much of this social work support is time consuming and set backs occur as such families are often difficult to help—perhaps due to the low intelligence of the mother and father. It is, however, essential that such after-care work be carried out, otherwise the family inevitably slips again into debt and the problem is never solved.

Initially many homeless families are housed in sub-standard housing and then progress towards normal council housing. This is usually arranged once the family has paid off any rent arrears and has shown themselves capable of managing their own affairs. Even at this stage, such families will need much support from social workers, family service units, health visitors and others.

Prevention of homelessness

The prevention of homelessness is in many ways more important than its treatment. There are two special problems, (1) the avoidance of large rent arrears, and (2) the support and help given to homeless families immediately after their rehousing. The avoidance of large rent arrears involves a number of actions which should be taken by housing and social services departments without having to resort to eviction. The following are important:

(1) An early warning system after a few missed payments should be instituted to enable special arangements for rent collection to be made, and for social services advice to be sought.

(2) If rent arrears are still accumulating, housing authorities should check whether the tenants are eligible for rent and rate rebates.

(3) There should be a vigorous pursuit of rent arrears and this should include selective visiting in certain areas to prevent the arrears becoming greater.

(4) If there are serious family and social problems, it may be possible for the Social Services Department to assist by payments of rent arrears, using the powers of Section 1 of the Children and Young Persons Act, 1963.

(5) If the family is receiving supplementary benefit, then this will contain a sum equivalent to the rent (the rent element) and arrangements can be made in suitable cases for this to be paid direct to the local authority.

(6) Transfer to cheaper accommodation to help reduce the rent problems. Care has to be taken in such cases to see that there is not undue concentration of families in social difficulties.

Family planning (see page 43) in all homeless families should always be carefully considered as too many children at too short intervals in any family are likely to aggravate problems. In the most intractable problem families, it is best to arrange a domiciliary family planning service to ensure the mother receives correct family planning advice, otherwise few will attend clinics (see page 44).

Bed and breakfast accommodation. In some urban areas, there is a grave shortage of temporary accommodation and families have to be housed for the time being in 'bed and breakfast' accommodation. This arrangement *must* be made by the Social Services Department (under the Children and Young Persons Act, 1963). It is always an unsatisfactory expedient and housing authorities should always attempt to rehouse such families as quickly as possible.

CARE OF UNSUPPORTED MOTHERS

The care of the unsupported mother (including the unmarried mother) is also the responsibility of social services departments who can make arrangements, often in conjunction with voluntary bodies, for the residential care of some mothers. As with other types of homelessness, it is important to do everything to educate the mother to prevent further problems. It follows from this that *the unmarried mother needs a considerable amount of supporting social work*; most will also require much advice and teaching which is best arranged by social workers in conjunction with the health visitors (see page 42).

HOSPITAL SOCIAL WORKERS

In the reorganization of 1974, the control of hospital social workers was transferred from the health services to local authority Social Services Departments. The number of hospital social workers has steadily increased in the last 25 years and their tasks have altered. At present there are approximately 2200 hospital social workers and most of these work in district general hospitals or in geriatric and paediatric units. Those who work in psychiatric hospitals are usually specially qualified *psychiatric social workers*.

There are four main areas of work for hospital social workers:

(1) **Medical casework** concerned with the adjustment of the patient and his/her family to the patient's disease. This is the largest and most important aspect of hospital social work. It mainly involves working with the patient in hospital (including in-patient and out-patient work) but may also necessitate the hospital social worker visiting the patient's home. All types of cases are covered, work with children including non-accidental injury cases; much work is also undertaken with the elderly, many of whom live alone and are consequently very vulnerable (see page 209). Terminal cases are included, especially carcinoma. Illness in the parent of a one-parent family often produces many extra difficulties which the hospital social worker will try to solve. Another important group of cases are accident patients and especially those suffering from chronic disabling diseases including rheumatoid arthritis. Many social problems occur in mental illness and the role of the hospital social worker in such cases is often a crucial one.

(2) **Environmental help**—arranging how the patient's home can be improved to help him/her cope with the illness. This may involve the complete rehousing of the patient or the adaptation of the home either structurally or by the introduction of certain aids.

(3) Arrangements for **immediate assistance to the patient or his/her relatives.** This includes financial help, convalescent arrangements, provision of escorts or accommodation for relatives visiting dangerously-ill relatives.

(4) **Liaison** with various other social work agencies (including the Social Services Department of the area where the patient lives) to enable long-term care and rehabilitation of the patient.

18 SOCIAL SECURITY

A very wide range of Social Security benefits are available and most patients that the nurse deals with in her practice will be entitled to one of these benefits. Social Security has become very complicated and to make things even more difficult for the student, most governments are constantly changing the range and amount of allowance payable. It is, therefore, *important that every nurse understands the basic* allowances or benefits which are available, and also *consults the excellent booklet published by the Department of Health and Social Security* currently (1976) called 'Family benefits and pensions' and obtainable free from local Social Security offices to check the latest details.

In this chapter, an attempt is made to introduce the nurse to the *range of* Social Security benefits available. The list given is not intended to be a complete one, but does cover the most important aspects of social security.

Benefits fall into three main types:

(1) Non-contributory

These are available to everyone who qualifies and do not depend on the individual having contributed for a set time into the social security system.

(2) Contributory

To qualify for these, two factors must be satisfied:
(i) that the individual has contributed a minimum number of weekly contributions over a set period of time, and
(ii) that his circumstances satisfy the requirements for each particular benefit.

(3) Provided the individual qualifies, **an entitlement to certain services** at no cost or at reduced cost.

NON-CONTRIBUTORY BENEFITS

There are nine main non-contributory benefits:
(*a*) Child Benefit
(*b*) Family Income Supplement
(*c*) Supplementary Benefits
(*d*) Attendance Allowance
(*e*) Mobility Allowance
(*f*) Non-contributory invalidity pension
(*g*) Pensions for persons over 80 years of age
(*h*) Guardian's allowance
(*i*) Various industrial injury benefits including injury benefit, disablement benefit, industrial death benefit.

(a) Child Benefit

From April, 1977, a new social security benefit called child benefit replaces family allowances. It is payable to *all* children including the first or only child. The children must be under school leaving age (16 years) or under the age of 19 and at school, college or university full-time. If the child is receiving non-contributory invalidity pension, he/she cannot also receive child benefit.

The claim for child benefit must be made by a person responsible for the child. Usually this will be the mother of the child (whether married or not). If the child lives with people who are not the parents but who share the responsibility, they can decide for themselves who should claim or ask the local Social Security Office. Child Benefit is tax free.

The rates of child benefit in 1977 are £1 for an only, elder or eldest child and £1.50 for each other child. Starting with the tax year 1977–78, child tax allowances will be phased out and their value added to the tax-free child benefit. Child tax allowances for children under 11 years of age will be phased out during the three years starting April, 1977, and the allowances for older children correspondingly reduced.

Child benefit is NOT payable for any week in which a child is in the care of a local authority or to a foster parent in receipt of a boarding out allowance. If a child returns home (for a holiday or on trial) child benefit will be payable for any completed week.

(b) Family Income Supplement

This is a benefit to assist families whose normal gross weekly income is very low. Anyone, including a single person, with at least one dependent child can claim *provided he or she is in full-time work* or, for a couple, the man is in full-time work (this means 30 or more hours per week). All children who are normally living with the claimant can be included if under 16 years or aged 16 and over if still at school.

The rate of supplement equals one half of the difference between the family's normal gross income and the prescribed amount decided by Parliament. In 1977, this prescribed amount was £39.00 for a family with one child plus £4.50 for each additional child. Family allowances and other sources of income—such as wife's earnings—are included in the total income but *the income of any child is not.* The maximum supplement (1977) is £8.50 per week for families with one child increasing by 50 pence for each additional child.

Family Income Supplement can be claimed on forms obtainable from local Social Security Offices or Post Offices. Details of the last five weeks' income will be needed.

Note: Any person awarded family income supplement is *automatically exempted from paying prescription, dental or optical charges; children at school are allowed free meals and children under five years and expectant mothers, free welfare milk and foods.*

(c) Supplementary Benefits

These are payable as of right to people in Great Britain who are *not* in full-time work and whose other income, whether from other benefits or from their own financial resources, is not enough to meet their requirements. These benefits, therefore, supplement other sources of income.

Supplementary benefits are divided into two types:

(a) *Supplementary pension* for persons over minimum pension age—60 for women, 65 for men

(b) *Supplementary allowance* for persons aged 16 and over but under pension age.

The calculation of supplementary benefits is complicated because it depends on the person's resources and requirements. *Certain income resources are disregarded—the first £4 of part-time earnings plus the first £4 of a wife's earnings, the first £1 weekly of any occupational pension and up to £4 weekly of disablement and war widows pensions. The disregard for one parent families is £6 weekly.*

If a man or his wife owns the house they live in, its value will be ignored. If a man and his wife and dependants have between them, capital of less than £1250, the income it produces will be ignored.

Minimum amounts are laid down for basic requirements—in 1977 these were £12.70 for a single pensioner and £20.65 for a married couple. To this is added:

(a) an allowance for rent,

(b) an allowance in certain cases for special expenses—special diet, special needs for extra heating or domestic help.

Claims should be made to the local Social Security Office.

It is *most important for the nurse to realize that many elderly persons without private means will qualify for special supplementary benefits for rent and extra heating* or *special diet* especially if they are ill or recovering from an illness. *Supplementary benefits are payable as a right* and care must be taken to point this out because many old people consider that to claim them is in some way degrading and makes them dependent on charity. This is not so and unless old people in need claim, considerable hardship is bound to occur.

Automatic entitlement to other benefits. People and their dependants receiving supplementary benefit are also entitled to exemption from payment of the charges (or to a refund of charges paid) for prescriptions, wigs and fabric supports supplied under the NHS, and NHS dental treatment and certain glasses; children under school age and expectant mothers are also entitled to free milk and vitamins; children at school do not have to pay for school meals; members of the family attending hospital for treatment may claim a refund of fares.

(d) Attendance Allowance

This is a tax free allowance for a person who because of his severe physical or mental disabilities requires the following assistance from another person:

By day: frequent attention throughout the day in connection with his bodily functions *or* continual supervision throughout the day in order to avoid substantial danger to himself and others.

At night: prolonged or repeated attention during the night in connection with his bodily functions *or* continual supervision throughout the night in order to avoid substantial danger to himself or others.

In 1977, a higher rate of £12.20 a week can be paid if one of the day requirements *and* one of the night requirements are satisfied for a period of at least 6 months. A lower rate of £8.15 a week can be paid if one of the day *or* night requirements is satisfied for a period of at least 6 months.

These requirements are strictly enforced and are dealt with by a single Social Security centre in Blackpool. Claims forms are obtainable from any local Social Security office.

(e) Mobility Allowance
This new allowance for severely disabled adults has already been described (see page 170).

(f) Non-contributory invalidity pension
This new non-contributory pension started in November 1975. It is a non-means tested benefit for people of working age who have been incapable of work for at least 28 weeks but who do not satisfy the conditions for contributory invalidity benefit (see page 228). In 1977, it was £9.20 per week plus increases for dependants.

(g) Pensions for people over 80
Anyone who is 80 or over and is not receiving a national insurance retirement pension or who is receiving a pension of less than £9.45 a week (1977)—£5.85 for a married woman—may qualify for a non-contributory retirement pension. The person *must* be at least 80 years old and at the time of claiming must normally live in Great Britain and have lived there for a period of at least 10 years in the 20 years ending on their 80th birthday or 19 Sept. 1971, whichever is the later. The current rate is £9.45 (£5.85 for married women).

(h) Guardians' allowances
A guardian's allowance is a payment to a person who takes into his family an orphan child. The age limits are the same as those for child benefit. Usually both parents must be dead, but the allowance can be paid on the death of one parent where the parents were divorced; or where the child is illegitamate or where the surviving parent is serving a long term of imprisonment.

One of the child's parents must have been a British subject who was born in the United Kingdom. If neither parent satisfies this condition, one of them must have satisfied a special residence test.

A guardian's allowance *should be claimed not later than three months after a child has joined the family.*

Child benefits are *not* payable in addition to guardian's allowance.

In 1977 the guardian's allowance was £7.45 a week.

(i) Various industrial injury benefits
Injury and disablement benefits. Payment to persons injured at work or who contract an industrial disease who are subsequently unable to work is covered by two main benefits:
(a) *Injury benefit* covering the first six months after the injury.
(b) *Disablement pension or gratuity* for any permanent disability after six months.
(a) **Injury benefit** is payable during incapacity for work for the first 26 weeks

from the date of accident or industrial disease (usually excludes the first three days). After 26 weeks, anyone still unable to work can get invalidity benefit. Injury benefit is claimed in the same way as sickness benefit.

Injury benefit for those over 18 years of age in 1977 was £15.65 per week with increases for dependent adults and children (as with sickness benefit). *note*: Injury benefit is *not* paid for pneumoconiosis or byssinosis; for both these diseases, disablement benefit can be paid from the start and sickness or invalidity benefit can be paid in addition for anyone unable to work.

(*b*) **Disablement benefit.** The amount of disablement benefit depends on the extent of disablement as assessed by a medical board.

Disablement of 20 per cent to 100 per cent is taken as qualifying the individual for a **disability pension** which, in 1977, varied from £25.00 per week for 100 per cent disablement to £5.00 per week for 20 per cent disablement for adults over 18 years of age. For disablement under 19 per cent and under, benefit is usually paid as a **disablement gratuity.** From £166 for 1 per cent to £1660 for 19 per cent.

Disablement benefit can also be increased for various additional problems or reasons in the following ways:
Note: All amounts given are those in 1977.

Special Hardship Allowance—Up to £10.00 a week, as long as the benefit and allowance together do not come to more than £25.00 a week; if as a result of the injury or disease the claimant is unable to return to his regular job or cannot work at a similar job.

Unemployability Supplement is paid at £15.30 a week with increases for dependants (at invalidity benefit rates) for anyone who is permanently unfit for work as a result of injury or disease.

Constant Attendance Allowance is paid of up to £10.00 per week for anyone who needs someone to look after him and whose disablement is 100 per cent. In quite exceptional cases, this allowance can be increased to a maximum of £20.00.

Exceptionally Severe Disablement Allowance of £10.00 a week is payable to anyone who is in receipt of constant attendance allowance.

Hospital Treatment Allowance. This raises the benefit payable to 100 per cent rate, while the claimant is in hospital and receiving treatment for the injury or disease.
Note: For anyone who is incapable of working, sickness benefit or invalidity benefit can be paid in addition to disablement benefit unless an unemployability supplement is also being paid.

Invalid Care Allowance is payable to people of working age (16 to 60 for women or 65 for men) who cannot work because they have to stay at home to care for a severely disabled relative (i.e. someone in receipt of either an attendance allowance or a constant attendance allowance).

This benefit is taxable, but it is not means-tested and there are no contributory conditions. The person claiming benefit must live in this country and be:

(1) regularly and substantially engaged in caring for a severely disabled relative for at least 35 hours per week;
(2) not gainfully employed (i.e. any part earnings must not exceed £6 weekly); and
(3) not undergoing full-time education.

The rate of allowance is £9.20 per week and normally cannot be backdated for more than 3 months.

CONTRIBUTORY BENEFITS

There are nine contributory benefits:
(1) maternity benefits
(2) sickness benefits
(3) invalidity benefit
(4) unemployment benefit
(5) earnings-related supplement
(6) widows' benefits
(7) retirement pensions
(8) children's special allowance
(9) death grant

(1) Maternity benefits

There are two maternity benefits:

Maternity grant (in 1977, £25) which is *payable to all insured persons*. It is intended to be a contribution towards the general expense of a confinement.

Maternity allowance which is *payable to women who are or have been employed or self-employed* and have been paying the full flat rate contributions. It is usually payable for 18 weeks starting 11 weeks before the baby is expected. It cannot, however, be paid while the woman is working.

In 1977, the maternity allowance was £12.90 per week. In certain circumstances where the woman has dependants, it may be increased in amount.

Claim *must* be made on forms obtainable from local offices of Social Security for *maternity allowance between 14th and 11th week before confinement* and *from 9 weeks before and 3 months after confinement for maternity grant*. Benefit may be lost if a claim is delayed.

(2) Sickness benefit

Anyone normally employed or self-employed can claim sickness benefit for the first 28 weeks of any sickness (it is then replaced by invalidity pension—see below). Anyone who falls sick and is incapable of work should obtain from his doctor a medical certificate the first time he sees him. The certificate must be completed (making certain that full details of any dependants, e.g., wife, children are included) and returned to the Social Security office within six days of falling sick.

In 1976, the standard weekly flat-rate sickness benefit for a man or woman (except a married woman) over 18 years of age was £12.90 with increases of £8.00 for an adult dependant (including wife).

The weekly flat rate benefit for an insured married woman was £9.20 (this can be increased if she has an invalid husband or is living apart from her husband).

Flat-rate sickness benefit is not paid for the first three days of any spell of sickness or for isolated days of illness.

(3) Invalidity benefit

This normally replaces sickness benefit after 28 weeks of illness.

Invalidity pension replaces sickness benefit in all cases and **invalidity allowance** is added as an extra weekly payment to people who become chronically sick while they still have a large part of their normal working lives ahead of them.

In 1977, the invalidity pension was £15.30 a week with increases of £9.20 for an adult dependant. The wife of a man drawing invalidity pension can earn £35.00 a week before the increase paid for her is affected provided she resides with him.

Invalidity allowance depends on the age of incapacity—the earlier the incapacity the larger the allowance. In 1977 it varied from £3.20 a week for those whose incapacity started under the age of 35 years to £1.00 per week for those whose incapacity started after 45 years of age but before 60 years for men or 55 years for women.

Note: Earnings-related supplement (see below) is *not* payable with invalidity benefit.

(4) Unemployment benefit

This is paid only while a person is unemployed, capable of work and available to take a job.

Unemployment benefit which is at the same rate as sickness benefit includes increases for dependants. It is payable for up to 312 days in any period of interruption of employment. Once benefit has run out, unemployment benefit cannot again be paid until the claimant has been back at work and paid 13 Class 1 flat-rate contributions.

On the first day of unemployment, the claimant should register for work at an Employment Exchange and claim benefit. If under 18 years of age, he should attend the Careers Office (Youth Employment Office) if there is one in the district.

(5) Earnings-related supplement

This is payable after the first 12 days of a period of interruption of employment to persons over 18 years and under 60 years for women and 65 years for men who are entitled to flat-rate sickness or unemployment benefit or maternity allowance. This supplement lasts a maximum of 6 months and cannot be paid with invalidity benefit.

The amount of the earnings-related supplement depends upon the 'reckonable earnings' which must be at least £550 a year. In 1977, the maximum supplement payable on annual earnings of £3450 or more is £12.18 a week.

(6) Widows' benefits

There are two main types of widows' benefits. All widows, whose husbands' contributions are sufficient, qualify for a **widows' allowance** payable for six months. After this period, benefit is only given to widows with dependent children (**widowed mothers' allowance**) and to widows over 40 years of age (**widows' pension**).

Widows' allowance in 1977 was £21.40 a week (payable for the first 26 weeks of widowhood) with increases for dependent children of £7.45 for the first child and £5.95 for every other child.

If a woman is widowed when aged 60 years or over, she can get the allowance only if her husband was not a retired pensioner.

A widow may qualify for earnings-related addition for the same period as her widow's allowance where her husband had reckonable earnings of more than £550 in the income tax year relevant to her claim. The addition is calculated in the same way as earnings-related supplement.

Widowed mothers' allowance. After 6 months, a widow with a dependent child will get a widowed mothers' allowance. The basic allowance in 1977 was £15.30 a week with similar increases for children as with widows' allowance (see above).

(If the children have left school and are under 19 years of age and still living with the widow, she can get the basic allowance of £15.30 without additions for children.)

Widows' pension is paid to two main groups:

(a) to a widow if she does not qualify at the termination of her widow's allowance for a widowed mothers' allowance, and was over the age of 40 years when her husband died; *or*

(b) a widow after she ceases to be entitled to a widowed mothers' allowance if she is then over the age of 40 years.

In 1977, the standard rate for a widow's pension was £15.30 a week if she was over 50 when her husband died or when her widowed mother's allowance ended. Below the age of 50, the widow's pension ranges from £14.23 for a widow aged 49 to £4.59 for a widow aged 40 years.

Widow's benefits cease if the widow remarries or cohabits with a man as his wife. From 5th April, 1971 all widows over 60 can get a retirement pension of at least as much as the widow's pension they were receiving before they left work.

(7) Retirement pension

At 65 (60 for a woman) an individual who retires from regular work and satisfies the contribution conditions can get a retirement pension.

When a man reaches 70 (a woman 65) a pension is payable whether retired or not.

In 1977, the amount payable for retirement pensions is made up of:

(a) *Basic retirement pension* of £15.30 a week.

(b) Increases of £9.20 a week for a wife who is not entitled to a pension herself.

Extra pension can be earned by deferring retirement beyond 65 (60 for women).

Graduated pension may also be added in respect of any graduated contributions paid between 1961 and 1975 (when graduated contributions ceased).

Age addition of 25 pence is payable to all pensioners aged 80 or over.

(8) Children's special allowance

This is an allowance to a woman whose marriage has been dissolved or annulled if, on the death of a former husband, she has a child towards whose support he was contributing (or had been liable to do so) at least 25p a week.

In 1977, the allowance was £7.45 for the first child and £5.95 for every other child. Child Benefit is, of course, payable in addition (see page 223). This allowance cannot be paid if the woman has remarried.

(9) Death grant

A death grant is a sum payable on the death of an insured person or of the wife, husband or child of an insured person. It can also be paid on the contributions of a close relative in respect of a handicapped person who has never been able to work.

If the deceased person left a will, it is paid to the executors; otherwise it is paid to the person meeting the funeral expenses.

The amount varies with age. For an adult, in 1977, it was £30. It is reduced for younger persons and for men born before 5th July, 1893 and for women before 5th July, 1898.

ENTITLEMENTS TO CERTAIN SERVICES AT NO COST OR AT REDUCED COST IF THE INDIVIDUAL QUALIFIES

There is a general entitlement to certain services at no cost or at a reduced cost if the person qualifies in a special group. Examples include:

At no cost:
Prescription charges
Dental charges
Charges for optical glasses
Hospital fares
Free school meals
Milk and vitamins
At reduced cost:
Legal advice and assistance
Rent rebates
Rate rebates

Prescription charges

Medicines and appliances prescribed under the National Health Service are supplied free to the following persons on completion of the declaration on the back of the prescription form:

Children under 16.

Men aged 65 or over and women aged 60 or over.

Holders of exemption certificates:

Expectant and nursing mothers (i.e. mothers who have a child under 1 year old);

People suffering from certain medical conditions;

War or service disablement pensioners (for prescriptions required for their accepted disablements);

People or their dependants receiving supplementary benefit or family income supplement.

In addition, anyone who is not covered by the above exemptions, but whose income is below a certain level is entitled to exemption.

If anyone does not qualify but needs prescriptions frequently, it is possible to buy a prescription 'season ticket' covering all NHS prescription charges for either 6 months (cost in 1977 £2) or 12 months (cost in 1977 £3.50).

Dental charges

The following persons are exempt from dental charges:

(1) All children under 16.

(2) Young people aged 16 and over who are still attending school.

(3) Young people over 16 but under 21 who have left school (*except for charges for dentures or alteration and additions to dentures*).

(4) Expectant mothers.

(5) Women who have had a child within the previous 12 months.

(6) Persons and their dependants who are receiving supplementary pension or allowance.

(7) Persons in a family receiving family income supplement.

(8) Persons, and their dependants, who are exempt from prescription charges *on income grounds*.

(9) Persons in a family receiving milk and vitamins free *on income grounds*.

To claim exemption the patient will be asked to sign a declaration on the dentist's treatment form. Hospital *in-patients* are not charged for dental treatment or dentures.

Charges for optical glasses

Children under 16 and older children attending school full time may be supplied free of charge with glasses using NHS lenses in NHS frames from a special children's range. In addition no charge is made for standard NHS lenses for children over 10 using any other NHS frame but the appropriate charge is made for the frame.

Other persons who are exempt from most optical charges include:

(1) Persons and their dependants, who are receiving supplementary pension or allowance.

(2) Persons in a family receiving family income supplement.

(3) Persons, and their dependants, who are exempt from prescription charges *on income grounds*.

(4) Persons in a family receiving milk and vitamins *on income grounds*.

Anyone not in the above exempt categories and aged 16 or over can claim for help if he is in full-time work. Whether help is received or not will depend on the level of income.

Hospital fares

Patients. Hospital patients who are receiving supplementary benefit or family income supplement can have their fares to and from hospital refunded on production of their order book when they attend for treatment. Patients not receiving supplementary benefit may also be entitled to help with their fares, if judged by supplementary benefit standards, they are unable to meet the cost themselves. The hospital social worker will advise how to claim.

Visitors. A person who has to visit a close relative in hospital may receive help with fares *in exceptional circumstances.* He should enquire at the local Social Security office.

Free school meals

Free school meals are available for school children in families receiving supplementary benefit, family income supplement or are in special need because of low income. Enquiry at school or at the local Education Office will indicate the steps which any parent must take to obtain this help.

Milk and vitamins

Liquid milk (7 pints per week) or its equivalent in dried milk, Vitamin A, D, and C drops for children (2 bottles every 13 weeks) and Vitamin A, D and C tablets for mothers (expectant mothers 2 containers every 13 weeks; nursing mothers 5 containers in all) are available free of charge for:

(1) An expectant mother and all children including foster children under school age in families who are receiving supplementary benefits, family income supplement or are in special need because of low income.

(2) An expectant mother who already has 2 children (including foster children) under school age regardless of income.

(3) All but the first two children under school age in families with three or more children (including foster children) under school age, regardless of family income.

Free milk is also available for:

(*a*) Handicapped children aged 5 to 16 who are not registered pupils at a special school or ordinary school (7 pints per week).

(*b*) Children attending an approved day nursery or play group or with an approved child minder (⅓ pint each day they attend).

Any mother wishing to claim milk etc. should contact her local health visitor or child health clinic.

Legal advice and assistance

People of small or moderate means may obtain legal advice and assistance for little or no payment from a solicitor, as if they were fee-paying clients, on any subject usually dealt with by a solicitor. This includes giving advice, writing letters, drafting wills, obtaining opinions from a barrister, preparing a written statement to help someone who has to appear before an administrative or appeal tribunal and visiting a police station or prison.

This help does not extend to representation in proceedings before a court or tribunal but, if representation is needed for proceedings in court, either civil or criminal, the solicitor will advise his client how to apply for legal aid. Legal aid is not generally available for proceedings before tribunals.

Information as to how to apply for legal advice and assistance is available from Citizens' Advice Bureaux, public libraries or by post from The Law Society, 113 Chancery Lane, London WC21 1PL or from The Law Society of Scotland, 27 Drumsheugh Gardens, Edinburgh EH3 7YR.

Rent rebates and allowances

Most tenants (*except those already receiving supplementary benefit*) who find it difficult to afford the full rent may apply to their local authority for direct financial help. Local authority tenants who qualify receive a rent rebate which is deducted at source from their rents.

The amount of rebate or allowance is governed by 3 main factors, the tenant's gross income (including his wife's), the size of his family, and his rent (excluding rates and services).

People who are having difficulty in paying their rent should seek information from Citizens' Advice Bureaux or their Local Authority.

Rate rebates

Owner-occupiers and tenants (including those who pay rates as part of their rent) who are not receiving supplementary benefit can claim a rebate on their general rates from a local authority. Residents of commercial or mixed properties can qualify for a rebate on the domestic part.

Many old persons may qualify (see page 204). Anyone who is *in doubt whether he qualifies should always apply*. All applications are treated in the strictest confidence. Application forms and further details of the scheme can be obtained from the local council.

INDEX